Creative Composition

NEW WRITING VIEWPOINTS

Series Editor: Graeme Harper, *Oakland University, Rochester, USA*

The overall aim of this series is to publish books which will ultimately inform teaching and research, but whose primary focus is on the analysis of creative writing practice and theory. There will also be books which deal directly with aspects of creative writing knowledge, with issues of genre, form and style, with the nature and experience of creativity, and with the learning of creative writing. They will all have in common a concern with excellence in application and in understanding, with creative writing practitioners and their work, and with informed analysis of creative writing as process as well as completed artefact.

Full details of all the books in this series and of all our other publications can be found on http://www.multilingual-matters.com, or by writing to Multilingual Matters, St Nicholas House, 31–34 High Street, Bristol BS1 2AW, UK.

NEW WRITING VIEWPOINTS: 12

Creative Composition

Inspiration and Techniques for Writing Instruction

Edited by
Danita Berg and Lori A. May

MULTILINGUAL MATTERS
Bristol • Buffalo • Toronto

Library of Congress Cataloging in Publication Data
Creative Composition: Inspiration and Techniques for Writing Instruction/Edited by
Danita Berg and Lori A. May.
New Writing Viewpoints: 12
Includes bibliographical references and index.
1. Creative writing—Study and teaching. 2. English language—Rhetoric—Study and teaching. 3. Report writing—Study and teaching. I. Berg, Danita, editor. II. May, Lori A., editor.
PE1404.C69 2015
808.'.042–dc23 2014047895

British Library Cataloguing in Publication Data
A catalogue entry for this book is available from the British Library.

ISBN-13: 978-1-78309-363-2 (hbk)
ISBN-13: 978-1-78309-362-5 (pbk)

Multilingual Matters
UK: St Nicholas House, 31–34 High Street, Bristol BS1 2AW, UK.
USA: UTP, 2250 Military Road, Tonawanda, NY 14150, USA.
Canada: UTP, 5201 Dufferin Street, North York, Ontario M3H 5T8, Canada.

Website: www.multilingual-matters.com
Twitter: Multi_Ling_Mat
Facebook: https://www.facebook.com/multilingualmatters
Blog: www.channelviewpublications.wordpress.com

Copyright © 2015 Danita Berg, Lori A. May and the authors of individual chapters.

All rights reserved. No part of this work may be reproduced in any form or by any means without permission in writing from the publisher.

The policy of Multilingual Matters/Channel View Publications is to use papers that are natural, renewable and recyclable products, made from wood grown in sustainable forests. In the manufacturing process of our books, and to further support our policy, preference is given to printers that have FSC and PEFC Chain of Custody certification. The FSC and/or PEFC logos will appear on those books where full certification has been granted to the printer concerned.

Typeset by Techset Composition India(P) Ltd., Bangalore and Chennai, India.
Printed and bound in Great Britain by Short Run Press Ltd.

Contents

	Contributors	vii
	Foreword	xi
	Introduction	xv
1	On Essaying *Denise Landrum-Geyer*	1
2	Eat Your Spinach! Why a Blend of Personal and Academic Discourses Matter *Sara Burnett*	10
3	Writing by Creation, with Response, in Experience *Graeme Harper*	16
4	Give it a Taste: Serving Creative Writing in Small Doses *Abigail G. Scheg*	24
5	Wiggling Between the Forms: A Cross-Genre Approach to Writing *Dustin Michael*	30
6	Writing to Discover: Creative Nonfiction and Writing Across the Curriculum *Andrew Bourelle*	35
7	Creative Writing's Five Stages of Development: The Mind of the Creative Writer in the Composition Classroom *Jonathan Bradley and Sarah Gray-Panesi*	47
8	Sought-After Sophistications: Crafting a Curatorial Stance in the Creative Writing and Composition Classrooms *Rochelle L. Harris and Christine Stewart-Nuñez*	59

9 Audience Resurrected: Restoring Motive and Purpose to
   Creative Writing   77
   Michael Kula

10 Lending the Muse a Hand: Expanding the Role of Social
   Constructivism and Collaborative Writing in Creative
   Writing Pedagogies   87
   Rod Zink

11 Grammar and Creativity in Composition: An Unexpected Nexus   109
   Shawn Kerivan

12 Invention in Creative Writing: Explorations of the Self and the
   Social in Creative Genres   114
   Danita Berg

13 Teaching the Exploratory Essay as Pedagogy, Process and Project   129
   Sonya Huber and Ioanna Opidee

14 Beyond Argumentation: Toulmin's Model as a Dialogic,
   Processual Heuristic   138
   Debra Jacobs

15 Leave it to the Imagination: Service Learning as Part of an
   Undergraduate Creative Writing Curriculum   148
   Scott J. O'Callaghan

16 Show, Don't Tell: Using Graphic Narratives to Teach Descriptive
   Writing   154
   Tammie M. Kennedy and Tracey D. Menten

17 A First-Timer's Approach to Teaching in a Non-Traditional
   Setting   169
   Connie Langhorst

18 In It for the Long Haul: The Pedagogy of Perseverance   174
   Anna Leahy

   Index   182

Contributors

Danita Berg chairs the English department at Full Sail University. She received her MFA in Creative Writing at Goddard College and PhD in Rhetoric and Composition from the University of South Florida. She has published both creatively and academically and founded *Animal: A Beast of a Literary Magazine*.

Andrew Bourelle is an assistant professor at the University of New Mexico. His writing has appeared in scholarly journals, such as the *Journal of Teaching Writing*, *Currents in Teaching and Learning*, and *Computers and Composition Online*, as well as literary journals, such as *Hobart*, *Jabberwock Review* and *Red Rock Review*.

Jonathan Bradley graduated from Middle Tennessee State University in 2013. He was co-facilitator of MTSU's Creative Writing Group from 2010–2012, conducted creative writing workshops at multiple venues and has worked as a freelance fiction consultant and editor.

Sara Burnett is a creative writing MFA student at the University of Maryland where she teaches. She taught high school English, designs curriculum, and has a MA in English Literature. Her poetry appears in *Hinchas de Poesia*, *PALABRAS* and *Poet Lore*.

Sarah Gray-Panesi is a PhD Candidate in English at Middle Tennessee State University. She currently teaches Research and Argumentative Writing, and has taught several sections of Expository Writing while also editing *Scientia et Humanitas*, MTSU's research journal.

Graeme Harper, DCA PhD, is Dean of The Honors College at Oakland University, MI, following posts in the UK and Australia. He is Editor of *New*

Writing: the International Journal for the Practice and Theory of Creative Writing (Routledge).

Rochelle L. Harris, PhD, is from the Appalachian Mountains in Northwest Georgia where she currently teaches writing and literature at Kennesaw State University. Her publications appear in such journals as *Pedagogy, The Writing Instructor, symploke, Women's Studies Quarterly, Fourth Genre, Crab Orchard Review, Passages North* and *Writing on the Edge*.

Sonya Huber is the author of *Cover Me: A Health Insurance Memoir, Opa Nobody*, and a textbook, *The Backwards Research Guide for Writers*. She teaches in the Department of English and in the Low-Residency MFA program at Fairfield University.

Debra Jacobs is an associate professor of English in the rhetoric and composition program at the University of South Florida. She is a coauthor of *Four Worlds of Writing: Inquiry and Action in Context* (with Janice Lauer *et al.*) and she has published on subjectivity in writing in several collections, as well as in *JAC* and *Composition Forum*.

Tammie M. Kennedy is an assistant professor of English at the University of Nebraska at Omaha. She teaches courses in writing, rhetoric, film, and composition theory and pedagogy to both undergraduate and graduate students. She has published in *Feminist Formations, Brevity, Rhetoric Review, JAC, The Journal of Religion and Popular Culture, English Journal* and *The Journal of Lesbian Studies*.

Shawn Kerivan teaches writing at the Community College of Vermont. He is the author of *Creative Writing in the Real World: A Reader for Writers* (New Plains Press, 2012) and *Name the Boy: Short Stories* (Dan River Press, 2007).

Michael Kula is an assistant professor at the University of Washington, Tacoma. His work has appeared in numerous literary magazines, and he has recently completed the novel, *The Good Doctor*, based on the life of an early 20th century veterinarian.

Denise Landrum-Geyer is Assistant Professor of Language & Literature and Writing Center Coordinator at Southwestern Oklahoma State University. Her interests include creative nonfiction, composition theories/pedagogies, rhetorical genre theories and sharing creative and critical writing on her blog 'Essaying the Plains' (http://deniselg.com).

Contributors   ix

Connie Langhorst holds a BA in Creative Writing from Eckerd College and recently graduated from the Red Earth Low-Residency MFA Creative Writing Program at Oklahoma City University. A substitute teacher at St. Petersburg Collegiate High School, Connie has published her work in *Aspiring to Inspire*, *Animal*, *Eckerd Review* and *The Scarab*.

Anna Leahy's *Constituents of Matter* won the Wick Poetry Prize. She edited *Power and Identity in the Creative Writing Classroom* and teaches at Chapman University, where she curates the Tabula Poetica reading series and the journal *TAB*. She co-writes Lofty Ambitions blog <http://loftyambitions.wordpress.com>.

Lori A. May is a mentor in the University of King's College-Halifax MFA in Creative Nonfiction program and a faculty member of the Wilkes University MA and MFA writing programs. Her books include *The Low-Residency MFA Handbook: A Guide for Prospective Creative Writing Students* (Continuum, 2011), *Square Feet* (Accents, 2014) and *The Write Crowd: Literary Citizenship & the Writing Life* (Bloomsbury, 2014).

Tim Mayers, PhD, is an associate professor of English at Millersville University. His books include *(Re)Writing Craft: Composition, Creative Writing, and the Future of English Studies* (University of Pittsburgh Press, 2005) and *Reading the Networks of Power: Re-Thinking 'Critical Thinking' in Computerized Classrooms*, co-authored with Kevin Swafford (Columbia University Press, 1998).

Tracey D. Menten is an International Baccalaureate Theory of Knowledge teacher and CAS Coordinator at Omaha Central High School. She has taught in public high schools for 12 years and has four years of corporate curriculum instructional design experience. She has published in *English Journal*.

Dustin Michael holds a PhD in nonfiction writing from the University of Missouri. His work appears in *The Fourth Genre: Contemporary Writers of/on Creative Nonfiction*, and elsewhere. He teaches literature and writing at Savannah State University in Savannah, Georgia.

Scott J. O'Callaghan teaches at Columbus State Community College in Columbus, Ohio. Previously, he taught at Southern Vermont College. He received his PhD from the University at Albany, State University of New York, where he studied teacher response to student writing across one semester of college teaching.

Ioanna Opidee is an adjunct professor in the Department of English at Fairfield University. She holds an MFA from Fairfield University and her work has been published in various magazines and literary journals.

Abigail G. Scheg is an Assistant Professor in the Department of Language, Literature, and Communication at Elizabeth City State University where she teaches traditional first-year composition courses. Scheg researches and publishes in the area of online pedagogy and social networking.

Christine Stewart-Nuñez, PhD, is the author of five poetry collections: *Snow, Salt, Honey* (2012); *Keeping Them Alive* (2011); *Postcard on Parchment* (2008); *Unbound & Branded* (2006); and *The Love of Unreal Things* (2005). She is an Associate Professor in the English Department at South Dakota State University.

Stephanie Vanderslice, PhD, is an associate professor at University of Central Arkansas. Her publications include *But Can It Really Be Taught: Lore and the Teaching of Creative Writing*, co-edited with Dr Kelly Ritter (Heinemann, 2007).

Rod Zink is currently Director of Composition at Penn State Harrisburg, and received his PhD in English from Oklahoma State University. His teaching repertoire includes courses in Creative Writing, Composition Studies, Rhetorical Theory, New Literacies, Technical and Business Writing, as well as Writing in the Social Sciences and the Humanities.

Foreword

Tim Mayers and Stephanie Vanderslice

At last. The potential for synergy between creative writing and composition has been discussed and written about for as long as we can remember; a book such as *Creative Composition* is long overdue. And what a thought-provoking collection it is, going far beyond the usual tropes about the commonality between the two subjects to suggest whole new pedagogies and practices that can infuse both the creative writing and the composition classrooms. What interests us most about this collection, however, is the ways in which the essays themselves speak to and echo *each other* and the ways in which they echo the calls of Wendy Bishop, whose early work first began to suggest the intersections between Composition and Creative Writing.

The fields of Creative Writing and Composition would seem to have natural points of overlap that some teachers and scholars have tried to exploit over the years, though the different kinds of work in this area have perhaps not exhibited much cohesion (at least not with each other). However there are certain aspects of institutional and disciplinary history – i.e. that Creative Writing and Composition have grown into what they are today, more often than not separately from each other – that sometimes prevent bridges from being built between these two. The classroom, however, at least for those teachers who have some freedom to experiment there, is always a ripe site for new practices that then may 'trickle up' into larger disciplinary structures. The chapters in this collection all offer ways to combine 'composition' and 'creative writing' in classroom activities and assignment design – not merely by *importing* practices and assignments from one realm into another but by actually *blending* the concerns of both fields at a fundamental conceptual level. In 'Invention in Creative Writing: Explorations of the Self and the Social in Creative Genres,' Danita Berg shows us, for example, how theories of invention from composition can be both applied in the creative writing classroom and be used, as well, to demonstrate the contested teachability of creative writing as a subject. Jonathan Bradley and Sarah Gray-Panesi support the idea of creative writing as a teachable subject by actually documenting the developmental stages though which students progress in a creative writing course in their essay: 'Creative Writing's Five Stages of Development: The Mind of the Creative Writer in the Composition Classroom.'

In one of her landmark essays, furthermore, 'Suddenly Sexy: Creative Nonfiction Rear Ends Composition,' published in *College English* in 2003, shortly before her death, Bishop called upon teachers of 'composition and creative writing who care about student writers' to 'pool their knowledge, develop new pedagogies, create fresh possibilities.' Bishop believed that one of the ways this knowledge synergy could occur would be to allow creative nonfiction to 'infuse, improve and invigorate the teaching of composition' (259). As she relates, in the 1990s creative writers 'turned toward nonfiction while those in composition left the study of stylistics, coherence and cohesion to investigate disciplinary writing and cultural studies' (259). Making a sharp turn towards 'content and thinking in student essays,' the path of composition teaching moved away from the 'teaching of aspects of craft.' Perhaps this move away from craft (understood in terms of written language's surface features) and toward 'thinking and content' was a necessary attempt to disrupt a deep-seated societal (Current-Traditional) (mis)understanding about writing in which correctness is posited as some basic underlying structure of writing ability that must be mastered before writers can move on to allegedly more complex writing tasks. This meant that the composition classroom had ultimately been left with an 'eviscerated type of essay, not personal writing (too easy, too dangerous), not professional writing (too challenging) but school writing and research papers,' (265). However, now that the importance of thinking and content have been asserted, we can begin to look back at how matters of 'craft' understood now as more than merely ornament or purity, require our attention.

Enter Andrew Bourelle, answering Bishop with his essay, 'Writing to Discover: Creative Nonfiction and Writing Across the Curriculum,' by reminding us that creative nonfiction is a form of probing with writing, of writing-to-learn, so to speak. Many creative nonfiction writers, Bourelle tells us, write to find out what they know. Such practices are indeed a cornerstone of the writing across the curriculum movement. Denise Landrum-Geyer echoes Bourelle's observation with her own essay, 'On Essaying,' which asks us to consider 'teaching by treating the world essay as a verb instead of a noun,' and posit essay writing as a 'mode of thinking.' In 'Eat Your Spinach! Why a Blend of Personal and Academic Discourses Matter,' Sara Burnett underscores both arguments (and Bishop's) by articulating the need to 'broaden what constitutes academic writing to be more meaningful for students.' Finally, Rod Zink reintroduces the connections between creative writing and writing-across-the-curriculum (WAC) and in-the-disciplines (WID) by arguing for the place of collaboration in the classroom, as a skill building technique in the creative writing classroom and a career-modeling activity in the composition classroom. Both of these demonstrate the value of social constructivism in the writing curriculum.

Burnett broadens the issue itself, however, by, advocating for this blend not only because blurring genres can 'foster intellectual curiosity,' the kind that happens when 'essaying,' but also because, 'When we allow for a wider blend of genres and discourses in an academic research paper, we create possibilities and access real learning.' Moreover, by re-introducing the more academic idea of 'audience,' and making rhetorical situation more explicit in the creative writing course, Michael Kula argues in 'Audience Resurrected: Restoring Motive and Purpose to Creative Writing,' that we direct that 'real learning,' toward helping students act more like experienced writers, who, research shows, write with this audience awareness. Audience theory in Composition Studies has perhaps gone dormant after Lisa Ede and Andrea Lunsford's landmark essay. Kula's essay has the potential to kick-start or revitalize important discussions of audience in both Creative writing and Compositions on a theoretical and a pedagogical level.

Arguably, the most daring move in the book might occur in Graeme Harper's 'Writing by Creation, with Response, in Experience,' where he posits that in teaching toward a material product, much of creative writing pedagogy in recent history has been woefully misguided. Though rhetorically bold, what Harper is really arguing for is a return to the pedagogy of process, a pedagogy that honors, documents, and teaches the process of creation by understanding that 'writing is not merely its artifacts, writing is the acts and actions writers undertake; ... the critical activities with which we writers explain the world'. 'Writers,' Harper reminds us, 'spend most of their lives in what can be called the event of writing,' or the act of 'composition.' Interestingly, Rochelle L. Harris and Christine Stewart-Nuñez, in 'Sought-After Sophistications: Crafting a Curatorial Stance in the Creative Writing and Composition Classrooms,' suggest that a 'curatorial stance' in the creative writing and composition classes that may address Harper's criticisms about the materiality/product-based nature of writing pedagogy. Curating is a creative act, one that 'seeks existing knowledge and generates new knowledge.' By situating students as curators – in a museum archive and an art gallery – Harris and Stewart-Nuñez encourage their interaction with 'interviews, observations, surveys and archival artifacts' that makes available 'selection, choice and agency' to students in their own inquiries and spaces. This 'selection, choice and agency,' reframes students' relationships to the intellectual work of writing and research,' helping students to not only 'claim ownership' of their knowledge but also to be more 'readily able to do-in depth, successful writing.'

Anna Leahy's essay on teaching for resilience, 'In it for the Long Haul: The Pedagogy of Perseverance' also emphasizes not the materiality of product in the writing classroom but the habits of mind that facilitates creativity and success: perseverance. As Leahy points out, writers frequently extol the value of perseverance in a writing career, yet, if this quality is as 'important as [we] think it is, we must prioritize that capacity as a goal.' We must teach it, and in doing so, we will be re-focusing, as Harper suggests, on acts of creation rather than production.

All in all, *Creative Composition* more than lives up to its name, deeply exploring the connections between composition and creative writing in only the most innovative of ways, ways that will significantly enhance our teaching of the subjects and greatly expand our knowledge of and thinking about *both* disciplines. We believe it will stake a claim among the most important collections of writing theory and pedagogy in this early part of the 21st century, further expanding two growing fields and guiding us into an exciting future that as it continues to validate writing as a teaching, teachable subject.

Introduction[1]

Danita Berg and Lori A. May

> *We need to be crossing the lines between composition and creative writing far more often than we do. In fact, we may want to eliminate the line entirely.*
> – Wendy Bishop, 'Crossing the Lines: On Creative Composition and Composing Creative Writing.'

> *Know the rules well, so you can break them effectively.*
> – Dalai Lama XIV

In Wallace Stegner's book *On The Teaching of Creative Writing*, he states that it is the teacher's job to keep students writing. Students need proof that they can write, a belief in and understanding of their process, and, perhaps most importantly, enthusiasm for putting pen to paper. This is true, no matter what type of writing class the student is enrolled in. Yet we have found, in the various courses that we have taught, that there seems to be more enthusiasm, on the part of the instructors as well as the students, for certain kinds of writing classes over others. The first-year composition classes are tolerated, yet the 'creative' classes are anticipated.

Wendy Bishop, a leader in studying the crossover between creative writing and composition, writes in her chapter 'Crossing the Lines: On Creative Composition and Composing Creative Writing' that undergraduate writing curriculums need to be revised in order to reflect the troubling beliefs students hold about the writing process because they are confused when creative writing and composition are separated into different classrooms. She cites a journal entry of her own student, who stated she used the words 'creative writing' and 'composition' interchangeably, even though it could be 'a grave sin to use one for the other' (Bishop, 1990a). Based on her own education, the student decided that composition was an essay or term paper, and creative writing was 'anything you felt like putting down on paper' (Bishop, 1990a). This disquieting view of writing continues to be held by many students, which is of little wonder when one considers how the disciplines have been separated and taught in roughly the last one hundred years.

Forced Choices and Questions of Separation

As Danita finished her first decade of teaching at the college level, she continued to instruct both composition and creative writing classes. She held an MFA in Creative Writing from Goddard College and a PhD in composition and rhetoric from the University of South Florida, so she had a background in both writing disciplines. She was, and is, equally engaged in writing and teaching in both composition and creative writing, and has been for most of her teaching career, as a graduate teaching assistant at a large public university, a visiting professor of rhetoric and creative writing at a private liberal-arts college, an assistant professor of writing at Oklahoma City University, where she founded and directed the Red Earth Low-Residency MFA in Creative Writing program, and now as the chair of an English department where she directs the pedagogical techniques of a gamut of writing and public speaking classes. During her tenure of instructing and/or managing the craft of writing and communication, she taught classes ranging from first-year composition to graduate classes in writing pedagogy, and enjoyed them all.

She found it perplexing that, at many of the schools where she taught previous to OCU, creative writing and composition classes were, and are, instructed by different faculty members; she was one of the few teachers who 'crossed' between collegia to teach. Danita was informed that if she wanted to pursue a tenure-track position, she would have to choose between the two disciplines, as though they were separate from each other, even though the schools where she taught had need for her in both disciplines. Yet she did not want to choose between them.

When she was on the job market and looking at the advertised positions for tenure-track professors of writing, she found that most colleges advertised jobs for either composition or creative writing, as though they were unrelated. The split between disciplines was theory- and practice-based. Composition positions asked for samples of critical papers written on scholarly issues, while creative writing positions wanted proof of substantial publication in 'creative' genres. The job ads reflected the underlying assumptions that composition is a scholarly discipline and that creative writing, by contrast, is practice based.

The separation seems welcomed by writing instructors. Gerald Graff wrote, after reviewing the writing program at a major university:

> [T]he [creative] writers were almost all practice-oriented, hostile or indifferent to [literary] criticism, much less theory ... Each component [of the department] is beautifully and completely insulated from any danger of hearing the criticism of the other – and of course that's the whole point, isn't it? (qtd. in Myers, 1996)

Perhaps the separation is because those professors who write in 'creative' genres are treated differently from compositionists in the university setting. Creative writers exist in a 'privileged marginality' in higher academia, 'mostly left alone to do what they do best – write – and teach aspiring young writers the tools of their trade' (Ritter & Vanderslice, 2007). Authors of novels, poetry collections, and other genres considered 'creative' are treated like artists of the written work and rhetoricians like the workhorses, to teach the 'practical' genres of writing persuasive essays, research papers, and various professional and technical documents.

Like Danita, Lori taught both composition and creative writing courses and had similar experiences in recognizing the need for loosened boundaries across disciplines. When crafting so-called academic essays or fine-tuning their grammar skills, she found her students benefited from the exploratory freedom of creative exercises. When not focused on the rules of academia, student writers unburdened themselves, and were more apt to write meaningful and argumentative sentences when writing about something that mattered to them. Likewise, the creative writing student may enjoy the carte blanche of penning with imagination, but his words carry more weight when eloquently written, when the rules of good writing are recognized. Lori often called on the Dalai Lama's quote above, in both composition and creative writing settings, encouraging an awareness of the rules if only to know how to break them with purpose.

Together we wondered about this dichotomy: Why must the genres, and the teaching of them, be separate? Are the pedagogical approaches different? And can the approaches be merged so that students gain a better understanding of all of the processes, forms, and genres available to them in the writing process? What can we do to help students understand the creativity in writing, without separating the creative process, and the definition of what and who is 'creative,' into different classrooms?

Calls for Alliance

Questions like ours have been raised and explored for some time, whether in the vein of such compositionists as Peter Elbow, Donald Murray, and Ken Macrorie, who have decried the notion that composition should focus exclusively on teaching academic discourse, or in the even more revolutionary manner of such scholar/teachers as Wendy Bishop and Tim Mayers, 'crossover' academics who have backgrounds in both composition studies and creative writing. A leading voice in the championing of a greater partnership between composition and creative writing instruction, Bishop has long spoken on ways in which the lack of creative writing craft in the composition classroom unnecessarily limits the composition curriculum and the pedagogical practices found in the composition classroom. In 'Crossing the Lines,' she shares the thinking of another student that is indicative of the perception many students have about the difference between composition and creative writing classes: 'creative writing (is the) stuff that is done for fun, and composition stuff that the teacher makes you do' (Bishop, 1990a). As the title 'Crossing the Lines' suggests, Bishop calls for instructors of composition and instructors of creative writing to recognize the commonalities of the genres and skills they teach and to develop pedagogical practices accordingly. Besides improving pedagogical practices and the negative views students tend to have about the 'unpleasant task' of writing in traditional composition courses, crossing the line between composition and creative writing would, Bishop suggests, bring critical attention to the political arrangement in English studies according to which literature and literary criticism are privileged over composition and creative writing.

Tim Mayers makes the political goal of bringing composition and creative writing out from 'the shadow of their dominant (and often domineering) counterpart called literary studies' the central claim to his argument that 'composition and creative writing, at this particular historical moment, have much to gain by forming an institutional alliance and perhaps much to lose if they do not' (Mayers, 2005: 2). Throughout his book *(Re)Writing Craft: Composition, Creative Writing and the Future of English*, Mayers underscores the sense of urgency for creating this alliance now. Such urgency is indicated immediately by the epigraph that appears in the first chapter of his book, a passage from the introduction to *Rhetoric, Poetic, and Cultures: Refiguring College English Studies* by James Berlin:

> English studies is in crisis. Indeed, virtually no feature of the discipline can be considered beyond dispute. At issue are the very elements that

constitute the categories of poetic and rhetoric, the activities involved in their production and interpretation, their relationship to each other, and their relative place in graduate and undergraduate work. (Berlin, 2003: xi)

Sharing with Berlin and numerous other scholars (including Wendy Bishop, as noted above) the view that disciplines other than those connected to literature studies are marginalized in departments of English, Mayers suggests that their peripheral status is perhaps 'the most important thing composition has in common with creative writing' (Mayers, 2005). He notes that while there have been fruitful efforts to integrate composition theory and pedagogy in creative writing classrooms and, conversely, approaches to the 'creative' craft in composition classrooms, almost since composition and creative writing began to appear together (but as separate disciplinary areas) within English departments, it is now, when there is an 'increase in "crossover" scholarship' and more and more graduate students moving from one discipline to the other, that we are witnessing an especially 'fertile historical moment' for alliance and reform (Mayers, 2005: 103).

As crossover academics, we can attest to the disciplinary encampments within departments of English. In fact, we would suggest that the division between literary studies and the two 'production' disciplines of creative writing and composition is no more entrenched than the dividing lines between creative writing and composition. Likely, the marginality the two disciplines experience contributes to their separation. Lacking the privileged position of the alpha member, the marginalized members vie for a secondary position of importance with each other. The very fact that there are calls for greater alliance between the two disciplines reflects the extent of their present separation. While an alliance may be an ideal goal, we believe it is, at best, a distant goal. Any alliance requires a 'meeting of minds,' and we do not find that such a meeting has occurred.

Mayers is correct to note that some theory and pedagogy from either side of the aisle can be found on the other side, but we would characterize such occurrence as mere trickles. For crossovers like ourselves, the small amount of 'sharing' between creative writing and composition has not been enough to construct a coherent sense of professional identity. Continuing to feel the same split personality as a teacher of both creative writing and composition, we fully appreciate the sense of urgency Mayers finds in the present moment, but the most urgent priority of the moment is to occupy our dual identities with integrity, and here we use 'integrity' in the sense that Scott Consigny defined it in the well-known *Philosophy and Rhetoric* article 'Rhetoric and Its Situations.' Aptly enough, Consigny's definition concerned the 'know-how' of writing, the knowledge that enables a writer to utilize writing arts from one situation to another. It is that know-how that makes the teaching of writing possible in the first place. Aptly enough as well, Consigny's notion of integrity is offered in response to and criticism of the view of writing as a wholly creative act, an act by a writer who has no need to consider constraints other than those he or she creates or discover points of view or lines of development other than those he or she already has. We submit that such a view of the creative act of writing is commonplace in creative writing.

In *Released into Language*, Bishop remarks that it is composition that can be found to have 'borrowed effective teaching methods' from creative writing, but not vice versa. Further, it is composition, according to Bishop, that improves 'on those borrowings' (Bishop, 1990b: 125). It may be that debates continue in composition studies about personal versus academic writing, about self-expression versus audience, about voice versus the conventions of discourse communities – and certainly these sorts of issues do reflect ideological differences that would influence the extent to which a compositionist would embrace or reject an alliance with creative writing. But much in keeping with Janice Lauer's description of composition studies as a 'dappled discipline' (Lauer, 1984), compositionists by and large are open to utilizing theories and pedagogical practices derived from any number of disciplines, including creative writing.

Primarily we are concerned with giving students choices of genre from their earliest experiences of composing within the university setting, although we also consider how conjoining the disciplines in college students' earliest writing experiences helps students understand that writing has many functions beyond research and persuasion and that more than one genre can facilitate the teaching of such skills.

Note

(1) Danita Berg's work stems from her 2010 University of South Florida doctoral dissertation work, 'Re-composition: Considering the intersections of composition and creative writing theories and pedagogies.'

References

Berg, D. (2010) Re-composition: Considering the intersections of composition and creative writing theories and pedagogies. Doctoral dissertation, University of South Florida.
Berlin, J. (2003) *Rhetoric, Poetic, and Cultures: Refiguring College English Studies*. West Lafayette: Parlor Press.
Bishop, W. (1990a) Crossing the lines: On creative composition and composing creative writing. Presentation, Annual Meeting of the South Atlantic Modern Language Association, Tampa, FL, 15–17 November.

Bishop, W. (1990b) *Released Into Language: Options for Teaching Creative Writing*. Urbana: National Council of Teachers of English.
Lauer, J. (1984) Composition studies: Dappled discipline. *Rhetoric Review* 3 (1), 20–29.
Mayers, T. (2005) *(Re)Writing Craft: Composition, Creative Writing and the Future of English*. Pittsburgh: University of Pittsburgh Press.
Myers, D.G. (1996) *The Elephants Teach: Creative Writing Since 1880*. Chicago: The University of Chicago Press.
Ritter, K. and Vanderslice, S. (2007) What's lore got to do with it? K. Ritter and S. Vanderslice (eds) *Can It Really Be Taught? Resisting Lore in Creative Writing Pedagogy*. Portsmouth, NH: Boynton/Cook Publishers.
Stegner, W. (1998) *On the Teaching of Creative Writing: Responses to a Series of Questions*. Hanover, NH: Montgomery Endowment.

1 On Essaying

Denise Landrum-Geyer

I

In *The Oxford English Dictionary*, 'essay' has two entries – one a noun and the other a verb. The noun definition is one often associated with academic writing: 'A composition of moderate length on any particular subject, or branch of subject... said of a composition more or less elaborate in style, though limited in range.' I am more interested in the verb entry: 'to essay' is '[t]o put to the proof, try (a person or thing); to test the nature, excellence, fitness, etc. of; to practice (an art, etc.) by way of trial; To try by tasting; to try to do, effect, accomplish, or make (anything difficult).' In *Reality Hunger: A Manifesto*, David Shields (2011: 9) points out the Latin antecedent to the term 'essay': '*experior*, meaning "to try, test, experience, prove."' The verb definition of essay is an active process, one that values experimenting and working through ideas without necessarily arriving at a definitive conclusion. The emphasis is on doing, trying – testing – even if the attempt fails or leads down an unintended path. What would happen in our writing classrooms if we treated the word 'essay' as a verb instead of a noun? What if we encouraged student essaying?

II

I walk to and from campus almost every day, barring bad weather (which is common on the wide open plains of Oklahoma) or the necessary toting of heavy objects. As I walk the three blocks to my office, my mind often turns to teaching: on the way to campus, I think about lesson plans for the day, revising them in my mind as my iPod pumps music into my ears. On my way home at the end of the day, I reflect: what went well? What not-so-much? How will this experience feed into the next class period I have with these students? The act of walking allows me to catch my breath and work through my thoughts. I am essaying about teaching – journeying, trying, reflecting – each day. And it is that act of essaying I hope to pass on to my students, in first-year composition, creative nonfiction, peer tutoring, fundamentals of English (our basic writing course)... really, any class they have, with me or someone else. I want my students to essay, even as they frown when they are told to create *an essay*.

III

The essay is a bit of a lost genre: it seems to fall somewhere between creative writing and academic writing, what Ruth-Ellen Boetcher Joeres (1993: 152) calls a 'boundary form;' put another way, essays inhabit a space between literary and rhetorical genres, yet most of the writing assigned in college courses is labeled an 'essay' (Devitt, 2004). The word 'essay' has been co-opted by the educational establishment to describe school-based genres, most of which do not reflect the characteristics associated with essay writing outside of school walls: what most teachers call essays in the classroom are more accurately labeled as articles or themes, or at the very least a specific essay subgenre – the academic essay. But the classroom is not where essays developed as a genre; the essay is a genre that has evolved in the writing world as writers have used it for various reasons since at least the 16th century. David Shields (2011: 8) goes so far as to trace the essay's lineage from aphorisms:

> When read together, these collections of sayings could be said to make a general argument on their common themes, or at least shed some light somewhere, or maybe simply obsess about a topic until a little dent has been made in the huge idea they all pondered... Via editing and collage, the form germinated into longer, more complex, more sustained, and more sophisticated essayings.

If the genre's tradition is traced through Michel de Montaigne, who is often touted as the father of the genre[1], it becomes easy to see the fluidity of the form: essays often seem to incorporate aspects of other genres while they move along, focusing in particular on working through a writer's thought processes as opposed to offering the neat and tidy linear arguments often valued in academic writing (D'Agata, 2009). That being said, I realize that the Francis Bacon essay tradition, a more formal and rigid subgenre more closely akin to conventional academic writing, arose around the same time as Montaigne's *Essais:* according to O.B. Hardison's (1989) essay 'Binding Proteus: An essay on the essay,' Montaigne first used the word 'essai' between 1572 and 1580, while Bacon became the second person to use the term in 1597. Both Montaignian and Baconian essays have a similar interest in tracing experimental ideas; as Shields (2011: 138) puts it, 'Maybe every essay automatically is in some way experimental – not an outline traveling toward a foregone conclusion but an unmapped quest that has sprung from the word *question.*' The difference lies in the presentation of those ideas: Bacon's essays follow a specific, formal structure for the presentation of ideas, while Montaigne's informal and meditative musings are known for the seeming absence of structure (Lopate, 1995). Bacon composed essays; Montaigne essayed.

IV

My interest in essaying began as an undergraduate student. I enrolled in a creative nonfiction workshop with a special focus on personal essays. Though I was afraid of sharing my work with my classmates, the act of writing in this genre thrilled me. I didn't have to know the answers as I wrote. Writing was an answer. It wasn't that I would find the answers to my questions when I was finished, though. The importance was the act of writing. As bell hooks (1999: 13) suggests in *Remembered Rapture: The Writer at Work*, 'Writing is a way to clarify, to interpret, to reinvent ... we write because language is the way we keep a hold on life.' Writing was a way of thinking through, though I rarely (never?) found answers while I essayed along. Personal essays gave me perspective on my experiences without requiring me to compose a tidy explanatory narrative. I wrote conventional academic texts, too, and I learned something as I wrote them. The difference, though, was the focus: I learned about Jane Austen, Thomas Hardy, feminism, and sonnets when I wrote those academic texts. When I essayed, I learned about process, struggle – learning. Things got messy – and uncomfortable – and it was okay. I was holding on to see where I was going. I just needed to push along, to essay my way: 'The essay consists of double translation: memory translates experience; essay translates memory' (Shields, 2011: 61).

V

Essays often vary in the characteristics they hold, which can make it difficult to create a comprehensive definition. As G. Douglas Atkins (1990: 12) points out in 'The return of/to the essay,' '[t]he essay is a genre that flirts with all other genres,' and it is the bagginess of the genre that sometimes makes it difficult to distinguish between essays and other genres and, therefore, makes it easy for someone to label a text an essay, whether the designation is accurate or not (Devitt, 2004: 10). But I believe there are some consistent qualities in the genre that make it especially useful in writing classrooms: essays tend to be inquiry-driven even as they are digressive – to essay requires writers to come at a subject from as many angles as possible, even when those viewpoints are contradictory. It is the contradictions that make the journeying – the essaying – worthwhile, and the genre provides a space in which writers are encouraged to admit and work through contradictions, which is often discouraged in conventional academic writing. Most academic writing is structured in such a way that students must reach a conclusion/decision/agreement before they begin writing, so that it is easier to compose a thesis and refute counterarguments. Essaying, on the other hand, focuses on the process of finding those arguments, counterarguments, and positions, and putting them into conversation in one space. As Phillip Lopate (2013) points out, 'Argumentation is a good skill to have, but the real argument should be with oneself.'

VI

I double-majored in both English and French as an undergraduate student, and I was struck by how often I heard the word 'essay' or some variation in both English and French. In English classes, I was often tasked with creating something called an 'essay,' while in French classes, I was often told 'Tuessaie de parler en Francais. *You must try to speak (in) French.*' In one language, I created a polished object, while in the other language, I made an attempt, which sometimes succeeded and sometimes did not. Object and action. Or was it action and reaction?

VII

Essays are conversational: the genre invites dialogue between writers and readers, asking both parties to consider and reconsider their positions as they move through the text. Even more important than the potential for conversation between writer and readers, though, are the dialogic elements of essays that occur within the text as the writer converses with him or herself. Essays encourage writers to gather as much information as possible while the writer works her way through her ever-shifting opinions on a topic, allowing writers to take their time in unfolding a topic and examining it as closely as possible (Atkins, 1990; Boetcher Joeres, 1993; Lopate, 1995). As Montaigne (2012a) points out, 'we are, I know not how, double in ourselves, which is the cause that what we believe we do not believe, and cannot disengage ourselves from what we condemn.' We must acknowledge and work through the contradictions in essays. The nature of essay writing encourages an emphasis on thinking through, of asking Montaigne's (2012b) question, *'Que sais-je?* What do I know?' – it is an emphasis on the act rather than the final product.

VIII

I'm really good at starting things: I've started many writing, knitting, gardening, home improvement, and service projects. I find, though, that I hate the thought of coming to an end of most of these attempts (dissertation writing notwithstanding); I suspect that this desire to start without ending is a large reason why I am so attracted to essays, and it is also why I rely on essaying as a pedagogical strategy in my classes. It involves all the joy of starting without the mourning that comes when something has ended, because we can never really stop essaying on a topic once we've started. 'Show me what you are thinking, why you are thinking it, and how you got here,' I often say in conferences with students. 'Help me essay alongside you in this text; remember, though, that there is no such thing as a finished text, only a text with a deadline.'

IX

If we focus on the *act* of 'essaying' – of exploring a topic and journeying through the composing process – rather than focusing on the resulting *object* known as 'the essay,' I believe the essay can become a useful genre to teach in a variety of writing courses. Essaying allows instructors and students to reconsider how and why they compose texts. Focusing on essaying as a verb provides a venue through which student writers can not only explore unfamiliar topics but also become more aware of how they function as writers: the resulting discussions of process can be especially useful when discussing multimodal texts and the multiple literacies our students bring to the classroom. If writing assignments focused on the act of essaying, though, students could then 'show their work,' as they are often asked to do in math classes, because 'What happened to the writer isn't what matters; what matters is the larger sense that the writer is able to make of what happened' (Shields, 2011: 41–42). What's more, using essays as a space to work through contradictions also provides instructors a site from which to encourage discussions of invention, process, and the chaotic nature of writing, which can help students better understand how they create texts in a variety of rhetorical situations, for a variety of forms. As one of my students said after taking an essay writing class with me:

> [W]riting is a process: you learn that biking. You learn how to ride a bike. You learn how, you know? And you learn how to bake a cake. But I never really saw writing as a process. Yeah, I saw it as drafts and editing, that sort of thing, but it's a lot more than just drafting. From start to finish, it's a process. And it's a constant process ... and just recently, I learned that reading is a process, comprehension is a process. I HAD NO IDEA. And so, you know, the entire world's a process. (Landrum-Geyer, 2010: 135–136)

X

Recently, I read David Shields' (2011) *Reality Hunger: A Manifesto*, which is a nonfiction text that's been generating a lot of buzz in the creative nonfiction/essay/literary communities since it came out in 2011. The gist of Shields' (2011) argument is this: we are desperate for reality primarily because the lines between reality and fiction have become so blurred in literature and television – almost every medium, genre, or form – that we've become accustomed to accepting a poor copy of reality as reality itself. Of course, reality is contextual and ephemeral; my reality is not your reality, and each or our realities is influenced by what we read/watch/listen to/play/talk about/etc. This fact leads into another aspect of Shields' (2011: 209) text: he is loath to cite where the quotations in the text come from because, as he puts it, 'reality cannot be copyrighted.' In other words, there are so many influences that shape us (and which we shape right back), and those influences have influences, that we cannot always remember where the inspiration came from – what's important, though, is that it did inspire us, and we shouldn't be afraid to follow the inspiration – in writing, music, film, life. This is why plagiarism becomes a more complicated cultural construct that we like to admit in school settings. What's more, Shields (2011) repeatedly admits to preferring shorter nonfiction texts instead of novels, especially essays (in the

Montaignian 'attempt' or 'journey' vein) to novels because, in his estimation, it is the grappling with our personal realities – the meditations, reflections, philosophical meanderings – that matter, not the faithfulness to rendering details exactly as they happened. I wouldn't go so far as to say the novel is dead or that we no longer need fiction (and I'm struggling to decide where exactly Shields lands in this discussion), but I think this text speaks to the importance of essaying.

XI

In a February 2013 opinion column for *The New York Times*, Phillip Lopate explores the benefits of essay writing as a mode of thinking through the world around us. The column, titled 'The essay, an exercise in doubt,' is short but clear: 'At bottom,' writes Lopate (2013), 'we are deeply unsure and divided, and the essay feasts on doubt.' Lopate (2013) goes on to explain, while channeling Theodor Adorno, 'The essay's job is to track consciousness; if you are fully aware of your mind you will find your thoughts doubling back, registering little peeps of ambivalence or disbelief.' It's the awareness of process that I find most important as a teacher: historically, the essay has been seen as a genre that invites writers to write about writing. The power of essay writing goes beyond writing about writing, though. Essaying is a process in and of itself. It's a way of thinking that allows the writer to see his or her progress/process, which can be, as a student once told me, a 'critical epiphany' (Landrum-Geyer, 2010: 150) for writers who have not thought about their processes before.

XII

Sometimes I worry that I am falling into the long-denigrated navel gazing that is often associated with personal essay writing, and I grow concerned that I am encouraging that same potential for narcissism in my students. So what if my student can create an engaging essay about his final football game? What does that matter when it comes to living life as an engaged, responsible citizen? These questions, concerns, worries, are my essays as I journey along, reconsidering my pedagogical choices. I can only hope that my essaying about my teaching will model a framework for thinking to my students. Because a final football game can have larger significance if investigated from as many angles as possible – if, that is, the writer essays while composing his essay.

XIII

I don't mean to suggest that 'the essay' is the only thing we should be teaching in a composition classroom. There are many genres that students should experience in academic settings, and the number of genres grows daily as our ways of communicating with each other morph and change. I do believe that essays should be a genre that we re-consider in the classroom. Often, when a teacher tells a student to write an essay, he or she is really asking for a specialized subgenre – the academic essay. Occasionally, the teacher is asking for that age-old classroom genre, the theme. Very rarely do instructors ask students to create essays of the sort that actually live and breathe outside of classroom walls. The essay is, in fact, an organic genre – one that sprang from a need centuries ago, and one that has managed to stick around by adapting and evolving alongside its surroundings. When we misname the genre we ask students to create, we risk cutting off the natural progress of that form; despite the misuse of the word 'essays' in classrooms since the 19th century, though, actual essays – in all their wandering glory – have managed to continue on, pushing their way through, often under the radar of writers and educators. Essays haven't gone anywhere, despite our best efforts (and despite news to the contrary), because the life of an essay depends on the act of essaying. And we need to embrace that act in the classroom in order to help our students better understand the who/what/when/where/why/how of their writing(s).

XIV

'And I shall essay to be.' (Shields, 2011: 158)

Note

(1) Admittedly, there are many writers who can be considered precursors to Montaigne as essayists: In D'Agata's Table of Contents for *Lost Origins of the Essay*, Seneca, Plutarch, Theophrastus, and T'ao Ch'ien are all listed as potential essay fore-parents due to the ways in which they composed philosophical dialogues, treatises, and historical writings that included reflection on how the authors' personal positions fit into the larger historical narrative.

References

Atkins, G.D. (1990) The return of/to the essay. *ADE Bulletin* 961, 11–18.
Boetcher Joeres, R. (1993) The passionate essay: Radical feminist essayists. In R. Boetcher Joeres and E. Mittman (eds) *Politics of the Essay* (pp. 151–171). Indianapolis: Indiana University Press.

Boetcher Joeres, R.E. and Mittman, E. (ed.) (1993) *The Politics of the Essay: Feminist Perspectives*. Bloomington: Indiana University Press, 14.
Butrym, A.J. (ed.) (1989) *Essays on the Essay: Redefining the Genre*. Athens: University of Georgia Press.
D'Agata, J. (ed.) (2009) *The Lost Origins of the Essay*. Saint Paul, MN: Graywolf Press.
Devitt, A. (2004) *Writing Genres*. Carbondale, IL: Southern Illinois University Press.
'Essay', *Oxford English Dictionary*. See http://www.oed.com.libnet.swosu.edu/view/Entry/64471?isAdvanced=false&result=2&rskey=ff8rf1&; (accessed February 2013).
Hardison, O.B. (1989) Binding Proteus: An essay on the essay. In A. Butrym (ed.) *Essays on the Essay: Redefining the Genre* (pp. 11–28). Athens: University of Georgia Press.
hooks, b. (1999) *Remembered Rapture: The Writer at Work*. New York: Henry Holt.
Landrum-Geyer, D. (2010) Excavating the essay: A generic approach to understanding invention in the composition classroom. PhD dissertation, Miami University.
Lopate, P. (ed.) (1995) *Art of the Personal Essay*. New York: Anchor Books.
Lopate, P. (2013) 'The essay, an exercise in doubt.' *The New York Times*, opinion column, 16 February. See http://opinionator.blogs.nytimes.com/2013/02/16/the-essay-an-exercise-in-doubt/ (accessed February 2013).
Montaigne, M.d. (2012a) 'Of glory.' In D. Widger (ed.) *Project Gutenberg's The Essays of Michel de Montaigne*, online archive, 2012. See http://www.gutenberg.org/dirs/3/6/0/3600/3600-h/3600-h.htm (original work published 1572) (accessed February 2013).
Montaigne, M.d. (2012b) 'Apology for Raimond Sebond.' In D. Widger (ed.) *Project Gutenberg's The Essays of Michel de Montaigne*, online archive, 2012. See http://www.gutenberg.org/dirs/3/6/0/3600/3600-h/3600-h.htm (original work published 1572) (accessed February 2013).
Shields, D. (2011) *Reality Hunger: A Manifesto*. New York: Vintage Books.

2 Eat Your Spinach! Why a Blend of Personal and Academic Discourses Matter

Sara Burnett

Of any paper a student will write in a composition course, the most dreaded and the most weighted assignment is the academic research paper. To be proficient, a student must prove that he or she can: diligently study a subject matter; investigate, synthesize and evaluate sources; form an 'original' and cogent argument; and write a lengthy, clear paper with proper documentation which reassures the reader (the teacher) that there is no plagiarism. Under no circumstances should the first-person voice be involved. In fact, it would be better to hollow out the writing voice into something that resembles overcooked blanched spinach (if spinach can be used here as a metaphor because like spinach, this research paper is supposed to be good and healthy). Good for the student to write and endure and good for the teacher because there will always be something to correct. Why then do we, as teachers, wonder why we get saddled with a sack of limp, hard-to-swallow spinach to grade? How does the college research paper become the paper students least want to write, and the paper teachers least want to read?

We know what really happens. Even if teachers and students have good intentions for the research project, the truth is students will likely start the weekend before by skulking over to the library bemoaning cruel fate. They will dip into a few books or articles to retrieve some quotes out of context, string them together with a few sentences that sound erudite, and attempt to spice it up with a conclusion that is just an introduction reheated. The final embellishment is slapping on a pretentious title with a colon, like a slab of butter, as if it could give the paper real flavor. The truth is also, of course, that some students have worked very hard to choose sources, to take meticulous notes, and to write in a language that does not seem to fit well with what they are trying to say. The title alone might have taken them an hour to write.

What we have leftover from students and teachers is the same – a bitter taste for the academic research paper. It is a distant cry from the kind of paper designed to foster intellectual curiosity, to teach students how to research effectively, to demonstrate creative problem-solving and to make an original argument. To receive that kind of research paper, a teacher must be interested in teaching research and writing as a multi-step, recursive process of thinking, discovering, and making meaning and students must be vested in researching their topic and writing about it. To receive that kind of research paper, we must broaden what constitutes academic writing to be more meaningful for students.

When we allow for more blending of genres and discourses in an academic research paper, we create possibilities and access for real learning and writing to occur beyond the performative act of essay writing. When a student feels he or she is writing to fulfill an assignment, the research paper amounts to little more than an exercise, quickly produced and quickly forgotten. As David Bartholomae (1985: 403) writes in 'Inventing the University,' every time we ask a student to write for us, we ask the student to invent the university for the occasion. The student must adopt not only the academic language, but also 'the peculiar ways of knowing, selecting, evaluating, reporting, concluding, and arguing that define the discourse of our community,' a community privileged with voice and power that the student may not have been exposed to or have access to. In the classroom power dynamic, the teacher acts as the active giver/keeper of knowledge and the student acts as the passive receiver of knowledge. There is smaller range of opportunities for authentic engagement with texts when the paper is merely an invention for the occasion.

No matter how you define academic writing, it is always a response to texts, and as Joseph Harris (2006: 2) writes in *Rewriting: How to Do Things with Texts*, 'we expect a respondent to add something to what is being talked about ... to add to what has already been said.' Blending genres allows for a greater variety of ways whereby a student can delve into and react to text(s). It does not mean lowering standards and accepting poor substitutes for scholarly research and writing. Rather, it means lifting privileged barriers so students can access and respond to texts with greater ease, flexibility, and authority. It means viewing student as creators *and* receivers of knowledge. Blending writing is akin to the original intention of freshmen English, as defined by Sharon Crowley (1998: 54): 'to equip students with cultural capital that would accrue in polite society from their knowledge about America's literary heritage, and to give them *widely* accepted standards against which they could measure and develop their own good taste [italics mine].' The goal is not only to equip students for success in the university, but *outside* of the university as well. A specialized academic discourse may not serve students as well unless we broaden the terms of academic discourse.

Experience tells me, however, that merely allowing for more genres to constitute academic writing will not automatically produce scholarly writing or critical thinking in our students. There will still be the student who procrastinates or does not take the paper seriously and the student who tries too hard to speak in academic jargon. In addition to opening up what constitutes the research paper, students need two things to guide them in writing and searching: motivation and scaffolding. They need to be shown the moves that matter, as Gerald Graff writes in *They Say/I Say: The Moves That Matter in Academic Writing*, but they also *have to want to make* that move. Though you can scaffold material appropriately, the ways 'of knowing, selecting, evaluating, reporting, concluding and arguing' that Bartholomae (1985: 403) outlines, I have yet to find a method to instruct motivation. Motivation is intrinsic; it can't be forced, but I am suggesting it can be coerced – a teacher can make the paper matter to the student.

The heart of an academic research paper is inquiry. Writing for the sake of performance does not represent authentic inquiry. We need to bring back the obvious, but often overlooked element of research – the search. Ken Macrorie (1988: 14) writes in *The I-Search Paper* that the purpose of such a paper is not to state what has been stated, but to conduct a meaningful 'search to fulfill a need, not that the teacher imagined for them, but one they feel themselves.' Until a student's curiosity is peaked, until a student has a burning desire to find an answer or to solve a problem, they are not engaged with the search and have little reason to write with purpose.

Experience-based writing offers a way to make the process more engaging for the student and will provide more interesting reading. If a student can relate to text(s) on a personal level and can speak with a voice of authority on a subject matter, then the writing generally improves. At the very least, the student is critically thinking, reflecting, and responding authentically. It is much closer to the intent of academic writing than the deadened mimicked prose that often obfuscates meaning and learning. When we rely on only one mode of academic discourse, we have to ask what other discourses are silenced as a result? As Candace Spigelman (2004: 24) states in 'What is Personal Academic Writing?,' 'some compositionists now assert that personal writing, when adequately theorized, is consistent with critical and political efforts to "vocalize" previously silenced voices.' When we broaden the terms of academic writing, we open ways for these voices to speak and be heard. By focusing on the personal, we allow room for the student to subjectively and objectively reflect on his or her role in meaning making – the writing and the writer matter. The subjective part is the student's experience, while the research and writing constitute an objective part (insofar as any statement is completely objective). Taken together, the blending of the subjective and objective enriches and deepens understanding.

When experience-based writing leans too subjectively, however it carries concerns. An important distinction noted by Spigelman (2004: 24) is that this type of personal writing must be 'adequately theorized.' She aligns herself with Harris in this regard. Harris (2006: 10) is drawn to teaching students writing drawn to 'public life,' an 'intellectual prose ... about texts and ideas, culture and politics, that while associated with the academy, is not confined to it, that seeks instead to address a broader and more public set of issues and readers.' Personal academic writing therefore should not be confused with personal narrative, memoir, auto ethnographic writing, or opinion-based argument. Nor should personal academic writing be confused with an either/or stance: either you write in an academic voice in one section and personal voice in another. This is not a true blending of genres, although it is possible and even likely that a less experienced writer may begin with this clear distinction between the two in the paper.

When I taught a personal academic research paper in my classroom, students were initially confused with how much of their voice and experience should they bring into the paper and how much research should they include. This is a great confusion for a student to struggle with. I want my student asking these types of questions every time they sit down to write; that is to say, how much of what I write is subjectively-based? How much of what I write is objectively-based? There is no one answer and I do not pretend as their teacher to have one. We discuss possibilities together in conferences, in small groups, and as a class. In such a way, I am no longer the only active giver of knowledge and my students are not the passive recipients. We participate together in constructing knowledge, which displaces some of the power dynamic and allows for more opportunities to discuss and demystify writing. Teachers are better able to emphasize writing as a process in all its murkiness and infinite possibilities.

What my students' questions also underscore is that motivation and freedom to explore will not necessarily produce high quality academic writing. As Margaret Kantz (1990: 85) reminds us in 'Helping Students Use Textual Sources Persuasively,' a writer can handle only so many tasks at a time and writing a rhetorical argument may ask students to read at a higher level of difficulty, utilize task management skills and to plan effectively. I scaffold critical skills that still need to be taught such as how to research, analyze and respond originally to texts, as well as how to organize a complex argument and document sources, but since this paper begins with personal experience, some of the content and tasks are familiar already. This previous knowledge lessens the outcome of creating an academic-sounding, incoherent voice. Books like *They Say/I Say* offer students templates and advice on appropriating some phrases of academic language, that when used correctly are powerful ways to augment their arguments and ease into using academic discourse without overloading or confusing meaning. Students will be less encumbered by *how* they say their ideas, and may put more importance on the *originality* of *what* they say. Once a student is motivated, they are in a better position to figure out not only the appropriate blend of personal and academic voice, but also to struggle with unfamiliar tasks in a way that is good for them like eating a healthy, tasty side of well-prepared spinach.

Eventually with practice and scaffolding, students become more comfortable, but a successful paper may not happen on the first try. There is a good chance a student might write from engrained routines of summarizing sources, but the student will begin to think creatively and to appropriate the academic skills necessary to enter the academic conversation. New ways of thinking and writing take time to develop into habits. The most engaging contemporary writers are often those who blend professional, academic, cultural and more colloquial styles of writing to advantage their purpose. They are the 'intellectual prose' writers Harris (2006: 10) refers to who write in the *New Yorker* or *Harper's* magazines. A personal academic research paper is one example of how blending genres can empower and enable a student to write with a voice that wants to be read. In fact, writers who blend successfully are in a unique power position, because they are able to have their writing resonate on personal and intellectual levels to broad audiences. They are using real voice, and while real voice is difficult to determine, Peter Elbow (1981: 65) defines it well: 'real voice is not the sound of *individual personality* redolent with vibes, it is the sound of *a meaning* resonating because the individual consciousness of the writer is somehow fully behind or in tune with or in participation with that meaning.' It is writing that is powerful for what it says and how it says it. It is also more pleasing and enticing to read, write and teach than bland, overcooked spinach.

References

Bartholomae, D. (1985) Inventing the university. In M. Rose (ed.) *When A Writer Can't Write: Studies in Writer's Block and Other Composing-Process Problems* (pp. 403–415). New York: Guilford Press.

Crowley, S. (1998) The invention of freshmen english. In *Composition in the University: Historical and Polemical Essays* (pp. 46–78). Pittsburgh: University of Pittsburgh Press.

Elbow, P. (1981) How to get power through voice. In *Writing with Power: Techniques for Mastering the Writing Process* (pp. 62–67). London: Oxford University Press.

Graff, G. and Birkenstein, C. (2006) *They Say/I Say: The Moves That Matter in Academic Writing*. New York: W.W. Norton.

Harris, J. (2006) *Rewriting: How to Do Things with Texts*. Logan, UT: Utah State University Press.

Kantz, M. (1990) Helping students use textual sources persuasively. *College English* 52 (1), 74–91.

Macrorie, K. (1988) *The I-Search Paper: Revised Edition of Searching and Writing*. Portsmouth, NH: Heinemann.

Spigelman, C. (2004) What is personal academic writing? In *Personally Speaking: Experience as Evidence in Academic Discourse* (pp. 1–28). Carbondale: Southern Illinois University Press.

3 Writing by Creation, with Response, in Experience

Graeme Harper

Has much about the teaching of writing been wrong? For example, has much that has been achieved by writing students in college writing classes been achieved because we human beings are a creative species that uses words to communicate, not because of the pedagogies that have been employed? Certainly, much about writing teaching in universities and colleges in the USA and other countries is in essence about something other than writing. In fact, some of it is barely about writing at all.

Lovers of classical rhetoric might assume I am attempting some half-developed version of *apophasis or paralipsis* here, but I am not. Plainly stated, the teaching of writing when associated with what we most often call 'creative writing' has labored to develop pedagogies that have much to do with writing at all and has found itself defending positions about the discipline of Creative Writing that have become increasingly dubious, increasingly indefensible. It has stuck often with these, against logic and evidence and against the importance of establishing more engaged and productive pedagogies for teaching people to write creatively.

Before moving to consider what teaching strategies might better prevail, let us stop a moment and consider the positive and negative aspects of the much that has gone before. The problem lies in a struggle to understand and address what it is that we have been, and should be, teaching. This problem can be approached along three avenues of discussion.

First, we need to separate the ideal of teaching someone to become a published writer and the ideal of teaching someone writing. Publishing and writing are not the same thing and the modes, methods and attitudes adopted in one are not always appropriate to the other.

From around the 18th century until around the end of the 20th century the centrality of the publishing industries – even in the USA where medium-sized publishers have flourished, comparatively, in and around universities and in many of the States (compared, that is, to the United Kingdom which has had a more difficult time with such devolved publishing) – and this centralized system of publishing has meant that when writing teaching associated itself with a successful result it did so by suggesting publication as a yardstick and publication of a certain, often centralized, type. The fact that 'learning writing' and 'being published by a publishing house' are not, and have never been, the same thing has not stopped writing teaching developing everything from course publicity to course structures based on the notion that being published defines a level of learning.

Of course, it has to be said that it would be disingenuous to suggest there isn't *some* relationship between a level of learning and the possibilities of publishing when it comes to the teaching of any kind of writing. This is as clear as, say, the fact that a good musician will likely find a career as a performer or a good swimmer will likely win a swimming race. But it is incorrect to suggest a direct relationship between learning writing and publishing and it is concerning when pedagogies are suggested that make such a direct relationship between the core of writing teaching and writing learning strategies. Publishing is publishing – based in the market for products not experiences of making the work or works. Writing is largely the experiences of making something with words. Creative writing, while often associated with various forms of creative artifact with various forms of market identity and market expectation, is still writing – and writers spend most of their lives in what can be called *the event of writing*, not in the aspect of products or marketable material artifacts.

Since the end of the 20th century these points have been even more pressing because centralized publishing is now part of history. While it is true that the infrastructure of the publishing and bookselling industries has endeavored to keep control of modes and methods of disseminating works of writing the fact is that, since the middle of the final decade of the 20th century, if someone wishes to write (producing works of creative writing or any kind of writing) and distribute their work electronically via the World Wide Web – if they do so without reference to the financial, distribution or even critical apparatus of the publishing and bookselling industries as we have known them – then they can do so and do so increasingly easily. There has not been as big a challenge to the publishing industries, as we know them, as the current challenge – not since the birth of publishing. Combining print-on-demand, e-publishing, new modes of textual literary, new ideals of interactivity, new concepts of ownership of intellectual property, new creative and critical knowledge and new skills connected with these, new methods of lay and professional reference and response, what we have seen (and are continuing to see and feel) is a revolution in how we receive writing and the works of writing. Not in more than 300 years has it been so obvious that learning writing and being 'published' (whatever that might be seen to now mean) were ever only partly related – but that change or confirmation, however we feel inclined to define it, is only one part of this current revolution.

Second, when considering the positive and negative aspects of the much that has gone before in the teaching of writing we need to recognize that much that has been done in the name of teaching creative writing has in truth been done in the teaching of appreciating literature. One set of actions is not the same as the other set of actions.

You will read books by D.G. Myers (2007) and by Mark McGurl (2011) and others about the history of Creative Writing programs in American Higher Education. Both Myers and McGurl are excellent literary historians and whether my own historiography would begin at identical places to one or other of them is not relevant here. The fact is, both they and others have explored very well the formal identification and identity of Creative Writing programs in colleges and universities in the USA. Even the casual reader of such works will notice the relationship between the growth and development, and indeed passionate engagement with the support for and advancement of an American literary culture and the support for and advancement of creative writing teaching in American higher education. The arguments of Myers and McGurl and others is far more sophisticated and interesting than that makes their work sound, but at the core of things being reported and history being revealed is a belief in and commitment to an American literary culture.

With this in mind, it make perfect sense that the teaching of creative writing 'took off' in the USA in a way that was distinctive to it, while in the United Kingdom (and its closely related former colonies too) the discipline of Creative Writing in universities had a somewhat slower start. Forming a strong – a commanding – literary culture was at the heart of the embracing of classes in literature and is at the heart of the relationship between contemporary America's belief in writing teaching in higher education. The history is indeed far more complicated, but suffice it to say that this fact is plain.

This leads to my second background point: much about teaching writing in the English language (driven as it has been by the size and strength of the American interest) has not been about teaching writing at all but about coming to appreciate, pursue and promote literature. There is (and has not been) anything wrong with doing this, of course. In fact, those of us who believe passionately in the importance of literature can celebrate the fact that this has occurred. However, the teaching of appreciating literature, of coming to understand and explore literature, of believing in a literary culture, is not the teaching of writing – even if models of good literary artifacts, spectacular literary artifacts, play a role in the teaching of writing. Thus, though it is sensitive to many and tenaciously resisted to a considerable number, it has to be said that to teach the understanding of literature is not to teach writing. The two things are not the same.

The third and final stop on this background journey combines our visits to the two previous ports of critical call. Thirdly, that is, the teaching of writing has most often located itself in the material artifacts of completion. That is, not only has this informed a kind of pedagogic *tradition of materiality* – it has led by intention and understanding – it has led to teaching practices that have ignored the clearly activity-related nature of writing and have assessed, promoted and supported positions related to objects not events of writing. What might be called additionally a set of 'completionist' beliefs have determined much in this, beliefs in the linearity of a movement toward completed literary works, and the reality of writerly making and understanding has been either unrecognized or ignored.

So, for example, a Creative Writing program will require a submission of a portfolio of work to determine entrance into the program. But if this portfolio of work was to include a collection of notes and draft pieces of writing, doodles and scribbles, for example, would it be well received? If someone was to submit a work published by a well-known literary publishing house and another person submit a story they had completed but never published which of these submissions, in truth, would be better received by those selecting students for the program?

Writing is not merely its artifacts, writing is the acts and actions that writers undertake; writing is the creative and critical activities with which we writers explore the world and ideas and emotions and cultures and ourselves. The evidence of this is vast and individual and often unstructured, often only partly teleological, often not chronological, often layered and synthesized or even tumbled into place. But what if someone showed that fact when they submitted their work to be assessed in a university undergraduate program and someone else submitted a story published neatly in a well-known literary journal – which student's work would be graded more highly?

The practices of teaching writing have often been associated with a materiality and a sense of material result both of which have very little to do with the actual practices of writing and, in doing so and with due recognition of those who have pursued this because of a belief in the importance of literature, this focus on materiality has prevented a better engagement with the teaching and learning of writing as it was it can be, and in terms of what it can achieve. In essence, we have touted in course design and program structures and in the ways in which we have defined success in learning writing often exactly what we know *not to be* at the heart of the human practice of creative writing.

Many of us enter our fields in academe with the hope that we will build relationships and even find friends among our colleagues. While this might not be our primary focus, we like to believe that we will at least find likeminded people with whom we might advance our fields and with whom we might, indeed, share ideas and ideals. I fear, in what I have now said that I might have fewer friends now than I did 1500 words or so ago. I admit to some regret in that, because those who would disagree with my opening analysis have indeed also been those who have helped to empower and propel the discipline of Creative Writing – over the past 50 or 60 years, in particular. But I must, as I would with any friend or colleague, be at least as truthful as I am supportive and though writing learning and teaching has been increasingly popular we must address the realities of how we approach the teaching of (creative) writing. This will not be to the detriment of literature or to the demise of a belief in the beauty of the finished material artifacts of creative writing; this will not be to deny the cultures of the literary or the identities of those who find in literature something of their joy and expression of self and place and experience. But literature is not creative writing; publishing is not writing; finished material artifacts are not writing. These things are laudable and supportable and wonderful, but writing is human acts and actions, and to develop the teaching of writing we must now – now even more so because the world has changed to alert us more obviously to this – embrace approaches to the teaching of writing that make the most of its truthfully *human* dimensions.

Begin then with the concrete notion that writing is often inconcrete. Writing consists of abstractions and notions as well observations and facts; it bears itself in the realm of human dispositions, both individual ones and the attitudes of cultures, places and times. Writing is thus a synthesis of knowledge and understanding, feeling and analysis. It comes about because of situations and involves what I have called 'situational knowledge' (Harper, 2012: 107). Bring this to bear in our teaching and we approach a positive pedagogy for writing. Try this along these lines:

If form is defined by function, then explore the forms of human habitation that relate our human engagement with the world around us. A home, for example, can be a metaphor for a narrative; a journey in a car can be analogy for the reading of writerly intention in a poem. Treat the evidence of human creative and critical engagement as fluid and open. Do not fix a class on an object that is identified only by its material condition but make that writing class a place of aspect and attitude, give those individuals in it the goal of revelation and allow them the room to reveal to themselves the ways their writerly situation might or might not be enhanced by their evolving knowledge. By 'situation' I am of course referring to the *event* that is writing.

Do not assume text defines text. It is post-event to pick out a novel in its material form and suggest this novel defines novel writing. For sure, admiration of the artifact might return the admirer to the place, time and person of its composition but that material object is several steps away from the writer who created it, from the event of the writing. Have you ever wondered why writers' readings can slip into a strangely awkward set of rhetorical movements that appear to bear little relationship to the supposed emotional and dispositional connection of writer to their final work? This is because the writer is only partly connected to the object; what they are mostly connected to is its composition and to the compositional events this entailed. Assuming text defines text assumes object defines action – this is far from the case.

Introduce into the writing class objects of all kinds, form and function come in many materially evidential ways; but make the exploration of experiences more important still. Give the class active recognition for active behavior. Writing is action, and the pedagogies of inaction do nothing to improve it; the occasional focus on the post-event should not take away from the event itself.

Query reflection, question reflexivity. Reflection, by its very nature, is static. You cannot stop something still – as Henri Bergson (1911) once noted – without changing its nature. Reflection involves contemplation. Contemplation is not entirely negative, because the mind requires time, the mind requires opportunity, and the rushed life does not always provide this. But to solely reflect on work, to contemplate it as part of a method of understanding it, means denying the fluidity of the human narrative. The illogic of such denial cannot go unnoticed because everything we do in our lives involves kinds of movements, large and small. To reflect does not. Some might say that the positives of such reflection outweigh the negatives – but imagine those positives were incorporated into a wider set of actions, rather than sitting here on their own. That would be better. This we'll explore. Before that, however, what is wrong with reflexivity?

Reflexivity involves circularity. Considering, assessing, reapplying. The nature of this is said to thus evolve learning. To be reflexive is seen to be being applied, being engaged – because in being reflexive things learnt are applied to things considered. However, reflexivity misses the nature of writing which does not involve simple circularities, or benefit from self-referentiality. The 'creative,' if ever that word has best described human actions, operates by means of networks and associations, it is nothing if it is not open and incomplete. That is not to say reflexivity cannot be part of writing, only that it is incorporated into a wider set of actions. This we'll explore now.

Both reflection and reflexivity are incorporated in critical response. Critical responsive understanding (Harper, 2013: 283–285) is understanding to the task at hand – that is, it is situational – and it is understanding aiming to produce actions, and potential artifacts as well. To be critically responsive is to use reflection within a wider event; it is to engage in reflexivity but not as an end but in set of epistemological activities that are as fluid as they are significant.

A writing class, therefore, needs to be encouraged and supportive to be critically responsive. Responsiveness is not just one action but many. It is not just the act of responding to a material object or an observation or something that is done. It is the nature of being in the actions rather than outside of them. It is, after all, impossible to respond to something if you are not connected somehow to it. Responsiveness, thus, is human connection and it complex and intentional and at the heart of why we value writing.

Finally, teaching writing should always seek to empower, not disempower. Writing – that is writing inclusive of the specific instance of what we most often call 'creative writing' – is one of humankind's most ancient arts. It has appeared in most cultures and some point in history and has been enthusiastically embraced. Once, focusing here only on Western history, everyone in any location engaged in the arts, and the idea of 'the artist' would have seemed very strange – after all, we were all artists in our communities. As occupational names were established more in relation to industrial models so 'artist' or, specifically 'writer' became a declaration of occupation; but it should never have been devolved from the shared human interest in writing itself. To return to that positive aspect of our engagement with writing we need to teach that each and every action and result of writing can have value.

Place in a writing class the clear provision of value through human context and you place a positive force for learning right at the center of the learning environment. Make drafts, for example, a valuable part of learning (the words often heard around colleges 'Oh, it's just a draft.' reflect our previous obsession with completion not human action). Empower observations, ideas and the expression of thoughts that do not directly relate to the making of texts. Observations, ideas and expressed thoughts are verbal equivalents of actions and bring to the class the energy for the engine of the writing event. Take journeys, use movement, encourage getting beyond the frame of the room – a writing classroom defined by the shapes of 19th century classrooms (as many contemporary classrooms still maintain) is nothing more than a metaphor for restrictions.

That writing teaching is able to display certain kinds of evidence to suggest its historical successes, should not prevent us from rethinking what it can achieve. It is more difficult to question the successful on the basis of the nature of its perceived success than it is to question the unsuccessful by using evidence of its failure. But we must be truthful in our engagement with this considerable human practice. We must build on what we know to progress through what we can find out further. Teaching writing by engagement with writerly event and critical response and with the acts and actions of writing itself will enhance the achievements of learners and teachers alike, and bring to the fore what it is about this art and this form of communication which excites us so much.

References

Bergson, H. (1911) *Creative Evolution*. London: Holt.
Harper, G. (2012) Creative writing research. In D. Donnelly and G. Harper (eds) *Key Issues in Creative Writing* (pp. 103–115). Bristol: Multilingual Matters.
Harper, G. (2013) Creative writing research. In G. Harper (ed.) *Companion to Creative Writing* (pp. 283–285). Oxford: Blackwell.
McGurl, M. (2011) *The Program Era: Postwar Fiction and the Rise of Creative Writing*. Cambridge: Harvard University Press.
Myers, D.G. (2007) *The Elephants Teach: Creative Writing Since 1880*. Chicago: University of Chicago.

4 Give it a Taste: Serving Creative Writing in Small Doses

Abigail G. Scheg

As a first-year composition instructor, one of the elements of the course that I enjoy the most is that the students typically do not want to take the class. Some students feel that they are poor writers; some have been told in the past by teachers that they were poor writers; some actually do lack important skills to effectively communicate. Students often have many misconceptions about the first-year composition classroom and what it means to write or be a writer (Downs & Wardle, 2007). New college students can also struggle with balancing their personal interests or abilities to write with the new challenges of academic writing expected in the college environment (Lillis, 2001). Preconceived notions about what constitutes 'appropriate college writing,' or one's owns abilities often present challenges for composition instructors and their students.

However the students feel about traditional academic writings, I have found that all students can relate to other types of writing: poetry, music, stories, novels, movies and much, much more. Wendy Bishop explains that students often think of composition as 'an unpleasant task, while creative writing is perceived as more enjoyable' (Bishop, 1990). I do not make it an overt goal of my course, but I do strive to give students the tools to enjoy writing and associate writing with positive elements of themselves. I spend time in my classroom trying to encourage students to write in any way, genre or style that they find to be interesting, whether it is writing poetry, music, lab reports, tweets or text messages. I encourage them to consider *all* of their writing activities as writing without classifying them as 'academic' or 'nonacademic' writing. More specifically, I rarely have students say that they *like* to write, but if you look at their Twitter profile, they have written 56,000 tweets in a year that they have been using Twitter. I try to encourage them to continue writing, even on Twitter, with the reassurance that tweeting does count as writing, even though it may not be one of the genres most traditionally emphasized in college. One of the ways that I try to encourage my students to write is by offering short creative writing assignments with no limitations or wrong answers.

In my traditional first-year composition courses, we have writing benchmarks to hit throughout the semester: cause and effect, compare and contrast, narrative and description, research writing, and more. I have taught first-year writing at six different institutions, all of which required teaching and assessing these very traditional genres of academic writing. Oftentimes, working on these traditional genres does not allow for students to gain confidence in themselves as writers, as many students feel that they do not have the writing skills and experience to successfully plan and execute an academic paper. Likewise, having so many requirements to meet in a traditional writing course does not typically permit an instructor the time and leeway to try creative writing assignments in the classroom. In a typical composition course structured by required institutional assessments, there cannot be a devotion entirely to the creative process. Even though I significantly value the place of creative writing in the classroom, I am required to focus the semester on these traditional genres. Add to that challenge that the word 'poem,' draws significant moans and groans from the students as though they may fall out of their chairs, typically because they don't understand the freedom of it at first. Therefore, students are typically uncomfortable with academic writing because they may be wary of their abilities, and nervous about non-academic writing assignments because they do not consider themselves to be creative writers. So how can we encourage student writers?

I assign my students short doses of creative writing, typically at the beginning and end of class sessions. We do acrostic poems, freewriting, write letters to ourselves, haiku, and many other types of writing. By the end of the semester, students come to enjoy and look forward to these creative writing practices and expressing themselves in a new form. I start early to combat the idea that there are right and wrong answers with their writing.

Two of the types of short, creative writing exercises that I like to have my students try are poetry and freewriting. Poems do not have to rhyme, they do not always have to have a certain number of syllables, and they do not have to be thematically intense. Although many students consider poetry to be impossible to understand or too artistic a genre to work with, I just encourage them to try. With the first few creative writing assignments, students are hesitant. What if someone else's poem rhymes? Will they be made fun of if theirs does not? Are they *allowed* to freewrite about their relationship problems? Can they use swear words in the freewrite? Are they using the right word? Are they going to get a grade for this? Do they have to share this with the rest of the class? Am I going to share this with other people once they turn it in? As time progresses, though, these questions fade away. They can write about anything – good days, bad days, successes, failures, questions, uncertainties, anything. I tell them: Yes, if you're having a no-good very bad day and you need to use a swear word in your freewrite, you certainly are allowed. Just do your best with word choice and expressing your feelings. No, there is no grade assigned to this. No, you do not have to share anything with me or with other students if you do not want to. No, these documents will go straight to my office where I will write notes back to you and then I will promptly return your writing back to you.

As these questions fade away and the semester moves forward, students feel more confident in their writing and want to earn a grade for their creative writing. As they feel more confident, they want to share their writing with me and read it in front of the class. As they share their writing more, they want to improve their writing and they want to be the ones that read their pieces and everyone responds with 'Wow, that was really good.' Slowly, students develop confidence in themselves as writers. There were not grades attached to these brief writing exercises and they were just encouraged to be organic. Some of the writings are strong, others could benefit from revisions, and sometimes students are just rushing through the in-class exercise. Eventually, though, each one of my students develops *something* in which they develop pride.

Sometimes, with permission from the students, I collect everyone's writings, mix them together, and then anonymously read them. In doing this, sometimes the students claim their writings; sometimes they prefer it to stay anonymous. As with the previous parts of these assignments, I stress that there is no right or wrong answer. Some students do not even submit their writing if it is too personal, they do not want it included in the pile, or they do not want it to be read. Some students come up to me after class and share their writing with me one-on-one; some, when doing this, solicit feedback from me on their creative writings. It can be beneficial to share student writing to demonstrate that everybody writes differently; we use different tones, language, rhyme schemes, rhythm and structure. Being exposed to other students' writing develops students' comfort with writing a little bit more because it broadens the circle of acceptability and therefore 'good writing.'

I see the benefits of these short creative exercises as two-fold. One, it slowly builds the students' trust in me and in the classroom environment. While at first they may be hesitant of the process and nervous of ridicule, they quickly learn that there actually were no right or wrong answers on the assignment. When students become more trusting of me as an instructor, they are willing to write more and share more on future assignments. Likewise, when students become more trusting of the classroom environment, they are willing to share more with their classmates', learn from each other in terms of writing and perhaps even personally.

The second positive is that it builds students' confidence that their thoughts and abilities to write are welcome and respected. There are plenty of assignments in my class and others' that provide structure and rigidity in student expectations. Likewise, there are plenty of assignments that offer confusion, challenges, and potential for self-disappointment for students. By offering short creative writing assignments within the first-year composition class, we are giving our students a break from those traditional (and for many students, seemingly insurmountable) assignments to reaffirm their capabilities as unique individuals.

I also consider it a disservice in the first-year composition class to remain incredibly structured in terms of assignments and class times. As an example: a few years ago, when I was teaching at a community college, my classes were knee-deep into the research process for a service-learning project. My first class of the day met at ten in the morning and on this particular day, we were meeting in the library. When I arrived at the library, some students were crying, many were huddled together, and no one was working on their projects. In talking to the students, I learned that another student of the community college was murdered the evening before. Needless to say, our class session was over before it began. In lieu of the research project, I asked that students do a short freewriting exercise and submit it to my mailbox at some point in the day. Some of the class did not know the student who was murdered and reflected upon their 'free day,' the project, or their personal lives. The students that did know him, though, poured their hearts out onto notebook paper until their handwriting became scribbled and illegible.

This is an extreme example of using the immediate situation as a creative writing or composition prompt. However, it gave the students an outlet for their emotions and a willing audience to listen, hear them, and respond to their thoughts and concerns. I could have spoken to the students about their grief and moved forward with the class as I had planned it, but the positive potential of the writing outlet far outweighed the research process for their coursework. Later that week or the next week, I had several students thank me for that opportunity and not in a snide 'Thanks for cancelling class' way, but in a humble and honest way that said 'that was exactly what I needed.' Again, my creative writing assignments are typically not that Earth shattering or even important for the students, but they are a sweet relief from the mundane and sometimes tedious processes of research and academic writings.

I want to be clear on my message: in terms of academic writing requirements, I am one of the 'hard teachers.' In my class, we go to the library and books are still required for research, no matter your topic. Yes, those dusty things on the shelves – as one of my former students referred to them – are required even though we use the internet for everything now. My students accomplish a tremendous amount of research and writing in the class, more work than they sometimes feel is possible to even do in a semester's time. The short creative writing assignments are a way to take much needed breaks from the required writing assignments and to build upon students' trust in themselves, their writing and the course. Sometimes these are reflective assignments that tie directly to the traditional writing assignments of the class; other times they are just presented as a challenge to student writers to try a new genre or discuss a subject that they may not have considered before.

Some examples of short creative and personal writing assignments that my students have completed over the years:

- At the end of the semester, write a letter to yourself at the start of the semester and give yourself some advice.
- At the end of the semester, write a letter to someone who has helped and supported you throughout this semester and *give* that person your letter.
- Write an acrostic poem about midterms using the word 'MIDTERM.' Go ahead. Tell me how you really feel.
- If you could make a birthday present list right now, what would be on it and why?
- Write a haiku about your day.
- Write an acrostic poem using 'GROUNDHOG DAY' as your focus (or, insert any holiday here).

These are short, simple tasks that take up to 15 minutes for the students to complete at the beginning of the course. The appreciation of the students for caring about their thoughts, asking about their days, and supporting them with my individual feedback goes far beyond the class period and even the semester. When my students return to visit, email me semesters or years later and follow up with me, they typically thank me for teaching them the hard stuff like research that they *did* actually have to use in other courses. My students also tell me how much fun they had with writing when they didn't even think that could be possible.

References

Bishop, W. (1990) 'Crossing the lines: On creative composition and composing creative writing'. Presentation, Annual Meeting of the South Atlantic Modern Language Association, Tampa, FL, 15–17 November.

Downs, D. and Wardle, E. (2007) Teaching about writing, righting misconceptions: (Re) Envisioning 'First-year Composition' as 'Introduction to writing studies'. *CCC* 58 (4), 552–584.

Lillis, T.M. (2001) *Student Writing: Access, Regulation, Desire*. London: Routledge Press.

5 Wiggling Between the Forms: A Cross-Genre Approach to Writing

Dustin Michael

My first semester in college I bought a clunky, old Mazda pickup: reliable but bad in snow. It snowed hard one week, and when I came out of the university library after a study group session, I found that the truck had been plowed in and was buried doors-deep in a drift. When I finally dug my way through to it, climbed behind the wheel, and threw it in drive, nothing happened. A slick *ffwwwwwwwrrrr!* rose from the rear tires, but nothing else happened. Snowflakes *ticked*! on the roof like seconds, an irregular measure of time in this pale, cold, frictionless world in which I was trapped. I gunned it. *FFFWWWWRRR!* Nothing. No amount of gunning and revving would make the truck go.

Although it's been years since my truck-in-the-snow incident, I think about it every few months because I'm a writing teacher. The feeling of 'stuckness' students get when they've written all they think they can write about a topic (usually between the second draft and the final version) is the closest thing I know to the memory of those spinning tires on snow. It's not writer's block; there's no barrier impeding the paper's progress, no sense of an obstruction. In fact, it's the opposite. With writer's block, the trouble is that the engine won't start; it's a problem of *not* writing. 'Stuckness' happens when there's writing, but no traction. The writer guns the gas, but the wheels just spin and spin. On the page the ideas stand in place, frozen between the towering white snowdrifts of the margins. Students suffering from 'stuckness' lament that no matter how much they write on their topics or how many examples they list to support their theses, they seem to be simply repeating themselves, unable to advance. 'Stuckness' is when the student essayist who is trying to persuade the local government to further regulate emissions on the town's bus fleet argues that air pollution is harmful to plant life, then goes on to argue that it is harmful to animal life, then mentions that it is harmful to people, her figurative wheels spinning all the while over the same patch of 'air pollution is harmful' ground until at last, unable to recall anything else potentially harmed by air pollution, they skid to a halt.

I'm calling this 'stuckness' because, back when my truck and I were literally stuck in the snow and ice, a big, burly guy in coveralls happened to see me as he was walking his dog and offered to help, and he said he was glad he could 'unstuck' me. Here's how he did it: He got in, put it in reverse, gave a little gas, turned the wheel both ways, then stopped, put it in drive, turned the wheel both ways, stopped, and repeated the whole thing a bunch of times, wiggling this way and that. Every so often he'd lean out the window and yell 'Push!' and I'd push with the hand that wasn't holding his dog. At last, the dog and I watched in astonishment as the guy in coveralls wiggled my truck 'unstuck.'

That 'wiggling' technique is how I help 'unstuck' my composition students when they're writing, and I start it with poetry, namely Wallace Stevens' 'Thirteen Ways of Looking at a Blackbird' (1954). The students are going to 'wiggle' between the forms of poetry and nonfiction, and turn in every direction within those forms until they get traction on an idea and take off moving again. I use the Stevens poem because it's got a wintery kind of feel to it and just seems right. Plus it also has short stanzas students can easily read and quickly access, *and* it does the thing I want my students to do, which is take a whole bunch of mutually exclusive aspects of something (like the items students scrawled in the lists and webs and all the other prewriting exercises weeks before) and not just index them but show them at work – show them *moving*. For the composition pedagogy crowd, this is essentially David Rosenwasser and Jill Stephen's '10 on 1' exercise, in verse: a series of mutually exclusive points providing evidence or analysis on a single subject (Rosenwasser & Stephen, 2006). Their model calls for students to reduce an argument to its elemental particles and examine the many possible relationships between them individually, focusing on one at a time: one item of evidence and ten of its unique aspects, for instance – all on their assertion that discovering ten distinct points about a single issue is preferable to tracing the same point ten times (Rosenwasser & Stephen, 2006). It is a decent pedagogical underpinning for the exercise discussed below, as it explains the basic operation performed by the Stevens poem – the student reading – and mastery of that operation is the primary goal because it will enable students to identify, expand, and advance the inert ideas in their essays.

Briefly, here is the lesson plan: The goals are that composition students learn an effective means by which they can continue developing their drafts, and that they understand ideas are not only mutable across written forms, but that repackaging ideas into different forms (prose to poetry, or vice versa) can reveal insight about a subject that is both unexpected and valuable. The concrete objectives are that students will generate two original texts during this class period through collaborative writing and come away with a 'class poem' and a 'class essay.' As for materials, students need Wallace Stevens' poem, 'Thirteen Ways of Looking at a Blackbird.' In an attempt to avoid copyright issues, I find a collection of Stevens' poetry at the library and have students read aloud and pass it. I do the same for a secondary reading, Michael Finkel's *National Geographic Adventure* piece, 'The Ténéré Desert – 13 Ways of Looking at a Void,' which appears in an edition of *The Best American Travel Writing* series (2002). Of course, students will need pen and paper.

The lesson begins with complaints. Everybody's stuck. They've had their topics for weeks and several rounds of peer edit revisions have all been applied, but somehow, with two or three pages to go, the march of ideas has halted. In my mind, I hear the familiar *ffwwwwwwwrrrr!* of tires spinning on snow.

'Pretend for a moment,' I say, 'that I took away everyone's topic and said, "We're only writing about blackbirds now." How long could you make that essay? How many things could you say about blackbirds?'

'I'd probably start out with the history of blackbirds,' says a male student in the front row. 'Maybe talk about why they're important in today's society, except I don't really think they are.'

'There could be paragraphs on habitat, feeding, mating,' says a female student. 'Boring paragraphs,' chimes another.

'Why would you do that to us?' asks a male student.

'Here,' I say, 'is a poem.' I don't even bother to introduce Stevens, really. If anyone ever *would* ask about him, I might tell the interesting tale of a fight Stevens picked in Key West with a decades-younger Ernest Hemingway, who pretty much took Stevens apart like a composition teacher takes apart a student's sloppy first draft. But nobody ever asks. Besides, this is composition, not creative writing or American literature. In here, a text is a text is an argument.

We take turns reading the stanzas, stumbling through Stevens' words like lost travelers through a wintery woods. 'Equipage' and 'euphony' trip us like stones hidden under snow (Stevens, 1954). Then we read the poem again. We notice things we missed the first time through.

'He's talking like he's from the Bible in that one part,' a female student says.

'It's very cold in this poem,' another declares.

'In that section, it's kind of spooky. It *feels* scary,' says a male student.

'One has a logical fallacy,' says a student who's been paying attention all semester. 'Just because the river moves doesn't mean the blackbird moves too.'

'I think he's using the blackbird as a symbol for love, in a way,'
'Or a symbol for death. These blackbirds are everywhere he goes.'
I tell them I think that is the point. Blackbirds *are* everywhere. Ubiquitous. We pass them without noticing in parks and parking lots. They scramble for our crumbs with the pigeons and sparrows in outdoor cafes. Aside from the often-iridescent sheen of their feathers (and discounting the red-winged, yellow-headed, and tri-colored varieties), they are a dark, monochromatic bird of no remarkable size, song, or habit – a pretty dull subject, one would think. Yet when it comes to vivid, mutually exclusive approaches to that subject, Stevens turns out a baker's dozen.

On the board I write other deliberately pedestrian subjects as the students call them out: pencils, hair, money, cell phones, a bag of rocks. I tell them any subject will work, but we have to decide on just one. I tell them to pick the most boring one. Bag of rocks it is.

'What are some aspects of a bag of rocks?' I ask.

'You can use a bag of rocks as a weapon,' says the marine in the front row.

'They have them for people to use at spas,' offers a student who used to work at a resort.

'What about geologists in the field, getting samples, looking for natural resources?'

'You can buy those decorative candle sets, and there are bags of rocks in there.'

'What about rocks used for measurement in scales?'

'Or the ballast in old ships?'

I am writing these on the board as fast as I can, and soon it's entirely covered with ways of looking at a bag of rocks that range from religious references (rocks carried by members of mobs during public stonings) to scientific definitions (igneous, sedimentary, metamorphic). Noticeably, the class is impressed with how many ideas are up there, especially because the subject was chosen specifically because it was supposed to be a dead-end.

The students to go down the row and choose a perspective to write about, and at the board I cross options out as they get picked. The task now is for each student to write a stanza on the aspect of 'bag of rocks' she or he chose. It doesn't have to rhyme. It doesn't have to be any particular length. After a few minutes, everyone has finished writing and we go down the rows reading our new class poem, 'Twenty-Three Ways of Looking at a Bag of Rocks.' There is laughing and high-fiving. The stuck vehicle of creativity lurches slightly in the snow bank.

Here is the place to segue into the second phase of the lesson. I mention that we've just paid an homage to Wallace Stevens, and that we aren't the first – that there are many literary variations on his 'Thirteen Ways'

(Stevens, 1954) theme, and one I happen to like is Finkel's 'The Ténéré Desert – 13 Ways of Looking at a Void' (2002).The students and I pass the text around, reading aloud how Finkel conducts interviews of residents and travelers in the Sahara, each providing a unique (mutually exclusive) perspective, and a picture of the whole emerges that ends up, like Stevens' poem, greater than the sum of its parts (Stevens, 2002). I tell the students to skip down a few lines from the stanzas they just wrote and to convert their poetry into prose.

'Repackage the thought,' I say. 'Essay it up. Get the idea out and put it in a new container.' A female student asks if she can use the phrasing of one line from her poem in her essay because it surprised her when she wrote it. I tell her that's kind of what I hoped would happen.

In a few minutes, 23 thematically linked stanzas have become 23 paragraphs – disconnected paragraphs sans transitions, of course, but paragraphs nonetheless. This is the moment it hits home, when everyone realizes this collaborative essay they wrote about an impossibly dull subject was not only quick and fun to write, but, if it were assembled and developed, would far exceed the length requirement for the essay assignment they have been spinning their tires on.

That's when they realize their tires are no longer spinning. I see notebook pages fluttering and pens scrawling feverishly. They're 'unstucking' themselves. They've 'wiggled' out. Someone says 'Hey! I got it!' Then someone else says it, too. In my head I hear the sound of spinning tires catching, getting traction, and pulling free.

References

Finkel, M. (2002) The Ténéré Desert – 13 Ways of Looking at a Void. *The Best American Travel Writing*. Boston, New York: Houghton Mifflin.
Rosenwasser, D. and Stephen, J. (2006) *Writing Analytically*. Boston: Thomson Wadsworth.
Stevens, W. (1954) Thirteen Ways of Looking at a Blackbird. *The Collected Poems of Wallace Stevens*. New York: Alfred A. Knopf.

6 Writing to Discover: Creative Nonfiction and Writing Across the Curriculum

Andrew Bourelle

Robert Root and Michael Steinberg (2002: xxv), in the introduction to *The Fourth Genre*, state that creative nonfiction writers 'are those who like to delve and to inquire, to question, to explore, probe, meditate, analyze, turn things over, brood, worry – all which creative nonfiction allows, even encourages' and that the genre 'grants writers permission to explore without knowing where they will end up.' Creative nonfiction writers are both introspective and extrospective: They think critically about themselves but also about the world around them and they use writing not just as a means to *report* this critical thinking, but actually as a method to *do* the critical thinking. Because of its characteristics – informative, veracious, self-reflective, explorative, analytical – creative nonfiction is situated in an ideal position to overlap with the writing in other disciplines.

Writing Across the Curriculum theory tells us that writing in one academic discipline is different than writing in another. The writing produced in the fields of history, biology, or business does not resemble creative nonfiction in format, tone, presentation, etc. However, these disciplines do see the value in thinking and communication that is informative, self-reflective, explorative, etc. Therefore, a genre that explicitly wrestles with these aspects in writing is particularly well suited to teach these pedagogical ideas that are used implicitly in all disciplines.

The nexus of these shared values of writing, what makes creative nonfiction what it is, I would argue, is the genre's underlying emphasis on writing as a means of discovery. Creative nonfiction is a genre that explicitly and consciously embraces the belief that writing can be used to make discoveries. Creative nonfiction scholarship is full of writers discussing how they used writing – during invention, drafting and revisions stages – as a means of thinking about their topics. For example, Patricia Hampl (2002: 262), in her article 'Memory and Imagination,' says, 'It still comes as a shock to realize that I don't write about what I know: I write in order to find out what I know.' This perspective on writing has long been accepted in English fields, particularly in composition and rhetoric, where the idea is referred to as 'writing to learn.' However, such a belief has been a much harder sell in disciplines across the curriculum. Biologists, historians, and scholars in numerous other fields don't necessarily share this view of writing. While writer Donald Murray (1989: 4) says '[w]riting is not thinking reported, it is thinking,' scholars in other fields might not see it that way: they see the act of writing as the transcription of thought, not actually an act in thinking.

In this chapter, I will discuss ways in which creative nonfiction can be used to infuse and invigorate the teaching of writing in other disciplines, bridging the divide between English studies and writing across the curriculum. Writing, I will argue, is integrally and inseparably tied to thinking. Using writing as a means of thinking and a way of making discoveries is present in all disciplines, though this presence is often implicit or unconscious. I argue that because creative nonfiction explicitly embraces this characteristic of writing, the genre can be a valuable way to help students understand their own writing processes and develop critical-thinking skills – and therefore has value to disciplines outside of English studies.

I will first describe the WAC perspectives that will serve as the theoretical framework. Then I will describe the composition- and WAC-based concept of writing to learn, and I will redefine or re-envision this idea with a broader interpretation than it's sometimes given. I will compare writing to learn, as I define it, with the creative nonfiction-based idea of writing to discover. Ultimately, I will show that writing to discover valued explicitly in creative nonfiction supports the philosophy of writing to learn – writing as thinking – present unconsciously or consciously throughout writing, regardless of the discourse community.

Writing Across the Curriculum

Good writing is subjective and dependent upon context. Good writing is only good within its discourse community. Take an English professor's article from an academic journal and exchange it with a journalist's news article written on deadline. The English professor might accuse the journalist of using simplistic prose, a basic vocabulary, and no discernable style; the journalist might accuse the English professor of being unnecessarily verbose, using a circuitous organization and having a pretentious tone. When those same articles would be considered by the authors' peers, however, the texts might be lauded as excellent examples of good writing within those discourse communities. The same could be said about comparing various other documents written in practically every discipline.

Learning to write in those discourse communities is much like learning to speak, either initially, as a child, or like an adult learning a second or third language. It requires immersion. Writing is inexorably linked to speaking and thinking, and in order to think, speak, and write like a journalist, a biologist, an English professor, or a member of any number of other academic or professional communities, it takes an immersion into that community.

The work of Lev Vygotsky (1986) supports the theory of immersion into discourse communities. Vygotsky describes writing as 'the most elaborate form of speech' (Vygotsky, 1986: 242). 'In written speech,' he says,

> lacking situational and expressive supports, communication must be achieved only through words and their combinations; this requires the speech activity to take complicated forms – hence the use of first drafts. The evolution from the draft to the final copy reflects our mental process. Planning has an important part in written speech, even when we do not actually write out a draft. Usually we say to ourselves what we are going to write; this is also a draft, though in thought only. (Vygotsky, 1986: 242–243)

Vygotsky's theories of language and thought development have become influential to writing studies. In particular, Charles Bazerman (1988) has taken Vygotsky's theory and applied the same language-learning principles to learning in academic discourse communities. A new student learning an academic language is a neophyte, Bazerman says, much like the child Vygotsky describes learning language for the first time (Bazerman, 1988: 304). The neophyte must gain understanding of knowledge as it exists and is created within the shared community (Bazerman, 1988: 304). As the neophyte is immersed and is learning the discourse language, often her comments are interpreted through a broad and more charitable view than a fluent, fully socialized speaker of the discourse language would be allowed (Bazerman, 1988: 305). The fluent speakers provide scaffolding for the neophyte's language learning: 'As the neophyte gains control of the structured meaning/behavior system transmitted through the scaffolding, she starts to incorporate parts of the scaffolding in her own behavior,' Bazerman says (1988: 306). What Vygotsky described as the zone of proximal development in language learning, Bazerman calls the hierarchy of expertise in learning academic discourse languages (Bazerman, 1988: 306). 'An important moment in a child's development for Vygotsky is when the child starts to develop an internal language so that these self-instructions, regulating the child's behavior, go underground becoming invisible to observers and even eventually to the child,' Bazerman says. 'In this way, gradually the neophyte becomes socialized into the semiotic-behavioral-perceptual system of a community with language taking a major and multivalent role in the organization of that system' (306–307). In other words, the neophyte learns to not only speak but to think as a member of the academic discourse community.

Mark Waldo (2004), in *Demythologizing Language Difference in the Academy*, argues that academic discourses are like languages. Each is only truly intelligible by the members of its community, and to become fluent in an academic language requires immersion in that academic discourse community. As a native English speaker would immerse herself in the languages of Spanish or Chinese in order to become fluent, students must immerse themselves in the language communities of biology, business, engineering, philosophy, etc. Each language serves a purpose within its discourse community, Waldo states, and therefore the speakers of those languages can accomplish more than they could if only one language existed that was mutually understandable to the academy.

An important part of this immersion is writing. To be a member of an academic community, one must be able to write fluently in the discourse. Each academic discourse community has its own values, purposes, and forms for writing, Waldo states (2004: 6). English departments might value voice, vivid detail, and originality; however, biology departments might value having a clear statement of purpose and including data in the appropriate sections, such as abstract, methods, materials, discussion, and conclusion (Waldo, 2004: 147). Waldo states, 'What makes writing good in one discipline certainly does not make it good in another' (2004: 6). Nevertheless, I argue that some aspects of writing transcend disciplinary boundaries, including using writing as a means of discovery.

Writing to Learn/Learning to Write

Composition theory tells us that writing can be used as a means of discovery, of thinking – that writing is not simply thought transcribed into printed form. This idea has been coined into a phrase: 'writing to learn.' From the standpoint of composition teachers and scholars, brainstorming, freewriting, drafting, and revision are all seen as instruments of writing to learn. These are approaches to writing that help students discover that writing can lead to thinking. This is a foundational idea in the field of composition – where it becomes controversial is when it is applied to writing across the curriculum. As I described earlier, at the heart of WAC theory is the belief that each academic discourse community has its own disciplinary language, with specialized vocabulary, values, and structures for writing. To learn to speak, think, and write in a discipline requires immersion. This immersion, at least as it relates to writing, has been dubbed, in WAC circles, as 'learning to write' (or sometimes 'learning to write in the disciplines').

Susan McLeod and Elaine Maimon (2000: 577), in the article 'Clearing the air: WAC myths and realities,' argue that these are 'complementary rather than competing views.' McLeod and Maimon say that, in order to help instructors teach their students to learn to write in their disciplines, WAC administrators need to help those instructors establish their goals for the course and think of ways to help create writing assignments to accomplish those goals (McLeod & Maimon, 2000: 580). At the same time, however, McLeod and Maimon argue that writing-to-learn ideals should be a part of any WAC program. 'The purpose of writing to learn assignments – journals, discovery drafts, in-class writing – is to use writing as a tool for learning rather than a test of that learning' (McLeod & Maimon, 2000: 579). How this complements learning to write, they say, is that the instructor is more of a 'facilitator rather than a judge' (McLeod & Maimon, 2000: 579). They state, 'The discourse is that of a discourse community; the role of the teacher in this case is to act as the professional already involved in the conversation of that community, helping the novice, the student, enter that discourse community' (McLeod & Maimon, 2000: 579).

It's worth noting that not everyone agrees. Waldo, for example, argues that although writing to learn and learning to write 'might not be contradictory, they are not complementary' (Waldo, 2004: 11). Waldo defines writing to learn as expressive writing, freewriting, journaling, in-class workshops, and 'exercises requiring personal, authentic, and creative responses to course and material' (Waldo, 2004: 11). Learning to write, on the other hand, is 'learning and writing in the language of the student's discipline with its own values, purposes, and forms for writing' (Waldo, 2004: 11). Further, Waldo says,

> Learning to write, by definition, belongs to all disciplines. Writing to learn is a set of values for writing developed largely in the context of the discipline of composition studies. It belongs mostly to one discipline. Not shared across the disciplines, it cannot complement learning to write. (Waldo, 2004: 11)

I would argue, however, that the *idea* of writing to learn is a part of all disciplines, but not necessarily that the activities commonly associated with writing to learn belong to all disciplines. I believe that writing and thinking are so inexorably tied that writing is always an act of thinking, discovering, and learning. Scarcely anyone – whether she's a scientist, historian, or creative writer – has a paper, book, poem, or letter fully formed in her brain and then simply writes it out, word for word as it exists in the mind. Writers might have an idea of what they intend to say, but they do not have it mapped out word for word precisely as it will exist on the page.

Prior to going to graduate school, when I was a newspaper reporter, I had to compose articles on tight deadlines. I did not keep a journal, or spend time brainstorming or freewriting, or even compose through a series of distinctive drafts. I did not use composition-based so-called writing-to-learn techniques. However, I wrote to learn. I discovered – quickly! – as I wrote. And I did, even on deadline, go back through my writing and make revisions, editing for clarity and brevity and even making new discoveries. I did not use a process as prescribed in composition textbooks, but I used a process. And I have no doubt that as I wrote, I was writing to learn.

Writers might have an outline in their head, key phrases, introductory language, and parts of what they intend to write, but I doubt they know exactly what they're going to say. Even scientists writing lab reports, where they are simply trying to report on an experiment, would not, I argue, know *exactly* what they're going to say. The structure of the lab report – with sections for the materials, methodology, literature review, conclusion, etc. – might provide a framework for the writing, but this does not mean that the writing is simple transcription. They might not use the so-called writing-to-learn techniques of journaling, freewriting, brainstorming, etc. However, the writing still involves a process, varied depending on the writer, and thinking would be involved as the writing occurred. And if someone does in fact know exactly what she is going to say before writing, then I would argue that writing and thinking are so integrally tied that this is still a part of their writing process. As I said earlier, Vygotsky explains that planning is important in writing and allows for drafting, either on paper or a mental draft (Vygotsky, 1986: 243). So if people truly do know exactly what they want to write before writing it, I argue that the drafting happened internally. They write in their heads, and rewrite in their heads, before writing on paper.

Call it Vygotsky's mental draft, neuro-brainstorming, cognitive freewriting, or whatever you'd like, but writing still happens. Thus, I argue that writing to learn is always a part of writing. Writing to learn, therefore, is a cross-curricular idea, not simply a value for writing held by compositionists. Perhaps where I disagree with Waldo is in definition. The idea of writing to learn – writing as a part of thinking, as a means of discovery, as way of making knowledge – is not merely a concept that comprises activities such as brainstorming and expressive writing. Writing to learn, in my definition, is the idea that writing and thinking are so integrally linked that to write is virtually impossible to do without learning as one writes. Learning is a process that involves writing; writing is a process that involves learning.

Writing is, in a sense, another way of using Vygotsky's inner speech, of conversing with oneself – thus writing can be used for exploration, discovery, learning. Whether autobiographical prose or the exploration of another topic through the author's personal lens, creative nonfiction also emphasizes writing for exploration. Whether the author has set out to discover something about herself or she discovers what she thinks about a particular topic – or discovers she thinks differently about the topic than she previously realized – writing to learn is explicitly a part of creative nonfiction writing.

Creative Nonfiction and Disciplinary Writing

A strong comparison can be made between the idea of writing to learn and the creative nonfiction-based idea of writing for self-discovery. Robert Root and Michael Steinberg state that creative nonfiction 'grants writers permission to explore without knowing where they will end up, to be tentative, speculative, reflective' (Root & Steinberg, 2002: xxv). Root and Steinberg say that frequently writers of creative nonfiction find that their subject matter 'becomes the catalyst or trigger for some personal journey or inquiry or self-interrogation' (Root & Steinberg, 2002: xxv). In other words, creative nonfiction writers use writing to explore themselves or the world around them.

Writing to learn, as I've described it, exists in all writing. But creative nonfiction seems to be a genre where it exists more explicitly and more consciously than it might in other forms or genres. This isn't to say that writers of creative nonfiction writers necessarily embrace or practice the composition-promoted activities of freewriting, journaling, brainstorming, etc., more than other disciplines. Rather, the genre embraces an understanding that writing, whatever process the writer is using, is a way of thinking. 'Personal essayists,' Phillip Lopate (1994: xxvii) says in the introduction to *The Art of the Personal Essay*, 'are adept at interrogating their own ignorance [...] They follow the clue of their ignorance through the maze.' While it might be an unconscious activity of writing in various forms and disciplines, writing to learn is explicitly embraced as a conscious act in creative nonfiction.

It's possible, of course, for scholars from other disciplines, fluent in their specialized languages, to write nonfiction for other audiences. For an example, I'll describe the work of Deborah M. Gordon, a biological sciences professor at Stanford University who studies ants and theorizes about the broader implications of their behavior for nature in general. In her 1999 article 'Close

Encounters,' she describes how harvester ants have no leaders, no one ant in charge of knowing what needs to be done for the colony, yet they complete their tasks in such a way that it's for the good of the colony. And, she claims, the ants will change tasks if circumstances change for the colony. This is the main point of the article: task allocation. This information – the discovery being reported, the main news of the article – overturns the previous understanding that ants had specific jobs that they would perform for their entire lives. Consider the opening two paragraphs of the article:

> Every summer for the past seventeen years I have studied the harvester ants in a small patch of the Arizona desert. The ants live at the side of a rough paved road that runs through a flat valley between the Chiricahua and Peloncillo mountains at the state line of Arizona and New Mexico. An enormous sky surrounds an endless reach of land. The Chiricahuas, to the west, are so close you can see the patches of rock change color during the day. The Peloncillos, to the east and north, form a jagged outline in the distance. To the south the desert stretches eighty miles to the Mexican border.
>
> I stay at the Southwestern Research Station up in the Chiricahua Mountains. The station belongs to the American Museum of Natural History in New York City, and at the peak of the summer season fifty people might be staying there, mostly undergraduates who come to work either for the station or as research assistants for people like me. We get up at 4:30, when it is still dark, and meet in the dining room. Then there is some antlike milling around while people make their peanut-butter-and-jelly sandwiches to get them through the morning, collect their water bottles and clipboards, and pile into a van. It's about a twenty-minute drive down into the desert. (Gordon, 1999a: 24)

To me, I find this introduction interesting and compelling. She paints a beautiful picture of her work environment, gives a feeling of what life at the research station is like, and, in a sense, puts the reader in her shoes for what she's going to be talking about in the rest of the article. Personally, as a reader, I'm interested. You may, however, as you were reading the paragraphs, have wondered about the audience for the article, the purpose, the publication it appeared in. It wouldn't seem like fellow scientists would be interested in what the Chiricahua mountains looked like; they probably wouldn't care that the researchers prepared peanut-butter-and-jelly sandwiches at 4:30 in the morning. In fact, this essay appeared in *The Sciences*, a now defunct journal that contained scientific articles but for a broader audience, and it was later selected for the *Best American Science Writing 2000*. It is, I would argue, creative nonfiction. It contains the personal presence of the author, it reports on a scientific discovery but does so in a language everyday people can understand, and it contains vivid, creative imagery and an elegance to the language. But I would argue that it isn't the type of article that fellow scientists would want to read in their peer-reviewed journals.

Gordon (1999b) also published her findings concerning the harvester ant that same year in another source geared toward an audience more steeped in hard science, taking the explanation a step further to provide a model for task allocation based on the discovery. Here is the abstract at the beginning of the article, titled 'Interaction Patterns and Task Allocation in Ant Colonies':

> Social insect colonies must accomplish many tasks, such as foraging, tending brood, constructing a nest, and so on. Task allocation is the process that adjusts the numbers of workers engaged in each task. This chapter discusses how information from other individuals is used in task decisions, and in particular, how workers use the pattern of interactions they experience, rather than the content of messages received. Empirical studies of harvester ants led to a mathematical model of task allocation in which environmental stimuli and interaction patterns both influence an individual's tasks. I outline the main results from this model, and describe recent empirical work that begins to examine how interaction patterns contribute to task allocation in harvester ants. (Gordon, 1999b: 51)

This writing is actually fairly accessible to non-scientists; however, you can see the differences between this and the previous excerpt. In the first excerpt, in what I'll call the creative nonfiction version, Gordon takes her time to set the scene for the reader before moving into the research. In this the scientific article, Gordon includes an abstract at the very beginning that summarizes the article and explains, from the get-go, the significance of the discovery. The pronoun 'I' appears once here, although I don't think it's used again in the entire article. Further, the scientific report is partitioned into sections with clearly marked headings so readers can quickly find the information they're looking for. The abstract summarizes the important information at the beginning – in other words, she gets to the newsworthy information immediately. In the creative nonfiction version, published for a more general audience, the personal presence of the author – her voice, if you will – appears valued, as does description, imagery, clarity. The audience doesn't care if she gets to her point quickly.

The readers of *The Sciences* are likely intelligent, educated, and have an interest in science – and the same can be said for the readers of the *Best American Science Writing 2000* – but they aren't necessarily the specialists who would read about this experiment with the intention of testing it, or using her model in their own research. I may have been able to understand the abstract, but I get lost in the rest of the article. It becomes very technical, at least to me. Other scientists within Gordon's field would likely be able to interpret this very quickly.

I, as a reader, prefer the creative nonfiction piece. However, I do not, in any way, suggest that the writing is better. If I were a scientist also interested in the research of ant colonies, the creative nonfiction version likely wouldn't satisfy my curiosity about the subject. It would be too simplified for my specialized language. It doesn't go to the length of detail that I would need. This is not to say, either, that the writing of the creative nonfiction piece is inferior. Both are intended for different audiences who value writing differently; both are written with different purposes. Both accomplish those purposes (as far as I can tell), but neither is better than the other, I would argue. The articles are, in a sense, written in a different language.

However, I would argue that Gordon's practice of writing what I would call creative nonfiction helped her as a writer in general, regardless of the genre, context, and purpose. In a video interview with Gordon (2012) on Stanford University's Rhetoric and Writing program website, as part of a series of interviews exploring writing's connection to academic and personal success, she describes how writing and thinking are interrelated in her research process. She states, 'Thinking about my work and talking about my work and writing about my work are all different stages of the same process.' She adds, 'In writing, I have time to think and lay out an argument and put together my thoughts. Writing really helps me think.' Furthermore, she emphasizes that writing is important in all areas of academic scholarship. 'Sometimes my students in my classes are surprised that I care about the quality of their writing,' she states, 'but I'm always surprised that anyone could imagine that there could be any area of scholarship or any area of dealing with the world when we wouldn't care about how we write and about how we speak to each other.'

Gordon's example illustrates that while disciplinary language requires fluency – which she demonstrates in the scientific article – this fluency doesn't have to be exclusive or come at the expense of an author's ability to write for other audiences. In fact, I would argue that Gordon's practice of writing for a different audience in the creative nonfiction piece contributes to her abilities to write in her own. She states in the interview that students struggle to learn the language of their discipline, but that writing can lead to a better understanding: 'For students, for people starting out, when you have a lot of ideas thrown at you, and it's hard to see how they all fit in, then the words, the names, the jargon become a way of trying to learn to talk in this new world.' I argue that the type of writing done in Gordon's creative nonfiction example, where students write in a comfortable voice and explore the ideas they wrestle with, can act as a way of building a bridge to the more disciplinary writing demonstrated in her scientific article.

Conclusion

A strong comparison can be made between the idea of writing to learn (as I define it) and the creative nonfiction-based idea of writing for self-discovery. The word essay, after all, comes from the French term *essai*, meaning 'an attempt' or 'a try.' Creative nonfiction essays are attempts at writing for self-discovery, whether that discovery is about the writer or about the world she lives in.

Whether they're quickly typing news articles on deadline, plugging information into sections of a scientific lab report, or writing a memoir, students will – in some form or some way – be using writing to learn in their futures. Therefore, I argue that using creative nonfiction that explicitly values writing to learn can provide important educational insight for students, whether in writing classes, such as first-year composition, or courses within their majors. Even as students are learning their disciplinary languages within their majors, creative nonfiction writing assignments can still be used, especially in first- and second-year classes where the disciplinary writing hasn't been internalized. Such assignments could work as bridges toward the more specialized language used later, giving students practice writing about the subject matter and writing for discovery (or writing to learn).

To return to the example of Deborah M. Gordon, students should not be misled to think that the writing done in the first creative nonfiction example belongs in a lab report, but there would be no harm in asking students in a first- or second-year science class to write in such a manner before attempting the more specialized discourse evidenced by the second, more scientific example. Creative nonfiction assignments can be a part of the scaffolding provided by the professors, as students climb the hierarchies of expertise in particular disciplines. Creative nonfiction can be the bridge that helps students develop as writers in a new disciplinary expertise. In considering how to build this bridge, it's important that instructors recognize their goals for a particular course, as well as recognize their discipline's values for writing, when considering how to incorporate creative nonfiction into their pedagogies. However, what I hope I've shown is the potential for creative nonfiction to enrich the education of students even within classes focused on disciplinary expertise.

This chapter can serve as the beginning of a larger conversation about the pedagogical use of creative nonfiction across the curriculum. I encourage teacher-scholars to consider ways that they can use creative nonfiction writing assignments to help their students become better writers across academic curricula. Techniques often associated with writing to learn, such as journaling and freewriting, might not always be relevant to every writer in every discipline. A person's writing process is largely individual – what works for one writer may not work for the next. However, it's important to expose students to as many writing tools as possible. It's important for students to understand that writing and thinking are integrally related, and that using writing as a means of discovery, as creative nonfiction writers do, can help them not only as writers but also as thinkers. If writing to learn – as a way to *essai* for knowledge – transcends disciplinary boundaries, then creative nonfiction writing, either in composition courses or within academic majors, can be used to help students develop as writers and critical thinkers.

References

Bazerman, C. (1988) *Shaping Written Knowledge: The Genre and Activity of the Experimental Article in Science*. Madison, WI: University of Wisconsin Press.

Gordon, D.M. (1999a) Close encounters. *The Sciences*, Sept–Oct, 24–28.

Gordon, D.M. (1999b) Interaction patterns and task allocation in ant colonies. In J.L. Deneubourg, J.M. Pasteels and C. Detrain (eds) *Information Processing in Social Insects*. Boston, MA: Birkhauser Verlag.

Gordon, D.M. (2012) Writing Matters: Deborah Gordon. *Writing Matters: A series about writing's connection with academic and personal success* (video). Stanford University Program in Rhetoric and Writing.

Hampl, P. (2002) Memory and imagination. In R.L. Root and M. Steinberg (eds) *The Fourth Genre: Contemporary Writers of/on Creative Nonfiction* (pp. 259–268). New York: Pearson Education.

Lopate, P. (1994) Introduction. In P. Lopate (ed.) *The Art of the Personal Essay: An Anthology from the Classical Era to the Present* (pp. xxiii–liv). New York: Anchor/Doubleday.

McLeod, S. and Maimon, E. (2000) Clearing the air: WAC myths and realities. *College English* 62 (5), 573–583.

Murray, D.M. (1989) *Expecting the Unexpected: Teaching Myself–and Others–to Read and Write*. Portsmouth, NH: Boynton/Cook Publishers.

Root, R.L. and Steinberg, M. (2002) Introduction: Creative nonfiction: The fourth genre. In R.L. Root and M. Steinberg (eds) *The Fourth Genre: Contemporary Writers of/on Creative Nonfiction* (pp. xxiii–xxxiii). New York: Pearson Education.

Vygotsky, L. (1986) *Thought and Language* (A. Kozulin, trans). Cambridge: The MIT Press.

Waldo, M. (2004) *Demythologizing Language Difference in the Academy: Establishing Discipline-Based Writing Programs*. Mahwah, NJ: Lawrence Erlbaum Associates.

7 Creative Writing's Five Stages of Development: The Mind of the Creative Writer in the Composition Classroom

Jonathan Bradley and Sarah Gray-Panesi

Instructors assigned with the task of teaching creative writing require practical advice on how to approach student writers. However, while the mechanics of creativity are still being dissected, understanding the stages of development the creative writer progresses through during a student's career can shed light on the appropriateness of certain pedagogical approaches and allow instructors the means to better address each writer's individual needs. The development of these stages is the product of both personal experience and a survey of creative writing pedagogy. Scholars present each of these various stages in the pedagogy, mostly in isolation, to describe their students' behavior, such as the treatment of stage four in Cherryl Armstrong's (1986) 'The Poetic Dimensions of Revision' or stages one and five in Baptiste Barbot et al.'s (2012) 'Essential Skills for Creative Writing: Integrating Multiple Domain-Specific Perspectives.' These perspectives seem to differ, yet to those who have taught creative writing, they also appear to be an accurate representation of student performance. Therefore, it seems to follow that all of these scholars present valid portrayals of their students, except they are describing students in different stages of development. Through research, experience, and logical backtracking, these stages are named, ordered and described here.

The first part of this article outlines the five stages of development creative writers experience as observed by the authors ('Insertion,' 'Doppelgänger,' 'Self-indulgence,' 'Actualization,' and 'Reflection'), the difficulties each of these stages present to the creative writing instructor, and possible pedagogical strategies for approaching students navigating each of the five stages. The second section explores how understanding these five stages and their challenges can allow an instructor new avenues to work with students in a composition classroom.

Creative Writing's Fives Stages of Development

During the early stages of creative development, the initial exercise practiced is Insertion. In this stage, a young creative mind, usually that of a child, begins interacting with the idea of fictional worlds, though at this point the mind usually has not developed the practical skills of mass creation of new material. Therefore, in order to interact with these fictional worlds, the writer must utilize pre-formed worlds and roles in order to produce something new. Hence, a young creative mind will 'insert' themselves into pre-created role he or she has encountered in books, movies, television, or other outlets. For example, I knew a student once who wrote herself into an *American Idol* episode, taking on a thinly-veiled clone of that season's most popular singer and providing details about the emotional background of a song not present in the show. This process, described by psychologists as 'selective combination,' seeks to use the familiar to generate original ideas (Barbot *et al.*, 2012: 211). For those using this process, this adopted role can range from something broad, like a generic cowboy in a generic old west setting, to a more specific role as a particular character in a particular world. This stage of development is defined by little creation beyond plot elements; a young writer may decide and execute (usually through games of make-believe rather than writing) story conflict and resolution, though much of this created plot is also mimetic of the kind of conflict the writer has experienced previously in such pre-formed fictional worlds (e.g. a cowboy has to save a group of settlers from marauding bandits). While this first stage produces very little in 'original' content, it is fundamental in teaching the young creative mind how to manipulate conventions of storytelling and build a skill-set that will facilitate their later original creations.

Encountering students in the first stage of development would be rare unless the instructor is in a K-12 system, though that is not to say such students do not appear beyond this setting. Such writers can be identified by a tendency to retell stories that are familiar to them, always working within a world not their own. The young writer who consistently produces stories about young, ostracized children who discover they are in truth wizards or witches and part of some unknown secret world are working in this stage. For this example, the writer may borrow directly from the *Harry Potter* series, including elements like actual characters or places, or they may provide a false veneer, changing familiar names in order to feign originality. But in these examples, the language used along with the plot will almost always rely on a bank of pop-culture fodder to draw from, and everything from conflict and dialogue will seem familiar. The biggest difficulties in teaching students in stage one is their desire to stick with 'what they know' and a general fear of failing to produce something that others will enjoy. These difficulties can be countered by providing the student writing exercises that introduce unfamiliar elements to their pre-formed worlds to take them out of their comfort-zone. For example, an instructor could ask a student who writes all his or her stories about a beloved space-ship captain what would happen if, on routine patrol, the captain's ship came upon a massive, slumbering dragon in the depths of a nebula. Such a break in the familiar would require the students to work outside of established conventions and hopefully make such an act more comfortable for the future. Writers in stage one can also benefit from exposure to less-lauded works by their favorite creators to build confidence by illustrating that not everything someone produces will be well-loved. The upside to working with students in stage one is their enthusiasm and honest desire to partake in fictional worlds, even if they are not completely comfortable in that space yet.

The second stage, referred to here as the Doppelgänger phase, is the product of a writer's desire to live out a fantasy life through his or her fictional world. In this stage, the writer is usually still working within a pre-formed fictional world or at least one that very closely resembles a setting he or she is familiar with, but now the writer wishes to insert themselves not into a role, but as a kind of avatar into a fictional world. The writer becomes a character in the fictional world, usually in the form of an idealized version of him or herself. The writer may insert themselves in the guise of an already existing character, in which case their own personality and idealized traits will wholly replace those of the original character, or the writer will add themselves as an extra character. In general, though not always, this character lives a charmed life in which all conflicts can be easily overcome, delicate social situations are passed over and made simplistic in order to facilitate the doppelgänger's lauded status, and established plot or character traits are ignored or actively dismissed in order to allow for a fantasy world customized to the writer. In the fanfiction community, such characters are known as Mary-Sues or Marty-Sues, and their prevalence within the genre suggests they are not an aberration, but as this article suggests, a fundamental stage of development for many young writers. This stage of development produces more original content than stage one but usually lacks in character development, realistic plot construction, and adequate conflict to engage readers.

However, this stage is usually indicative of a mind willing to progress further in order to improve existing skills.

Writers in the Doppelgänger stage of development pose a number of issues for the creative writing instructor. Many students in this stage write stories in which the reader can never really engage with the characters because they are a little too perfect, too unrealistic, and conflict is only present in the most minor, unimportant ways. Encouraging writers to move out of this stage can be particularly difficult, as improvement usually requires writing more flawed or well-rounded characters, and some students, due to the nature of the doppelgänger, will take the criticism personally. When trying to help writers in stage two, one of the worst actions an instructor can take is to point out that a character is not well-rounded, as most students will immediately react negatively to what they perceive as a personal attack. Instead, exercises that introduce new, difficult conflicts for the character to face may be taken as a challenge for the young writer to overcome. For example, if a character is not realistic because the reader never believes he or she might actually fail at something, asking the student to write a story exploring how the character reacts to a failure could be beneficial. In addition, John D. MacDonald poses an exercise in which students describe a scene from ten different points of view, and this exercise could be particularly beneficial to students in this stage of development. MacDonald (1989: 85) states, 'This exercise begins to detach them from their previous ego-image of writing and takes them rudely into a world of character.' Exercises like MacDonald's are useful because they push writers into characters that the writer has less of a personal stake in. However, despite the difficulties presented by this stage, working with these students can be very enjoyable as they usually have a strong passion for the craft.

Stage three, or the Self-Indulgent phase, is similar to stage two in that missteps on the part of instructors can provoke withdrawal from writers who feel they are being attacked personally. The Self-Indulgent phase is marked by writers who care little for audience awareness, and because of this, 'these students then object to both feedback and assignments from their instructor' (Barbot et al., 2012: 211). At this point, most of these writers are working within their own creations, and although these creations may still seem reminiscent of works they are familiar with, stage three writers are generally more willing to form complex worlds and build characters that reflect a more sophisticated understanding of plot and character development. However, writers in stage three are not looking for constructive criticism, though they will assert vehemently that they are. Instead, writers in stage three are searching for praise and admiration, and they are easily discernible by the way in which they speak of their work. Writers in the

Self-Indulgent phase regularly comment that they only write for themselves and do not care what others think, despite their active search for an outside audience. They will also commonly assert that a friend or family member has read their writing and said it is fantastic, and now they have expanded their search for acknowledgement to a wider audience. The problem arises in the fact that, as the referent suggests, the writer's work is very self-indulgent. While some self-indulgence is a part of any writing, students in stage three construct stories that may make little sense to others or do a poor job of engaging readers because the writer has produced the entire story based on whether or not it is interesting to themselves, not considering whether others would find the story realistic or even pleasant to read. Additionally, because writers in this stage rarely want or are willing to let the outside world affect their writing, they usually do not care about conventions of genre and will often produce rehashes of stories told hundreds of times. But despite these drawbacks, writers in stage three usually experience a burst of creative energy that, given time and more experience, can become magnificent work later on.

Depending on the circumstances of the classroom, stage three students are usually encountered most often, and other scholars, such as Stephanie Vanderslice and Kelly Ritter (2011), have identified the traits of stage three writers as well, though Vanderslice and Ritter use a different classification system than the one employed here. The fact that stage three writers, more so than any other stage, have been addressed by other scholars reveals their prevalence in the field. Yet even though they are encountered most often, these students can be the most difficult to teach. They have generally placed a high value on their work, meaning anything but praise will be construed as an insult. In many cases, it is best to focus on only one issue with stage three students, even if the work has multiple, rather serious problems. In experience, providing only one major issue for the writer to deal with suggests in their mind that their work is almost perfect aside from a single problem, in which case they may be more willing to try to improve said problem. Once the writer has made strides to change one issue, the instructor can delicately introduce a second problem for the writer to focus on. While this method can work with many student writers, some can prove too hard-nosed, in which case the best strategy is to shift their perception of their work by encouraging them to submit their work for publication in paying markets. At first, stage three writers will have a tendency to blame their rejections on people who 'don't get my work' or a bias among editors, but after enough rejection slips, most students will come to accept that their work is not perfect and that valid demands can be made on an author who wishes to bring his or her work to a wider audience.

In 'Articles of Faith,' David Jauss (1989: 65) argues that creative writers 'must make friends with doubt. It is the imagination's greatest ally, for it forces you to consider possibilities – different word choices, rhythms, character traits, events and so forth – you would never consider if you moved too abruptly to closure and certainty ... great writers are almost always those whose doubts about themselves and their art are extreme.' This process of accepting doubt as one's friend is what happens during the transition from stage three to stage four: Actualization. The Actualization stage is common to encounter, though students in this stage are easier to deal with in the classroom. The Actualization stage is distinguished by writers who are more aware of their audience. Writers in this stage still understand the personal nature of writing but are looking to send their work into the world, and more importantly, want to build genuine connections with their readers. Stage four students have come to appreciate constructive criticism in a way that stage three writers still do not understand, and they will regularly take notes on any feedback they can get their hands on. They are generally a joy to have in the classroom, as they will actively listen and engage with the help an instructor provides. Their biggest drawback and the distinguishing feature that sets them apart from stage five writers is their lack of reflection concerning the feedback they receive. Stage four writers will regularly make the changes that readers suggest and actively attempt to improve their writing, but many do not yet value understanding why one sentence style works versus another. Their minds are turned toward improvement as opposed to understanding writing as a craft.

Writers in stage four pose few difficulties and usually make the class more rewarding for the instructor, since they show a great deal of enthusiasm and exhibit visible improvement in their work. However, developing their own internalized critical eye would allow these writers to edit and revise their work without relying as much on outside readers, resulting in a more mature, confident writer. One strategy to help push writers beyond stage four is to provide constructive feedback in the form of questions designed to engage the writer instead of simply providing the 'right' action to take. For example, instead of stating, 'This character's motivation in this scene is not convincing. You need to detail their friend's death earlier in the story to have their reaction here seem natural,' ask, 'Do you think there is something odd about Jeremy's reaction here? It rings a bit false, and I'm wondering if we're missing out on an important aspect of who he is. What do you think?' In addition to this type of response, discussions about the craft of writing with stage four students can help get them engaging beyond what needs to change.

Finally, stage five writers, referred to here as Reflective writers, are not only beneficial to the instructor to have in class but also to his or her fellow students. Unlike stage four writers, Reflective writers have developed their critical eye and are usually willing to help others with their work by providing good feedback. They still receive feedback willingly and benefit from it, and they are usually thoughtful about writing, asking questions that can engage others in the classroom and encourage reflective thinking. Such writers generally pose little to no difficulties for a creative writing instructor. It is important, however, to remember not to neglect these writers. They are present because they still desire to be a part of a community of writers and want to share and improve their work, so they deserve that opportunity.

With these stages outlined, it is important to provide some caveats to them. First, these stages are not exclusive from one another. A writer can straddle the line between two or rarely even three of these stages at a time, so it is valuable not to approach this as an either/or situation. Writers will not always progress through these stages in order either, and certain writers might skip a stage completely (stages 2 and 4 are the most commonly skipped).The stage a student is in also should not be used to judge the quality of his or her work; students from any stage can produce quality work, and it is important not to lose sight of this fact. And finally, perhaps the most important concern for the creative writing instructor is the mix of these stages that will be encountered. No class will consist of all stage three students and depending on the classroom, a group of students could have writers from all five stages. Being able to identify which stage an individual student is in can ensure that he or she is receiving the needed motivation to continue improving as a writer.

Creative Approaches in the Composition Classroom

A student's first forays into composition are not unlike the beginning stages of a creative writer's journey. Indeed, it is this very similarity that has caused composition scholars such as Wendy Bishop, Judith Harris, and Joseph Moxley, among others, to question the common belief that creative writing and composition must be taught through separate pedagogical approaches. Even students often mark the distinction between creative and 'non-creative' composition by describing the former as enjoyable, and the latter as boring (Bishop, 1994). However, these lines of distinction begin to break down when students such as Bishop's (1994: 181) Fran learn that writing about topics that interest them can be just as much fun as crafting stories or poetry. While the students Bishop (1994: 181) discusses in her essay experience epiphanies related to the similarities between creative writing and composition, Bishop herself experiences her own as she recognizes that it is 'more productive to cross the line' between creative writing and composition pedagogy 'than to create a separate teaching persona on either side.' Having established a framework for measuring a student's capacity for creative writing, we now prepare to cross the line as well.

For many students, the composition classroom is a place of boredom and insecurity – a place where basic writing skills, rather than individual writers are the focus. The problem, Lea Masiello (1994: 208) suggests, lies in our emphasis on skills rather than 'the development of identity and confidence' in our composition students; 'imaginative invention activities,' according to Masiello, are highly effective tools for building the composition student's confidence in his or her writing, and discovering one's identity both as a student and a writer. In this section of our project, we consider how the imaginative activities used to move students through the five stages of creative writing development can be employed to the same or similar effect in the composition classroom. Furthermore, the theoretical foundations described in the first part of this study are usefully applied to the composition student here to more fully elucidate the extent to which the pedagogical approaches in the two classrooms can and should overlap. Notably, the composition classroom context explored in this project follows a 'career writing' approach in which the instructor crafts assignments that allow the student to explore and experiment with writing that they may consider more 'valuable' than the usual expository or argumentative essay found in freshman composition classes. Specifically, assignments should ask the student to engage in writing styles common in his or her own field of study.

Interestingly, while students find value in the writing they produce on websites, blogs, and social media, most do not actually consider themselves to be 'authors,' especially not in the scholarly sense of the term. Students entering creative writing classes will almost certainly be more apt to think of themselves as writers and also to find value, be it emotional or economical, in the work produced in these courses. Additionally, many students enrolling in creative writing classes may see themselves someday becoming professional, or at least paid, writers. In other words, creative writing students are more likely to see the connection between their writing and the writing they will do in the 'real world' because they are already doing it every day. Our challenge as composition instructors is to help students recognize the relationship between the 'real world' and the writing we ask them to produce for our classes. Crossing the line between creative writing and composition pedagogies allows us to do precisely that while simultaneously offering them the chance to 'Insert' themselves into the processes of 'career writing' development.

The five stages of creative writing development often begin when a student is still a child. While one would not normally encounter an Insertion stage creative writer at the college level, college composition instructors are almost certain to encounter several such writers in this stage as it pertains to expository and 'career writing.' Like children imitating their favorite fictional characters, upon determining a career path, young adults often attempt to model themselves on the form of a successful 'actor' in that role. A young man decides he wants to build the next computer company and begins wearing black turtlenecks and deconstructing computers a la Steve Jobs. However, he most likely does not engage with the less glamorous side of building a multi-billion dollar company, the writing side. He sees the spotlight, but chooses not to explore the shadows surrounding it. The task falls to the composition instructor to coax the budding writer out of his comfort zone, so he does not miss the opportunities waiting for him in the unknown.

Students in the Insertion stage of their career writing development, like creative writers in this stage, tend not to consider the conflicts that must be resolved prior to reaching a 'happy ending,' or how those conflicts provide body to an otherwise flat story. Students may imagine themselves lauded for saving a company from the brink of economic ruin or inventing the next 'flugalbinder'; however, they do not consider that once the company is safe the board of directors will demand explanations or that the lab supervisor will require a report once the flugals are bound. While we might ask a creative writing student in this stage to imagine new conflicts for his or her characters to overcome, we might invite a composition student to research and examine some of the conflicts faced by people working in their chosen field and determine how they might respond to them.

Building on the work of Roland Barthes, David Bartholomae, and James E. Seitz, Chris Drew and David Yost (2009: 34) assert that though it is often seen as 'removed from the normal work of composition,' role-playing exercises offer students a chance to imitate the language of academic discourse. Drew and Yost (2009: 35), unfortunately, confine their study to an examination of how creative writing exercises in composition classrooms 'could give students an early step toward appropriating academic discourse.' In contrast, our approach expands this examination to determine how incorporating these exercises allows students not only to engage with the specific discourse community into which they may enter upon graduation, but also to engage with the global discourse community in which they will certainly become a part.

Now that the student has begun to engage with the inner workings of their chosen career world, they, like the creative writer, move to the Doppelgänger phase. Anthropology majors may watch *Bones* religiously while a Fashion Design student might imagine winning *Project Runway*. Though not all composition students will have an ideal persona upon which to model their own, they will, no doubt, at least have an idea of the career path they wish to travel which lends itself well to writing exercises at this stage. Particularly problematic for the composition student in this stage, though, is the fact that, often, students imagine a fictional world as a reality: Kathy Reichs *is* Temperance Brennan and murders really are solved in the space of one day. As with the creative writing student in the Doppelgänger stage, the goal of an instructor working with a composition student in this stage is to help him or her insert more reality into an otherwise unbelievable world. However, the composition instructor must be careful here not to foist so much reality onto the student's ideal world that he or she chooses to abandon it.

While the creative Doppelgänger may be asked to write his or her character's failure, an assignment for the career Doppelgänger might ask him or her to interview someone in their discipline to find out what it is really like to work in that field and then produce a diary or journal entry as if they had just worked a 'day in the life' of that job. Asking medical students to interview a medical professor about possible jobs in that field will not only allow the students the opportunity to network with faculty in their discipline, it will also offer them a dose of reality not to be found by watching *Grey's Anatomy*. Furthermore, a med-student is much more likely to accept feedback regarding mistaken perceptions of the daily life of a medical doctor from someone with first-hand knowledge of being one. Finally, an active participant in the student's chosen field is likely to present that reality in such a way that, while sobering, can also be encouraging.

The Insertion and Doppelgänger stages of writing for the composition student have been attached equally to the students' growing knowledge of themselves as writers and as 'actors' in their chosen career fields. However, as the path to career awareness may stray from that of writerly self-awareness, the similarities between creative and career writing development become more pronounced from this third stage on. Some college students may never reach this stage, but those who do are both some of the most challenging and most rewarding students to engage with. Convinced of his or her writing prowess, the Self-Indulgent writer will often profess that he or she has always done very well in English, and, indeed, stage three composition students will often produce excellent writing. However, attention to such details as assignment guidelines and audience will often be lacking. When working with Self-Indulgent writers, the focus shifts from what types of assignments to offer to what type of feedback to provide in order to coax the student to recognize the importance of outside influence on both career and creative writing.

While critique of the stage three writer's work must be approached with care, it must be approached if the student is to develop a world-view compatible with success in the global marketplace. The block-by-block approach detailed for critiquing creative writers in this stage can be usefully employed here as well. Like creative writers, composition students at this stage often place a high value on their work, which, while it makes critique appear insulting, also provides an opportunity for instructors to leverage the paper's strengths in order to point out its opportunities. Also, as with creative writing students in this stage, encouraging the student to submit their work for publication in your university's research journal or another undergraduate research journal will offer the student the chance to learn that journal editors do not refuse work because 'they don't get it.' Fiction or nonfiction, an audience can and will make demands on authors, and seeing the same notes come back from multiple reviewers will teach the student a lesson that no single set of comments from a composition instructor could provide.

Having progressed through the first three stages of development, the career writer arrives at stage four with an understanding of the importance of the rhetorical situation that allows him or her to produce original, audience-aware work of above average quality. Like the creative writer in this stage, the Actualized writer understands the importance of feedback and has a true desire to succeed with their writing; however, he or she has yet to develop the critical eye necessary for reflection. Rather than offering deep revisions, asking students to go back over previous feedback and use it to revise this new draft can force them to consider the comments for their value to them as writers as opposed to their value for their writing. This style of constructive feedback can prompt evolution from an Actualized to a Reflective writer and will be useful for composition instructors as they help their students move to stage five.

Reflective writers in a composition classroom mimic those in the creative classroom. Reflective students will often be more apt to help their fellow students read and revise their own work, and just like their creative writing counterparts, Reflective composition students are not just eager for feedback, they are starving for it, and will seek it out wherever they can find it. The desire to continue to improve their writing has taken root and will not be easily rid.

With the five stages of creative writing development in mind, instructors in both the creative writing and composition classrooms are better equipped to help students develop as writers. Compositionists continually study how students develop into accomplished essayists in order to improve their pedagogy, and it is equally important for creative writing scholars to devote this same kind of study to our students, especially considering that such studies can be beneficial to all writing instructors. Therefore, we offer this work as a stepping off point and encourage other creative writing scholars to further define or revise our theory in order to better develop a practical system of instruction.

References

Armstrong, C. (1986) The poetic dimensions of revision. New Orleans LO: Conference on College Composition and Communication. Paper presented at the Annual Meeting of the Conference on College Composition and Communication (37th, New Orleans, LA, 13–15 March, 1986)

Barbot, B., Tan, M., Randi, J., Santa-Donato, G. and Grigorenko, E.L. (2012) Essential skills for creative writing: integrating multiple domain-specific perspectives. *Thinking Skills and Creativity* 7 (3), 209–223.

Bishop, W. (1994) Crossing the line: On creative composition and composing creative writing. In W. Bishop and H. Ostrom (eds) *Colors of a Different Horse: Rethinking Creative Writing Theory and Pedagogy* (pp. 181–197). Urbana: NCTE.

Drew, C. and Yost, D. (2009) Composing creativity: Further crossing composition/creative writing boundaries. *The Journal of the Midwest Modern Language Association* 42 (1), 25–42.

Jauss, D. (1989) Articles of faith. In J. Moxley (ed.) *Creative Writing in America: Theory and Pedagogy* (pp. 63–77). Urbana: NCTE.

MacDonald, J. (1989) Guidelines and exercise for teaching creative writing. In J. Moxley (ed.) *Creative Writing in America: Theory and Pedagogy* (pp. 83–89). Urbana: NCTE.

Masiello, L. (1994) Voices from the writing center: It's okay to be creative – A role for the imagination in basic-writing courses. In W. Bishop and H. Ostrom (eds) *Colors of a Different Horse: Rethinking Creative Writing Theory and Pedagogy* (pp. 208–216). Urbana: NCTE.

Vanderslice, S. and Ritter, K. (2011) *Teaching Creative Writing to Undergraduates: A Practical Guide and Sourcebook*. A. Smith and T. Smith (eds) Southlake: Fountainhead Press.

8 Sought-After Sophistications: Crafting a Curatorial Stance in the Creative Writing and Composition Classrooms

Rochelle L. Harris and Christine Stewart-Nuñez

As writing teachers, we search for places where student writing shifts from just-okay to in-depth wrangling with rhetoric – an unexpected paragraph of insight, a source more intuitively connected to a research topic, or a reach to metaphor. We strive to intervene when stereotypes about writing hamper intellectual work, when composition students insist on idealized academic scripts that 'flow' from one 'unbiased' point to the next and when creative writing students assume successful works rest on abstractions. In two of our recent classes, such shifts began to happen, and we explored the elements that facilitated such movement. We both involved our students in public history spaces: Christine's students conducted research in a museum archive, and Rochelle's students visited an art gallery to study arrangement. We both balanced traditional approaches to creative writing and composition with alternative approaches. In earlier assignments Christine's students wrote poems based on personal experience, and Rochelle's students wrote an eight-page academic essay; in later assignments, Christine assigned archives-inspired poems, and Rochelle assigned research-based collage essays. We immersed ourselves in interdisciplinary investigations of the use of research in creative writing, the discipline of Public History, archives and historiography, Museum Studies and exhibit theory, the collage genre, and the canon of arrangement. The role of the curator surfaced as important. In the curator's role we find a metaphor for a relationship a student-writer can have to writing and research; this *curatorial* is a specific epistemological perspective with which students approach inquiry by reframing the materials of research and composing as a collection from which students draw to both create and convey meaning. The role of curators, in a museum environment particularly, is to conduct inquiry into theory; collect and study artifacts; research; and design exhibits for museums, galleries, and historic sites that create interactive, critical engagement between the exhibit materials and visitors. When translated to the spaces of a writing classroom, a *curatorial stance* can enhance the teaching of writing through creative, data-grounded inquiries and a critical, multivocal ethic that emphasizes discovery, connection, and arrangement. We focus on inquiry and arrangement as two ways in which a *curatorial stance* reframes students' relationships to the intellectual work of writing and research, and we argue, such a stance encourages a sophisticated relationship with writing that enables students to claim ownership of their own writing.

For this article, we discuss the role of the curator, the *curatorial stance* in each of our classes, and an invitation to imagine how this metaphor might be taken up in writing pedagogy. We selected the student writing with which we work because it represents some of students' best practices in successful texts. Christine chose to address techniques used across several poems by Rebecca, Karissa, Brianna, and Thomas in her Spring 2011 Creative Writing course while Rochelle selected one exemplar piece and reflections from her Fall 2011 and Fall 2012 Composition II courses. Students gave us permission through signed, informed consent to discuss their writing and use their real names.

Curating Disciplinary Contexts

In both Creative Writing Studies and Composition Studies, scholar-teachers study, define, and debate the role of research in writing classrooms, to which the curation can add a new angle. Creative writing practitioners call for a more substantial emphasis on research in pedagogy to counter the lore, recycled stories, and important – but often narrow – insights from personal experience (e.g. Bizzaro, 2004; Healey, 2009; Mayers, 2009). Kimberly Andrews (2009: 250) argues that creative writing needs a 'hybrid discourse, one that allows [practitioners] to code-switch between the discourse of craft and the discourse of scholarship.' Some practitioners frame research as a bridge between craft and scholarship. Emily Orley (2009: 159, 160), for example, juxtaposes 'creative modes alongside more traditional academic forms' as an effort to address 'how to produce rigorous scholarly research about artistic practices without losing all the creative and imaginative impulses behind the work that existed in the first place.' Shady Cosgrove (2009) argues that research can help creative writing students address issues of representation, and Natasha Sajé (2009) takes up this issue as well, explaining that 'ethical difficulty arises when poets write about subjects superficially. Poets must know their subjects better than their best readers.' Clearly, the discipline values the development of research practices for students as they write creatively.

Compositionists discuss both the value of research as well as students' reactions to the research essay, an assignment that can inhibit the very intellectual work it is designed to encourage. Students still believe they cannot use 'I,' cannot have an opinion, can only use sources directly on a topic, and must make citation and flow the most important decisions even though writing theory has already exposed the inequities, ideologies, and hierarchies implicit in the traditional research paper (e.g. Davis & Shadle, 2000; Heilker, 1996; Hood, 2010).Teacher-scholars respond by designing innovative assignments that broaden understandings of the role of research, ranging from composing multi-genre texts, conducting service-learning projects with community-based programs, and using digital mediums: electronic portfolios, blogs, social media, and wikis (e.g. Balzhiser *et al.*, 2011; Coogan, 2006; Costello, 2011; Pullman, 2002; Romano, 2002; Weingarten, 2011). Yet, in all of these projects, students and teachers encounter resistance – sometimes from law enforcement, students, institutions and/or their own training (e.g. Blitz & Hurlbert, 1998; Crawford, 2005; Welch, 2005). Even in ethnographic research, a well-tested methodology in composition, difficulties can arise as students try to find, analyze, and trust non-library sources. A *curatorial stance* does not eliminate these difficulties but suggests another strategy for teachers to work within such difficulties.

That stance can prompt in-depth intellectual work in writing and research. Curators manage museum and gallery exhibits, build collections, make documentaries, develop curriculums, conduct historic preservation projects, maintain archives, and work with all levels of government and the private sector as consultants (e.g. Evans, 2010). Consistently asking large questions of small spaces, curators privilege the belief that history and cultural memory matter in how people go about their daily lives (e.g. McDaniel, 2004; Hawkins, 2010). Curators regularly work in archives, also a key site for historiographers. A growing number of compositionists draw on historiography and/or archives as sites to build new research and writing frameworks for students (e.g. Enoch, 2011; Kirsch & Rohan, 2008; Norcia, 2008). Our framing of the *curatorial stance* includes attention to how and where artifacts are gathered yet emphasizes the relationships a student can build with research objects – be it library sources, artifacts, gallery paintings, blog posts, text messages, experiences or memories – through inquiries that privilege multiple perspectives in and on the research gathered. A *curatorial stance*, then, shaped by these intellectual and disciplinary expectations can open up epistemologies, demand attention to methodologies, and provoke sophisticated inquiry and composing.

Student as Curator

As Christine walks into South Dakota State University's Agricultural Heritage Museum, a brick building south of the equestrian barn and west of the Dairy Bar, she mentally prepares to teach research in a creative writing course. *A student could write about this*, she thinks, eyeing the main gallery's centerpiece, a sixty-five horse-power steam engine weighing 20,600 pounds. Nearby, she sees a nursing bra patented in 1899 by a man from Deadwood, a child's two-in-one cloth doll, and a myriad of 19th-century tools. As she inhales smells of decaying paper, dust, oil, and wood, she chuckles. *This is the perfect place for students to confront what they believe to be true about writing poetry and conducting research,* she thinks. Eight hundred miles away at Kennesaw State University, Rochelle follows a fine arts curator across the hardwood floors of the Sturgis Art Gallery. White walls hold portraits, photographs, paintings, and prints from the Senior Art Student Exhibition series. In one corner, 17 kites silkscreened with monkeys, giraffes, an octopus, and a walrus float out of a tattered, cardboard box. Students across the room line up face-to-face with wooden masks. Her research and writing class undulates through the gallery and its texts, creating pools of students around a stormy canvas of a ship at sea and a continuous tide past the inexplicable pile of human hair on the floor. She wonders, *Will students see the arrangement choices in these exhibits? Can they translate those choices into textual arrangements for their writing?* Although we planned our visits to public history spaces to challenge students' composing choices, we came to understand that students' new relationships to texts became the real goal. As we studied the dynamics of that relationship, we discovered that crafting a *curatorial stance* for students involves an understanding of the epistemologies, critiques and applications of curatorial work.

A curator seeks existing knowledges and generates new knowledges about the sources and objects under study. Paul Chaat Smith (2008: 133) at the National Museum of the American Indian, sees the curatorial role as composing a narrative space that 'uses objects to provide an experience you cannot have any other way ... [and] generates controversy, questions, discussion, and yes, argument.' In that role, the 'creative effort' of research is emphasized as curators not only gather information but also create frameworks in which to generate new knowledge about the objects, histories, and data involved in an exhibit (Alloway, 2010: 221; Thomas, 2010: 6–7). Curating both scaffolds and complicates the research process by inquiring into a variety of possible facts, metaphors, information, ideas, and tensions about a subject for visitors to be 'active agents in the construction of knowledge' (Moser, 2010: 22). This methodology for research inquiry provides insight into inviting students into this work. As Christine's students interact with scrapbooks, journals and clippings, they respond to, ask questions of and focus on connections with artifacts from South Dakota's history. As Rochelle's students move through the gallery, they look as both visitor and writer to translate visual text arrangements into ways of writing. Generating an experience in the research process that mirrors an experience in the curated text – be it exhibit, essay, or poem – is creative, grounded in data, and dialogic, allowing those new frameworks of composing to take shape.

Taking responsibility for the ethics of research is part of crafting a *curatorial stance*. Since curators control the content of exhibits, determining the center and the margin of the ideological map (Ramirez, 2010: 22), this gaze can be complicit with the literal and metaphorical theft of artifacts from their contexts as well as institutionally sanctioned (often reductive) 'catalogs of meaning' (Powell, 2008: 122). Such critiques make the curatorial role troubling. Yet, if curators can generate the energetic dialogues Chaat Smith advocates, curators can become part of the critical project reframing public history spaces for debate, in what Janet Marstine (2007: 305) describes as the ongoing transformation of museological spaces from 'temples to forums.' This dialogism encouraging critical conversations is exactly the kind of intellectual work we desire in writing classes.

Curating both scaffolds and complicates traditional research processes by asking students to gather a variety of source-objects from multiple perspectives in, as Nichols Thomas (2010: 7) describes, a 'happening upon' openness. In an exhibit on Renaissance Italian texts, university students selected the objects to display, chose the theme, wrote the labels in both English and Italian, and installed a nine-case exhibit at the library. Students at the Tang Teaching Museum created the *Many Different Heavens* exhibit, which focused on Neolithic Irish and West African astronomical knowledges, as a critique of the Eurocentric focus of the professionally curated *A Very Liquid Heaven*. These exhibits reveal students' 'discovery of [an] intellectual and artistic voice' (Marstine, 2007: 7), acquisition of technical skills, and increased subject area knowledge (Falke, 2007: 221). Likewise for writing students, seeing the materials gathered in research as the objects of a collection that students draw on to both create and convey meaning invites students to inquire, discover, argue, connect, and arrange.

Poets in Christine's Class Adopt a Curatorial Stance

As my students gather around the table of artifacts at the 'As Soon as the Chores are Done' (2011) exhibit in the Agricultural Heritage Museum, they pick up white gloves, ready to shift to a *curatorial stance*. For the Poetry and Primary Research Project, I have asked students to write two poems inspired by research conducted here, and I know most of these students associate research with search engines and databases, not archives and exhibits. Yet many scholar-teachers regularly define research in ways that emphasize discovery and the creation of new knowledge, and I share these definitions with my students. Philip Gerard (2006) sees research as 'a habit, an attitude of open-minded alertness . . . It entices you into the public arenas of history and politics and catches you up in the shared public memory of a place, a community, a region. And ultimately . . . it leads you back through a new route into yourself.' Brenda Miller and Suzanne Paola (2004c: 162) stretch research to cover 'anything that takes you out of the realm of what you already know.' I want the archives to pique my students' intellectual curiosity and yield material for their poems.

After I frame the assignment, Carrie Van Buren (2011), the Museum's curator, demonstrates archive etiquette and explains the collection's history. 'Often, a person calls us because someone in her family has died and they don't want to throw away the photographs, diaries, etc. This scrapbook,' she says, holding up an eagle-embossed album, 'was sent home right before the war ended with the soldier's belongings.' She pauses. We let that story sink in; the soldier himself did not return. The details these artifacts offer encourages the kind of specificity readers of poetry value. As I learned with the 'writing from memory' work at the beginning of the course, many students compose first in abstractions. Designing a lesson that asks students to write in concrete language (as opposed to 'translating' thought into imagery) facilitates the writing of more effective poems.

As the students explore the artifacts, I reframe what material can 'inspire' poetry by asking them to observe closely. 'Pay attention to detail,' I coach, circulating around the table. 'What does it look like? Smell like? What shape is it? Does it have texture? The right detail can add believability.' Their pencils begin to move. Ben copies the shorthand in 'Hal's' journal so he can try to decipher it later; two students read the Christmas cards, cartoons, newspaper clippings, poems, and letters in the soldier's scrapbook (Hubbard, 2011;

Johnson, 2011). I hope this research facilitates a richer thinking about the intersections among personal, community, state and regional histories as well as how those farming histories cover indigenous histories.

I continue to instruct, asking students to use analysis and imagination to become active agents in the construction of knowledge: 'Listen to the artifacts. What stories do they tell? Don't they tell? What do they tell us about the ways people communicated, loved and died? Do you see tension in them?' Dani motions me over. 'This is a woman's garden journal,' she says. 'It notes what she planted and where. Her iris never seemed to grow and she quits trying right around the time Francis dies. Do you know who that is?' (Cummins, 2011). Her question seems rhetorical, and she turns back to the journal. In her poem, Francis becomes a beloved son who dies young. As the class ends, most of the students commit to a primary resource. Three students pour over Esther Brown's (2011) scrapbook and argue over how many suitors she entertained. Another student interviews Carrie Van Buren about a quilt's history. A few students study exhibits: replicas of farm kitchens and barns where they can gather plastic eggs from plastic hens and 'milk' water from a life-sized cow. I feel excited; already students have learned how to conduct basic archival research, and most have begun to ask questions. I hear two women discuss historical artifacts they possess – letters of a grandparent and great-grandparent. The buzz of discussion is rare for these reserved students.

The next week I see how this research influenced their writing processes when I walk around during peer response time. In trios, students talk about their artifacts: Addie's autograph book, Hal's daybook, embroidered handkerchiefs, and photographs taken in 1909 at a campus-sponsored dance (Harris, 2011; Hubbard, 2011). 'I identified the kind of shorthand Hal used,' Ben says, demonstrating his openness to discovery. 'But it's an old kind, and the library's copy of that kind of shorthand is missing. Odd, don't you think?' A few feet away, Brianna talks about constructing new knowledge by giving Esther Brown's (2011) spurned suitor a voice. Libby, too, seems interested in Esther Brown as a character. 'She always had men vying for her affection,' Libby says. The students discuss imagery, both in terms of where they need more and what those additions could be. I use their discussions of further research to integrate a mini-lecture about the differences between 'academic research style citation' and 'creative research citation.' Drawing on the advice of writer-teachers like Sondra Perl and Mimi Schwartz (2006), I outline the ways that creative writers can ethically acknowledge their source material, choices they have for their final portfolio of writing.

Drafts of the students' poems reveal the various ways students used their primary resources. Several students, like Rebecca, find a fragment of archival text to inspire additional research. 'Cindy Allison, Oysters, Ten Dollars' is Rebecca's twelve-line poem that conveys the oysters' journey from a New York City manufacturer to Cindy Allison's Thanksgiving table. Rebecca took the grocery store log entry (the title of her poem) and observed what other customers bought around the same time, which spurred her own inquiry into historical American Thanksgiving menus (Jaton, 2010). She used this research to flesh out the imagistic details in her poem. Karissa integrates visual imagery and exhibit descriptions. Her 'Washday on Monday' borrows words and phrases from Norman Thomsen's washbasin display, 'Growing Up on a Farm in the Thirties.' In another poem, 'Tackling Fall Chores,' she gives 'old house displays' a contextual narrative by showing glimpses of a family doing daily farm chores (Kuhle, 2011). Furthermore, Karissa demonstrates how she negotiated research, narrative, and imagery with the other writing techniques we discussed in class, namely the repetition of sound: 'Water and dib-dab of carbolic acid tackled / the cobwebs. Floors, mud-streaked, called / for sweeping and hands-on-knees mopping.'

When I receive the portfolios, students' inquiries and texts demonstrates excellent research and poetry. At least one-third of the students developed a line of inquiry that incorporated information from three, four, and five additional sources and demonstrated effective craft choices. In 'The Old Shanty,' inspired by the 'Hodges-Shanck Claim Shanty,' Brianna extended her research beyond her observations (Kunf, 2011).Using a website that specializes in finding graves, she found information about the shack's inhabitants to incorporate into her poem. Similarly, in a poem narrating a scene of two lovers parting, Brianna includes 'handkerchief history and lore' in which the handkerchief symbolizes surrender. She also used literary allusion to add additional layers. In her reflection work, Brianna writes: 'I took the idea of how the handkerchief in *Othello* was used to trick Othello into becoming jealous, as he came to believe that Desdemona was unfaithful. In Esther's letters, there were many men in her life, some at the same time.' Using an artifact as metaphor, she creates knowledge, deepens the meaning of the archival object, and suggests its possible historical and contextual significance.

Thomas's work exceeds my expectations because his process led him to investigate additional primary resources that offered new contextual information for his artifact. His poem, 'Adison, Not Addie,' narrates 'a day in the life' of Adison Harris, incorporating details from historical atlases, county histories, and the 1880 US Census (Cleberg, 2011). In his reflection, Thomas writes: 'Through the synthesis of census records, names of the classmates who signed the autograph book, and the name Eldora, Iowa, found in the book, [I have] identified that "Addie" was a boy named "Adison," not a girl named "Addison," as the book is currently attributed.' His in-depth inquiry resulted in a revision of the original assumptions about the archival artifact – the child's autograph book – demonstrating new knowledge creation. And his reflection reveals a transformation of attitude that allowed for lasting learning: 'At the Ag Museum, I wasn't engaged at all ... but this passed as soon as I began looking into the census records and clustering classmates into Eldora in the 1880s. I got excited because I knew things that no one else knew.'

In addition to untangling ideas about what constitutes the intellectual work of writing poetry and the critical work of conducting research, the Poetry and Primary Research Project encourages a broader understanding of what can constitute undergraduate student research, especially at a land-grant university where the dominant discourse for research occurs in the language of science and engineering and where undergraduates, if included in research, are often 'bean-counters,' document checkers, or the *subjects* of research conducted by others. This project, however, begins with student inquiry and careful observation, two important research skills. It disabuses students of the notion that research is just facts pasted into the body of a paper; instead, researched facts can be used as metaphor, as evidence that encourages a reader of literature to 'suspend their disbelief,' and as concrete details that appeal to readers' senses; these give students more rhetorical choices for how to use research. This project also requires students to digest the research so that they deliver new knowledge in their voice or a speaker they create for the purpose of the poem; in other words, it discourages the 'patchwork' effect I often see in more traditional kinds of research papers. Finally, many students claim their creative work as their 'own' more often than traditional kinds of research papers because they have drawn the research across their imaginations and experiences.

Curating the Research Collage in Rochelle's Class

At the Senior Art Exhibition (2011) in the KSU Sturgis Gallery, my students ponder a grouping of three paintings, trying on their new roles as curators by focusing on arrangement. 'What does this mean?' half-laughs Julie J. about one of the paintings that features a woman with pre-surgical, incision lines – dotted spheres around areolas, broken arcs on thigh and cheek. In places, torn canvas has been pressed back together, edges uneven. Sentences start and stutter, students' lips sewn shut against the image. Men glance into this alcove and veer away; women stand with faces of repulsion and fascination. This exhibit is one of the reasons I've brought the class to the gallery: to see how different enactments of arrangement craft meanings and how the *curatorial stance* enables that epistemological work. Students are at the end of a semester-long inquiry project in this Composition II course; they've written proposals, exploratory essays and a formal research essay. Now, they have the final assignment of the course, a collaborative collage essay. The collage does not replace the research essay with its clear arguments presented in discipline-specific formats; the collage provides a space to think through the rhetorical tensions students encounter in the research essay. Students often feel obligated to perform academic formats in the stranglehold of the five-paragraph script, in which one paragraph lasts for two pages, analysis suffers as 'bias,' or organization withers under the dictates of 'flow.' Since collages rely on juxtaposition, accretion, and arrangement instead of formal essay markers such as thesis statements, transitions, and topic sentences, the collage is another way to teach, and study, the rhetorical exigencies of academic writing. Students shift to a *curatorial stance* when they disassemble their existing texts and trawl them for pieces to contribute to the collage, seeing how new arrangements open up new insights into their topics.

Looking at the paintings in the gallery, I say to Julie J., 'What if the largest picture is an innocent girl who's wearing the bear hat and silly socks? Then there's this picture that's bugging us; I want to call it the way society critiques a woman's body. Then there's the final picture; it's horizontal, more comfortable. What about this story: She was innocent, had a moment of doubt, and she ultimately chooses her own body.' Eyebrows lift and heads nod.

'But what about the lemons on the background of the last painting?' Brittany asks. 'I mean, they're *lemons*, sour.'

'What if it went the other way,' Julie N. says, frowning and gesturing. 'Here's the woman. Then she goes to the doctor and gets all surgically changed. Then, she winds up younger-looking and happier.'

'That's cool,' says Madi.

'And difficult,' I say, wanting to argue yet appreciating the rhetorical analysis. 'I do think it's powerful how you have to decide what the order is. Different order, different story. *How* the paintings are exhibited is central to what meaning we make.' I pause. 'How might you write a collage essay based on this technique?' Madi and Julie J. stare at me. Julie N. and Brittany look thoughtful, turn back to the paintings.

In the gallery and in the assignment, I emphasize arrangement as a key curating practice, and students rhetorically analyze the overall organization of the gallery, specific vignettes of art, and the 'path' taken through the exhibit. I hear students discuss why an artist put Santa Claus by the cats in a painting, why the hair and barstool are placed so that visitors have to walk around them, and how the oversized canvas filled with golden stars in a maroon sky can be seen from anywhere in the gallery. Arrangement orders the 'visual, spatial, and material elements of an environment' (Dean, 1996: 32) to craft a 'space where visitors encounter curated representations' (Kratz, 2011: 38). By making decisions ranging from the selection of artifacts, theme, catalogs, and labels to architecture, wall color, lighting and event security, curators craft an intercultural, interdisciplinary space that exposes the debates and tensions in the subject under study (e.g. Ferguson, 2010; Kratz, 2011; Moser, 2010; Parman, 2010). In Composition Studies, too, arrangement is an essential element. As a canon of classical rhetoric, arrangement refers to how one orders the parts of a discourse; in more recent discussions, arrangement is framed as a function of genre (e.g. Devitt, 2004). Drawing on this long history and the scholars who argue for the essay as a dynamic form (e.g. Goldthwaite, 2003; Heilker, 1996; Lopate, 1994), I emphasize the collage's reliance on arrangement to reframe composing as a set of epistemological choices and encourage students to take ownership of their learning.

An essay by Julie J., Julie N., Jason, Madi and Brittany demonstrates how the *curatorial stance* yields a sophisticated arrangement that marks such ownership. This group began composing in the exhibit, becoming part of the exhibit themselves as they sat in a semicircle under a row of handmade paper books. I prompted students to look for connections and themes, experiences and contrasts. Students learned a strange diction of 'vignettes,' 'crots,' 'dingbats,' 'section breaks,' 'scenes,' 'interruption,' 'accretion,' and 'juxtaposition' to describe their rhetorical decisions (e.g. Elbow, 1997; Gallagher, 2000). Later, in the basement classroom with its banks of computers, I pick up the group's draft and read with that open-ended attention I have for all new collages, waiting for a strange zig or an odd zag as the essay begins to piece together different bits into one text. I explain the layering I see starting and the story I build based on the order they've chosen, a story that currently ends with a stark (yet stereotypical) description of a child in Africa. I ask, 'Is that the journey you want me to have as a reader? To start a search and end up starving and alone?' They look at me with glimmers of understanding, with frowns. I shift to a more rhetorical way of describing this work. 'It also looks like you kept each of your sections intact, one at a time. A collage needs more than five arrangement decisions.' This clicks for them, and we discuss possibilities as the students finally get down to the business of arranging: copy/paste, splice, embed, experiment with section breaks, brainstorm section headings, discover different ways to visually cue a shift, dive back into individual texts for more material, and recognize an emerging focus. Like the curators who create relationships between objects in an exhibit, the possible organizations students try requires reinterpreting each vignette, quote, or description. Students use such terms as 'mixing up,' 're-puzzle,' 'interlock,' 'weave,' 'mesh,' and 'back-and-forth' in their reflections to describe this composing;

they draw on the familiar term of 'story' to describe their writing goal of making 'connections.'

The group's finished essay demonstrates how a text can both create new knowledge from existing knowledges as students master the technical skill of the collage format and make a deliberate (albeit implicit) argument. 'Our Journey' (Jones et al., 2013) introduces a search for 'home' and then offers a series of experiences that reframe the concept, suggesting that home is multiple, global, local, and requires the construction of family. Nichols Thomas (2010: 10, 8) argues that the best exhibits in museums 'offer their audiences problems instead of solutions,' that the specific objects in an exhibit should provoke viewers to ask 'what these categories and distinctions might mean, where they come from, where they mislead, and where they remain useful or unavoidable.' Simply by starting the essay in a spinning moment of introspection as Julie J. (Jones et al., 2013: 96–97) searches a crowd for her birth mother – *'This is silly,* Julie would tell herself. She is miles away and the chance of running into her at Six Flags is absurd' – the students plunge readers into this search for 'home' and its uncertainty, creating the problem that readers must resolve.

Then, students make two key moves in the middle of the essay that reframe the idea of 'home.' First, Julie N. (Jones et al., 2013: 99) describes her fellow passengers on a trip to Haiti – 'filmographers from Columbia and Argentina who didn't speak a lick of English and were as hairy as cavemen but as kind as kittens, a well renowned American photographer, four American teenagers, and even a famous Mexican actor' – as she disembarks. By dislocating readers from the US – where Brittany had solidly embedded them with questions about the Coles Street Housing Project and the expectations any United States citizen should have of her neighborhood – and explaining the mixed feelings of terror and welcome that accompany the Haiti trip, Julie's vignette is a stark contrast to Madi's childhood memory. In the next vignette, Madi (Jones et al., 2013: 100–101) recreates the scene of being at home and receiving a *National Geographic* picture book for Christmas with a picture of a starving child in Africa: 'At first she thought, *This cannot be real.* But upon reading the photograph description, Madi learned it was real. It's still real.' However, that scene takes place in a typical suburban American home, inverting the expansion movement of the essay by pulling the questions, energies, terrors, and welcome of the entire globe back into the daily, lived spaces of an individual. Madi doesn't argue directly for a specific definition of home; the students communicate the effort it takes to understand families and homes through arrangement.

The final two sections of the essay demonstrate how this *curatorial stance* allows students to take ownership by using arrangement to add a redefinition of 'family' to their reframed 'home.' Jason (Jones *et al.*, 2013: 101–102) has a lengthy vignette narrating an interview with his employer and his father, the owner of an industrial fabrication company. The notions of family from Julie J.'s and Madi's vignettes that readers bring to this section become more nuanced as Jason describes family members who are also colleagues. He then introduces a cast of characters from his workplace, a non-biological family: Dixon the Machinist, Arthur, Ted full of 'dirty humor,' Louis, and Phillip the 'fast mover.' Jason describes the factory's machines – press brakes and quarter inch shears, turret punch machines and CNC burn tables – as the fabricators follow 'the project all the way through to the end. It's their own process; it's their own art form.' To this layered idea of family, Jason adds an emphasis on fabrication – on building a product from scratch with talented, idiosyncratic people – that becomes a metaphoric blueprint for how to address the difficulties raised in the essay: hunger in African children, destruction and loss in post-earthquake Haiti, and the questions of *who am I* and *who are Americans* and *what is a home*. The collage ends by returning to Haiti as Julie N. (Jones *et al.*, 2013: 102) wakes up on an ordinary day in a resident's small home to the smell of baking bread: 'Julie opened her eyes and suddenly knew exactly where she was.' The dialogic movement across the layers – and across the gaps – fills a simple ending scene with nuanced, simultaneous meanings. Julie was in a home changed-yet-familiar, filled with a 'family' both genetically connected as well as encompassing a plane full of strangers, residents of a Georgia street, men from a factory, a foreign country and people never met on another continent.

The collaborative collage assignment shows how a specific focus on a rhetorical element can illuminate the intellectual work of writing. 'Our Journey' not only earned a successful grade in the course but also won the 2011 KSU 'Emerging Writers' contest – judged by *Brevity* editor Dinty W. Moore and included publication in the contest journal – because these writers accepted the invitation to take up a new relationship to composing. In end-of-course reflections, students consistently focus on insights about arrangement and meaning: 'Arrangement, whether it is linear or not helps identify precedence of information. It helps build up smaller ideas into the overall picture.' This willingness to re-see arrangement as non-linear – as a deliberate choice to be made, not a script to follow – is evidence of students seeing their texts as their own. Students contextualized the study of arrangement in the collage retrospectively, re-seeing each previous writing assignment from that vantage point. As Alex explains:

> I didn't realize how organization can change the tone or message of an essay. Like in our first essays we were telling a story. The reader needed

to move with the author through the space we were writing about to get a good sense of how the place looked. ... And then of course we all had trouble organizing the research essay after gathering our notes ... Now with the collaborative essays everything about flow and organization has been flipped upside-down ... The point is – arrangement can make or break an essay, so it is very important to consider the material, audience and the statement your essay is making to help decide how it should best be arranged.

The authors of 'Our Journey' (Jones *et al.*, 2013) describe their insight as simply learning 'how to see' – how to see their inquiries, composing, arrangement, the collage, and each other as they 'felt for one another when we read what each of us had written throughout the semester.' The intellectual space of the collage demanded sophisticated rhetorical work in which student learning emerged from selecting their purposes, arranging their research, and crafting texts that encompassed dialogic points of view.

Curating Pedagogies: An Invitation

In taking up a *curatorial stance,* our students transformed their resistance to two of the most intimidating, and potentially frustrating, aspects of writing – research and arrangement. Such a stance doesn't neglect the wonderful elements of writing pedagogy already present in our classes – portfolios and reflections, journals/blogs, discussion, peer response, drafts and feedback, rhetorical analysis and studies of argument and craft. The stance is a metaphor and an entry point, a different invitation for students into that dynamic, generative space that academic research can be, a space where disciplines like creative writing, rhetoric and public history can coalesce to provide new insights into familiar pursuits. Emphasizing curating gives some heft to the invitation into this intellectual work where students stand in the middle of competing tensions, make choices and understand how and why those choices work the ways they do. Students in our classes did not see research as a network of quotes demonstrating correct citations and did not assume texts followed scripted, ideal organizations. Like the exhibits that deliberately craft critical conversations with their visitors, we saw students make hard composing choices when given the invitation to do so. In this spirit, we ask our readers, and ourselves, to consider this question: how can assignments be created or revised to invite students to take up a *curatorial stance*?

Two approaches suggest themselves. First, how might primary research be included in (existing) assignments? Reframing 'research' by introducing primary research into projects can encourage students to re-think their relationships to research and its purposes. Primary sources – interviews, observations, surveys, archival artifacts – can be found in many spaces, both tangible and digital. Places that hold archival possibilities in particular include the student union, dorms, faculty offices, student annuals, display cases, public libraries, city or county administration buildings and historical societies. The staff members at historic sites and museums have experience with different research techniques. Second, how might arrangement enhance the intellectual work of an (existing) assignment? Emphasizing arrangement can reframe students' understandings of how and why texts are composed. Arrangement can be accentuated in an assignment by having students make room for a specific kind of source, concept, or visual. Changing the genre of an assignment to one with a heightened attention to arrangement, designing workshops in which pieces of an assignment are composed separately so that students determine organization, and adapting a non-written model –like an exhibit, a city, a piece of art – as a structure for a written assignment can open up a *curatorial stance* for student writers. To include primary research and/or emphasis on arrangement in our classes, we scheduled visits, crafted new assignment documents, designed workshops to teach unfamiliar material, and created space in the class for conversations supporting students' writing.

Poet and teacher Priscilla Uppal (2007: 48) captures a sense of the pedagogical work at the heart of the *curatorial stance* when she writes, 'If students arrive with limited experience and a restricted range of response to authorship, the task of the creative writing teacher first and foremost must be to give them exercises that *expand and open* their creativity.' If we replace the word 'creative' with 'critical thinking,' then Uppal also describes what a composition teacher could be doing. And, if a teacher believes, as we do that academic inquiry is an inherently creative act, then no words need replaced for Uppal to describe what composition and creative writing classes could be doing. The *curatorial stance* offers a means of approaching writing and research across a breadth of rhetorical situations, and this is the best of what we do as practitioners of writing: we study, synthesize, theorize, orchestrate, and take action on the materials and texts with which we come into contact. Through its emphasis on inquiry and openness, a *curatorial stance* demands students ask questions about artifacts, texts and the information emerging from them while reminding students of the ethics of research and meaning-making. Through its emphasis on arrangement, it affirms students' choices as they seek their own sophistications in their writing. We know that some writing goals will get missed with this stance but we hope those goals are ones that should be deemphasized, those that require students to memorize containers for writing instead of curating for themselves the texts that reflect their discoveries and knowledges.

References

Alloway, L. (2010) The great curatorial dim-out. In R. Greenberg, B.W. Ferguson and S. Nairne (eds) *Thinking about Exhibitions* (pp. 159–165). London: Routledge.

Andrews, K. (2009) A house divided: On the future of creative writing. *College English* 71 (3), 242–255.

As soon as the chores are done. (2011) Exhibition based on *Bob Artley's Book of Farm Chores: As Remembered by a Former Kid*, 2003. South Dakota State Agricultural Heritage Museum. Brookings, SD: SDSU.

Balzhiser, D., Grover, M., Lauer, E., McNeely, S., Polk, J.D., Zmikly, J., Holmes, C., Porter, E., Saucier, C. and Swearingen, T. (2012) 'The facebook papers', *Kairo* 16 (1). See http://www.technorhetoric.net/16.1/praxis/balzhiser-et-al/ (accessed March 2012).

Bizzaro, P. (2004) Research and reflection in English studies: The special case of creative writing. *College English* 66 (3), 294–309.

Blitz, M. and Hurlbert, C.M. (1998) *Letters for the Living: Teaching Writing in a Violent Age*. Urbana, IL: National Council of Teachers of English.

Brown, E.M. (2011) College Years Scrapbook, 1918–1924. Acc# 83:43:02. In As soon as the chores are done, South Dakota State Agricultural Heritage Museum. Brookings, SD: SDSU.

Cleberg, T. (2011) Adison, not addie. Student poem.

Coogan, D. (2006) Service learning and social change: The case for material rhetoric.' *College Composition and Communication* 57 (4), 667–693.

Cosgrove, S. (2009) WRIT101: Ethics of representation for creative writers. *Pedagogy: Critical Approaches to Teaching Literature, Language, Composition, and Culture* 9 (1), 134–205.

Costello, L.A. (2011) The new art of revision? Research papers, blogs, and the first-year composition classroom. *Teaching English in the Two-Year College* 39 (2), 151–167.

Crawford, I. (2005) Playing in traffic: A timely metaphor for postmodern ethnography and composition pedagogy. *Composition Studies* 33 (2), 11–23.

Cummins, L.S. (2011) Farm Ledgers, 1917–1933 & 1944–1975. Acc# 2008:038:01. In as soon as the chores are done, South Dakota State Agricultural Heritage Museum. Brookings, SD: SDSU.

Davis, R. and Shadle, M. (2000) 'Building a mystery': Alternative research writing and the academic act of seeking. *College Composition and Communication* 51 (3), 417–446.

Dean, D.R. (1996) *Museum Exhibition: Theory and Practice*. New York: Routledge.

Devitt, A.J. (2004) *Writing Genres*. Carbondale, IL: SIUP.

Elbow, P. (1997) Collage: Your cheatin' art. *Writing on the Edge* 9 (1), 300–313.

Enoch, J. (2011) Remembering sappho: New perspectives on teaching (and writing) women's rhetorical history. *College English* 73 (5), 518–537.

Evans, J. (2000) What is public history. *The Public History Resource Center*, September. See http://www.publichistory.org/what_is/definition.html (accessed 16 November 2011).

Falke, M.V. (2007) The student as curator: Real world lessons in the humanities. *International Journal of the Humanities* 5 (2), 215–222.

Ferguson, B.W. (2010) Exhibition rhetorics: Material speech and utter sense. In R. Greenberg, B.W. Ferguson and S. Nairne (eds) *Thinking about Exhibitions* (pp. 175–190). London: Routledge.

Gallagher, C. (2000) If this were not a collage: A collage. *Writing on the Edge* 11 (2), 33–42.
Gerard, P. (2006) The art of creative research. *The Writer's Chronicle* 39 (2). See https://www.awpwriter.org/magazine_media/overview (accessed February 2012).
Goldthwaite, M. (2003) Confessionals. *College English* 66 (1), 55–73.
Harris, A. Autograph Album, 1880–1882. Acc# 78:10:02. In As soon as the chores are done, South Dakota State Agricultural Heritage Museum. Brookings, SD: SDSU.
Hawkins, P.S. (2010) Naming names: The art of memory and the names project aids quilt. In R. Greenberg, B.W. Ferguson and S. Nairne (eds) *Thinking about Exhibition* (pp. 133–158). London: Routledge.
Healey, S. (2009) The rise of creative writing and the new value of creativity. *The Writer's Chronicle* 41 (4). See https://www.awpwriter.org/magazine_media/overview (accessed February 2013).
Heilker, P. (1996) *The Essay: Theory and Pedagogy for an Active Form.* Urbana, IL: NCTE.
Hood, C.L. (2010) Ways of research: The status of the traditional research paper assignment in first-year writing/composition courses. *Composition Forum* 22. See http://compositionforum.com/issue/22/ways-of-research.php (accessed July 2012).
Hubbard, H. (2011) Diary, 1896–97. Acc# 78:162:08. In As soon as the chores are done, South Dakota State Agricultural Heritage Museum. Brookings, SD: SDSU.
Jaton, R. (2010) Cindy Allison, oysters, ten dollars. Student poem.
Johnson, A. (2011) Soldier's Scrapbook, 1941–1944. Acc# 2002:25:02. In *As Soon as the Chores are Done*.South Dakota State Agricultural Heritage Museum. Brookings, SD: SDSU.
Jones, J., Wilkins, J., Hernandez, M., Ngo, J. and Adkins, B. (2013) Our journey, their world, our canvas. *Emerging Writers* 3, 96–103.
Kirsch, G.E. and Rohan, L. (2008) Introduction: The role of serendipity, family connections, and cultural memory in historical research. In G.E. Kirsh and L. Rohan (eds) *Beyond the Archives: Research as a Lived Process* (pp. 1–9). Carbondale, IL: Southern Illinois UP.
Kratz, C. (2011) Rhetorics of value: Constituting worth and meaning through cultural display. *Visual Anthropology Review* 27 (1), 21–48.
Kuhle, K. (2011) Washday on Monday and Tackling fall chores. Student poems.
Kunf, B. (2011) The old shanty and The handkerchief. Student poems.
Lopate, P. (1994) (ed.) *The Art of the Personal Essay: An Anthology from the Classical Era to the Present.* New York: Anchor.
Marstine, J. (2007) What a mess! Claiming a space for undergraduate student experimentation in the university museum. *Museum Management and Curatorship* 22 (3), 303–315.
Mayers, T. (2009) From creative writing to creative writing studies. *College English* 71 (3), 217–288.
McDaniel, G.W. (2004) At historic houses and buildings: Connecting past, present, and future. In J.B. Gardner and P.S. LaPaglia (eds) *Public History: Essays from the Field* (pp. 233–255). Malabar, FL: Krieger.
Miller, B. and Paola, S. (2004) *Tell It Slant: Writing and Shaping Creative Nonfiction.* New York: McGraw Hill.
Moser, S. (2010) The devil is in the detail: Museum displays and the creation of knowledge. *Museum Anthropology* 33 (1), 22–23.
Norcia, M.A. (2008) Out of the ivory tower endlessly rocking: Collaborating across disciplines and professions to promote student learning in the digital archive. *Pedagogy* 8 (1), 91–114.

Orley, E. (2009) Getting at and into place: Writing as practice and research. *Journal of Writing and Creative Practice* 2 (2), 159–171.

Parman, A. (2010) Exhibit makeovers: Do-it-yourself exhibit planning. *History News*. See http://www.utahhumanities.org/files/MII-Exhibit-Makeovers.pdf (accessed July 2012).

Perl, S. and Schwartz, M. (2006) *Writing True: The Art and Craft of Creative Nonfiction*. Boston: Houghton Mifflin.

Powell, M. (2008) Dreaming Charles Eastman: Cultural memory, autobiography, and geography in indigenous rhetorical histories. In G.E. Kirsh and L. Rohan (eds) *Beyond the Archives: Research as a Lived Process* (pp. 115–127). Carbondale, IL: Southern Illinois UP.

Pullman, G. (2002) Electronic portfolios revisted: The efolio-project. *Computers and Composition* 19 (2), 151–169.

Ramirez, M. (2010) Brokering identities: Art curators and the politics of cultural representation. In R. Greenberg, B.W. Ferguson and S. Nairne (eds) *Thinking about Exhibitions* (pp. 21–38). London: Routledge.

Romano, T. (2002) Teaching writing through multi-genre papers. In R. Tremmel and W. Broz (eds) *Teaching Writing Teachers of High School English and First-Year Composition* (pp. 53–65). Portsmouth, NH: Boynton.

Sajé, N. (2009) 'Poetry and ethics: Writing about others.' *The Writer's Chronicle.* See https://www.awpwriter.org/magazine_media/overview (accessed February 2012).

Senior Art Exhibition II. (2011) Sturgis Library Art Gallery. Kennesaw, GA: Kennesaw State University, November 22–December 6.

Smith, P.C. (2008) Critical reflections on the our peoples exhibit: A curator's perspective. In A. Lonetree and A.J. Cobb (eds) *The National Museum of the American Indian* (pp. 131–143). Lincoln: Nebraska UP.

Thomas, N. (2010) The museum as method. *Museum Anthropology* 33 (1), 6–10.

Uppal, P. (2007) Both sides of the desk: Experiencing creative writing lore as a student and as a professor. In K. Ritter and S. Vanderslice (eds) *Can It Really Be Taught?: Resisting Lore in Creative Writing Pedagogy* (pp. 46–54). Portsmouth, NH: Boynton/Cook-Heinemann.

Van Buren, C. (2011) *Etiquette in the Archives*. Class lecture, Creative Writing I from South Dakota State University, Brookings, SD. 3 February.

Weingarten, K. (2011) Authoring wikis: Rethinking authorship through digital collaboration. *Radical Teacher* 90 (1), 47–57.

Welch, N. (2005) Living room: Teaching public writing in a post-publicity era. *College Composition and Communication* 56 (3), 470–492.

9 Audience Resurrected: Restoring Motive and Purpose to Creative Writing

Michael Kula

To begin, let's set the scene. Outside there's a breeze, and the trees in the quad are just beginning to show hints of the yellows and browns that will come when the weather fully turns later in the month. But for now, the leaves are still mostly green, and it's warm out, clear sun in fact, as it always seems to be these first days of the new academic year. In front of me, the desks are arranged in a circle, positioned so the students will face mainly each other, and it's a sight some of the students groan to as they enter, realizing there's no back row, no place to hide if they expect to sleep or doodle or text on their phones not-so-discretely.

The class is Introduction to Fiction Writing, and as each student takes their seat, the circle is filled in, leaving 20 or so faces staring back at me eagerly or nervously or sometimes with a blend of both. Then, before going over the syllabus or even introducing myself, I begin the hour by asking the students to pull out a pen and paper. It's a writing class after all, so let's write. A free write. Startled, the students rifle through folders, elbow neighbors for an extra pencil, and once they're settled again, I scribble the question on the board and ask them to write their response. *Why do you want to write fiction?*

To this, some of the students will nod, tuck their heads and go at it without delay. Others, however, will linger without moving for a minute or so, staring at me or out the window at those leaves fluttering in the wind. In their hesitation, I like to think those students are in deep thought, contemplating the very essence of the artistic impulse that's brought them here; but I'm wise enough to know it's probably not that. Instead, from experience, I expect that what most of them are thinking is that they don't necessarily *want* to write fiction at all – what they *want* is an easy A or just a break from their regular schedules filled with macro-this or micro-that – but this, they surely imagine, can't be what I want to hear. So instead of being blunt and honest, they try to please me, writing something vague about how much they like books or how much they've always enjoyed writing stories.

When everyone has finished, their pencils and pens snapped down on the desks, I begin on one side of the circle, asking each student to read what he or she has written and for the most part, they're all the answers I expect, the same ones I've heard year after year whenever I've used the prompt. 'I write fiction because it's a great escape from the stress of life.' Thank you, next. 'I want to write fiction to explore my imagination.' Interesting, next. 'I want to write fiction to express the feelings I have inside.' Very nice, next. 'I write fiction because I enjoy putting together stories.' Excellent, thank you.

I'm not entirely sure when I began using this prompt, though I know it was early in my career when I was still feeling my way with classroom management. I suppose it seemed a good way to decentralize the class, to get the students talking right away. A good old-fashioned icebreaker. And for that purpose, it's always functioned just fine. However, with each passing year of using the prompt, with each semester of listening to all those variations of the same responses, I felt myself beginning to tune out, even grow strangely aggravated as the students shared their answers. But why? Outside of the classroom, that question – why do you want to write fiction? – is really an interesting one, perhaps one of the hardest questions for me or any artist to answer. Why do we do this? Why do we *want* to do this? And in thinking about it, I knew my students' responses were all fine answers. There was no reason for me to expect any deeply self-analyzed understanding of their motives for choosing the subject, since I'm certain if I were asked the same question at twenty, I probably would have said something very similar. So why did their answers trouble me?

Fast forward a few years now. I moved schools. A new crop of students. Different demographics. Different trees out the window. Surely, I thought, things would be different here if I asked that same question. *Why do you want to write fiction?* But, no. Once again, every year, it was the same thing, versions of those same answers. 'I want to write fiction to express things that aren't real.' Interesting. 'I want to write fiction because I can be creative and do whatever I want with it.' Nice. 'I want to write fiction because it will be fun to use much more of my imagination.' Thank you. Again, there was nothing inherently wrong in any of these responses. After all, in writing fiction, I like to use my imagination. I like to be creative. I enjoy putting stories together. So what was the problem?

And then, I met *her* – let's call her Jennifer – an adult student, a nursing major who'd returned to college after several years of a career and several more years of raising a family. As I would later find out, at the time of my class she was working part-time and juggling a home life with two sons in elementary school, and looking back on it now, for her, that question was a particularly good one. With everything else she had going on in her life, why in the world did she want to write fiction? Her answer: 'I want to write fiction because as a mother I have always told my children stories. Sometimes there's a moral, sometimes my stories are just for entertainment, but either way, I want to improve, so I can reach my kids better.' On the surface this initially seemed no better or worse a response than any of the others I'd received; yet that night as I pulled out and reread those freewrites at home, it hit me. It was one of the first answers I'd seen – or at least that I could recall – that explicitly mentioned anything about having an audience and having an outward-looking purpose at the core of her motivation to create fiction. In her response, Jennifer demonstrated an understanding of what I'd always assumed was obvious to my students: that we write fiction in order to say something to or do something for an outsider, whether it be to present a moral or an idea or perhaps simply to evoke some emotional response. Like any other genre or rhetorical mode, at the end of the process, there is a reader, an audience, and if we fail to recognize this, then we are missing, perhaps, the entire point of the endeavor. Yet with the exception of Jennifer's, the rest of the responses in that class only commented on the things the students *liked* about the creative writing process: 'I want to write fiction because I can be creative and do whatever I want with it.' Or on the things writing in a creative genre did *for* them: 'I write fiction because it is a great escape from the stress of life.' Removed from the context of my class, these responses could just as easily be applied to journaling or keeping a diary as to fiction writing and with this I realized that my opening day icebreaker had inadvertently uncovered a significant issue with the way my students approached the class, not to mention a major oversight in the way I'd been teaching the subject.

After that, for the next several semesters, I continued to use my opening prompt, only now I paid more careful attention to assessing how little awareness of audience my students had when expressing their motives for writing fiction. Indeed, as I have attempted to study it more formally – collecting and logging my students' responses each semester – I've discovered just how much of an outlier Jennifer's insightful answer had been. To this day, on average less than 10% of my students ever comment on the importance of the reader or the role of the audience in explaining their motive for writing fiction, and most of them simply express something along the lines of those self-centered and self-interested reasons I've heard for years. But, you might be wondering, so what? What's the problem here? What's wrong if our students fail to see their writing as audience-directed and their motives are driven more by what the writing does for themselves, than by what it does for a reader? And in a way, you'd be right. Certainly it's a good thing that our students connect personally with the material, and it can obviously be helpful if they enjoy it on some level. However, as I see it, by letting this mindset go unchallenged, we allow our students to forget that the reader expects something from them, or as Kurt Vonnegut (1999: 12) put it in his first rule for writing a good short story, that their writing should 'use the time of a total stranger in such a way that he or she will not feel the time was wasted.'

Indeed, we can see evidence for this same idea in a recent interview with Sherman Alexie. When asked essentially the same question I ask my students on day-one of my course – why do you want to write? – he responded by saying: 'The fact is, I want to move rooms full of people. I want to move someone sitting alone under a reading lamp. I want to move someone sitting on a beach. I want to make them laugh and cry' (Alexi in Case, 2012). Now, does Sherman Alexie also enjoy being creative? Of course. Does he also want to sell books? No doubt. And does he want the economic benefits that come with that success? We could assume so. But are those his motives for *why* he writes? Clearly not. His motive, in its purest rhetorical definition, is to reach his audience, to move them. This, as Matthew Parfitt (2012: 111) states it in the Composition handbook *Writing in Response*, is his work's 'basic purpose and reason for existing.'

Fortunately, as the field of Creative Writing has undergone growth in the scholarly inquiry into its pedagogy and practice, we do not need to rely simply on the suggestions of Kurt Vonnegut or the anecdotes of Sherman Alexie to see that addressing questions of motive and audience awareness with our students would be a good thing. Thankfully researchers have begun to study this same issue more rigorously, and in one case, researchers in Great Britain set out to measure precisely how much consideration fiction writers gave to their audience when writing. Using professional authors as their subjects, each of whom had published at least one book of fiction, Evers and Kolle (2012) conducted controlled interviews and then coded the authors' responses in an effort to isolate moments that demonstrated their level of concern for their audience. The results these researchers found after analyzing the data, while somewhat preliminary at this point, are important for my argument in two ways. First, they (Evers & Kolle, 2012: 14) found that the writers they interviewed thought 'more about their audience than they admit(ed).' And second, perhaps even more helpful for us to consider in our work with emerging writers, Evers and Kolle (2012: 16) found that the 'more experienced an author is, the more he/she is aware of his/her audience and also of what kind of impact the audience has on them and their writing.' From these findings, if we reconsider my students' responses to my free write, we can assume, in light of the first point, that many of the students do have some awareness of audience as part of their motive, even if not explicitly stated. We can also assume, in light of the second point, that there is likely to be a relationship between the level of audience awareness in our students and their level of experience with writing, as Jennifer's experience with her children might further support. To this, some might argue that there is nothing we can or should do about it: the audience awareness will develop naturally in our students as they gain more experience. As writing teachers though, I believe that it is our role to expose students to the best practices of the field, and if it's been documented that the most advanced writers demonstrate a high level of audience awareness, then don't we owe it to our students to teach toward that ends, rather than simply assuming the awareness will develop on its own with time and practice?

Armed with this new insight and inspired to challenge my students to resurrect their awareness of audience as part of their motive to write, I turned to the books around me for help. One by one I scoured the creative writing textbooks on my shelves, looking for any that offered insights and practical guidance for working with my students on audience. To my disappointment and only partial surprise, there was little I could find. The best, if not only, material I found that directly related to audience and motive was in Wallace Stegner's (2002) landmark book, *On Teaching and Writing Fiction*; but beyond that, none of the indices or tables of content in the more practical-oriented textbooks had any sections dedicated to teaching motive or purpose or even audience. Then, in examining each one more closely, I found that there were only superficial references to the 'reader' or to the workshop 'participants,' and most of these passages were concerned with smaller issues than motive, things like how to make characters believable and when to include backstory to help the readers follow a story.

My own observations about this have been shown more fully in Christine Peter Cucciare's (2008) large-scale study of pedagogical approaches to the subject audience in creative writing classes. In her research, Cucciare (2008: 29) analyzed the contents of the most common creative writing texts and confirmed what I had seen: 'Within books and articles on creative writing, few authors address audience ... explicitly.' She continued her research beyond the textbooks and analyzed the syllabi from dozens of creative writing courses across the country, and again she (Cucciare, 2008: 120) found the same results that the role of audience, even loosely defined, was directly addressed in far less than half of the class syllabi. This, at least, offered me some solace as I realized I had not been alone in my relative neglect of the subject. Unfortunately it still didn't offer me any help, and for that, I had to look toward my other classes, those in academic writing.

During the semester I first began searching for a practical way to address audience in my creative writing classes, I was teaching a section of composition – a course almost exclusively focused on argumentation at my university – and in the midst of working with that class on developing rhetorical strategies to counter reader opposition, it hit me. Couldn't this – reader opposition – be seen very much like the issue of disbelief in fiction writing? Aren't the questions I heard my students voice in a workshop about how a certain character or event in a peer's story wasn't believable, identical to the objections my composition students raised when I asked them to challenge the logic of an essay's argument during a peer review? And don't we, in fiction, have to anticipate the ways our audience will doubt the verisimilitude in our stories, the same way we, in argumentation, have to preemptively defuse our counterarguments? I realized then that the help I'd been seeking had been right in front of me the entire time. To resurrect audience awareness – in its macro sense – I could look toward rhetoric for help, since as Cucciare (2008) showed, the subject is far more often found in composition and rhetoric texts, than in those of creative writing. I suspect this will change in the coming years as our field grows continually more reflective in its scholarship of teaching, and I hope the practical suggestions I outline now, each adapted from more rhetorical approaches, will be part of an ever-expanding dialogue about how, not to mention why, we should address audience and motive in the creative writing classroom.

So, how have I done it? Well, to be honest, with considerable trial and error; but fortunately also, with some solid success:

1. Make it Explicit

As I have experimented in my fiction classes, one of the most effective techniques I've found is the simplest: make it explicit. By this I mean that we should be up front with our students about those big questions about audience, purpose, and motive, the same way we are in our academic writing classes. How many of us ever stop and ask a student why his or her short story should even exist? I do not mean this question in its largest, most theoretical sense – i.e. why should art exist? – but rather on an individualized level. In my academic writing classes, I have introduced this concept to students by using two words: so what? As I have found, many of our beginning writers come to a Composition class thinking that the goal of academic writing is simply to parrot the thoughts and ideas already put forth by others, and not to make new contributions of their own. In my classes, I spend considerable time and energy trying to teach my students that they should seek to say something new, that readers should care about what they are saying, and when I conference with my academic writing students, I feel at times like a broken record with this question. *So what?* Why should someone read your argument and not the primary sources from which it draws?

It might at first seem harsh and perhaps even combative to ask a student fiction writer this question. *So what? Why should I bother reading this?* Yet when asked in a supportive way, I've found it very helpful. I should note that the question has been most effective for me when I've used it as part of the revision process. I've found that when I've asked it too early, when students are still writing first drafts of their stories, young writers inadvertently get the idea that they need to be writing about something serious, which, I think, is over playing the hand and can have a tendency of causing a young writer to freeze and lock up, thinking that the material they'd been planning to use isn't important enough. I've found instead, that the question can be particularly helpful after a round of workshopping, when students are going back to the drawing board and genuinely re-seeing their stories. By that point they've already established an artistic vision in their early draft, and rather than prompting a sort of writerly stage-fright, the question has a way of inspiring them to look deeper into the work and help them recognize important themes and ideas that arose organically in the draft, themes and ideas an audience could easily be made to care about.

2. The Rhetorical Situation

A second way I've worked to be more explicit with my students about audience and motive is to fall back on the key terms and concepts of my academic writing classes. In teaching argumentation, I regularly frame their assignments around four terms: idea, evidence, audience and purpose. In those classes, I spend a great deal of time showing the students how nearly any writing task – from a love letter to a grocery list to chemistry lab report – can be analyzed through these concepts. Strangely, until recently, it was an approach I'd never taken with my fiction classes.

Having now done so, I've found that by drawing attention to these concepts in creative writing, my students are able to transfer some of their knowledge from academic writing and more easily analyze the component parts of their drafts. For example, by framing plot and character as evidence, my students are better able to see that those parts of the story must serve some greater ends, some purpose, and in order to understand that purpose, they need to consider audience. As I often put it, in order to know how best to say something, you need to know *to whom* you are saying it (audience) and *why* (purpose). During the many times I've used this approach, I've watched as my creative writing students have sat in nearly stunned silence as they realized that while they'd enjoyed writing the draft and thought it successful on many levels, they'd never stopped to consider to whom they were writing or why.

3. The Metaphor of Conversation

Inspired by one of the traditional ways the field of rhetoric has framed argumentation, I have begun to borrow the metaphor of conversation and apply it to short fiction. What does this mean? In my composition classes, I will often have students read several arguments that speak back to each other about similar issues (an idea central to popular rhetoric texts like *Ways of Reading* and *They Say, I Say*) and then ask my students to situate themselves within that on-going conversation about ideas. In their reading, my students are *listening* to what others have to say, and in their writing, as they formulate their own arguments, those voices my students have read then become part of the audience as they seek to make their own new contributions to the conversation.

So how might one begin to frame fiction writing in this way? How can it be seen as a *conversation*? One example would be the way I have addressed the issue of coming-of-age stories with my classes. I have noticed through the years that it is one of the most common themes my students explore in their work. In this case, I use the metaphor of conversation to frame the discussion after having my students read several professional stories that deal with coming-of-age. After that, I ask them to consider what each author is *saying* about the process of maturing. For example, in the past I've used Joyce Carol Oates' 'Where Are You Going, Where Have You Been?' along with Leonard Michel's 'Murders' to show how each story is *saying* something different about the way we come of age. In the Oates story, for instance, the climax comes when the young narrator chooses to walk out the front door of her house, knowing full well that she is headed for danger. In the Michels story, the climax is built around a young boy who goes exploring and eventually watches his friend slip to his death off a rooftop. If we reduce each climactic moment down to its central action, we could see how, while obviously simplified, the Oates story could be read as an argument that coming-of-age is a conscious choice, that we freely step into adulthood aware of its dangers. On the other hand, the Michels story could be read as an argument that the movement toward adulthood is more accidental than deliberate, a slipping. Both actions are verbs of motion, and when reduced in this way, each could be read to represent a distinctly different worldview for how we come of age. By highlighting this with a student who has written a similarly themed story, I might ask them to consider what their story's climactic action is saying about how the character is coming-of-age and how that action contributes to the ideas already put forth by their *audience*, of which the Oates and the Michels are a part. This approach, of course, is not limited to working with students who've written coming-of-age stories. From my experience it can be adapted easily no matter what ideas or thematic content our students are exploring in their work, and whether they are interested in issues of love or violence or any theme common in the undergraduate course, by steering them to other professional 'voices' in the conversation, we can bring the students face to face with their audience and challenge them to reconsider their understanding of the motive behind their stories.

Obviously the approaches offered here are but a glimpse of what is possible as we seek to bring more attention to the ways our creative writing students understand audience and motive in their writing. By offering them, it is my hope that others will recognize that we can and should do more work with our students in these areas. Since creative writing teachers frequently teach academic writing courses along with the creative genres, it should serve also as inspiration for us to look for pedagogical guidance from the academic arena and experiment with our students in these and similar ways. In his chapter on 'The Writer's Audience,' Wallace Stegner (2002: 83–84) rightly pointed out that, unlike visual artists who can have the benefit of literally standing by and watching the impact their work has on a viewer, writers lack this opportunity, since our audience 'is not a crowd, but single individuals in armchairs (who are) absolutely faceless.' For our students, the problem is even greater. For them, their audience is not only faceless; but they often fail to even recognize that those armchairs and occupants exist. As teachers, it is our responsibility to combat this, and by challenging our students to resurrect their audience and understand that reaching them is an essential component of the art form, we can help them deepen their motive beyond the self-interested and self-motivated levels and in doing so, help them see how their writing, ultimately, should matter.

References

Case, N. (2012) Silence is the deadliest thing: Sherman Alexie in conversation with Niko Case', article in *belivermag.com*. See http://www.believermag.com/issues/201202/?read=interview_alexie_case (accessed February 2013).

Cucciare, C.P. (2008) Audience matters: Exploring audience in undergraduate creative writing. PhD thesis, Bowling Green State University.

Evers, K.J. and Kolle, L.T. (2012) Fiction writers and their audience: A qualitative phenomenological inquiry into who novelists write for. Paper presented at *Poetics and Linguistics Association Conference* Malta. See http://www.pala.ac.uk/resources/proceedings/2012/evers-kolle2012.pdf (accessed February 2013).

Parfitt, M. (2012) *Writing in Response*. Boston: Bedford/St. Martin's.

Stegner, W. (2002) *On Teaching and Writing Fiction*. New York: Penguin Books.

Vonnegut, K. (1999) *Introduction to Bagombo Snuff Box*. New York: Berkeley Books.

10 Lending the Muse a Hand: Expanding the Role of Social Constructivism and Collaborative Writing in Creative Writing Pedagogies

Rod Zink

Ever since the slow transition from the oral tradition to the advent of writing, and the eventual conceptualization of authorship, the act of creative writing in particular has been predominately viewed as an individual act. Today, the perception of creative writing in most genres (with the notable exception of a few such as screenwriting, etc.) is solidly rooted in the convention of authorial ownership and the individual production of texts. Even so, creative writing instructors routinely utilize techniques borrowed from social construction and collaborative pedagogies. For example, classdiscussions of creative writing works by established authors are a type of social heuristic aid to the 'collaborative' development of student knowledge and skills in the components, principles, and techniques of the creative writing craft, or what Kenneth Bruffee (1984) terms 'normal discourse.' Similarly, included in Bruffee's definition of normal discourse would be 'peer review,' another collaborative activity reflected in the contemporary social constructivist based 'writers' workshop,' and commonly incorporated into the pedagogies of today's creative writing courses and seminars. And yet, because of our entrenched perception of individual authorship in creative writing, we rarely utilize any additional social-constructionist or collaborative pedagogical conventions commonly incorporated into other writing courses.

Collaboration in the creative writing classroom does not necessarily, for example, typically include many collaborative group workshop activities outside of peer review. More significantly, perhaps, our pedagogies almost never utilize collaborative writing exercises and projects such as those routinely incorporated into professional writing courses in other disciplines such as business, technical writing, communication, the social sciences and scientific fields. Group workshops and the type of collaborative writing where participants establish and negotiate meaning with the aid of a community of knowledgeable peers, is what Richard Rorty (1979) would refer to as the collaborative process of 'socially justifying belief,' a major feature in successful collaborative and social construction based pedagogies. Indeed, social constructivism has been successfully incorporated in writing courses outside of creative writing, but is seldom ever fully implemented or utilized in ways other than peer review workshops and discussion exercises in them. Even if we fully embrace the view of creative writing as predominately an individual act, utilizing such 'skill building' collaborative group workshop and writing exercises in the classroom setting offers learning opportunities and student development in writing technique and theory proven successful elsewhere, but that have traditionally remained untapped for use with creative writing.

As the director and an instructor within a composition program that includes specialized writing courses in several professional fields in addition to freshman composition, I have often felt that the traditional approaches I took when teaching creative writing were simply not as productive as the more expansive social-constructivist collaborative exercises I utilize as a predominant feature of my other writing courses, where the development of student collaborative writing skills is a listed course objective and desired outcome. Instead, as with the majority of us, I approached teaching creative writing differently, within certain boundaries not to be crossed out of respect for the value we still place upon the romantic ideal of the solitary writer and the entrenched beliefs regarding individual authorship and ownership we cling to as part of the current paradigm in the creative writing profession.

Underwhelmed by the development of my student creative writers over a semester when compared with my other writing students, however, I became convinced they would develop more if I could find a way to move beyond the use of class discussion and peer review in my courses, and utilize modified versions of the collaborative and social constructionist features so successful in my other writing classes. With those goals in mind, I set about reworking my teaching approach in my creative writing courses to include more collaborative activities to enhance student skills without endangering the mighty power and delicate nature of each writer's individual creative expression and each student's sense of authorship as 'owner' of his or her work.

What follows is an account of a pilot study I conducted to gauge the potential of increasing the role of group workshops and incorporating collaborative writing exercises into an introductory fiction writing class. My own reflections as an instructor, and experiences as a former student writer, are supplemented by the presentation of survey results obtained from students in the course.

My Own Story as Instructor and Writer

As is often the case with many of us, my own experience as a developing student writer initially informed and strongly influenced my initial approach to teaching creative writing. I must say, I absolutely loved the writing courses I took as a developing student writer. Along with what I now recognize as social constructionist peer workshops, my creative writing classes were composed of immersion through reading in whatever genre of writing we were creating in the course, as well as discussion and imitation of the writing we were exposed to. I have to admit, at that early stage in my development as a creative writer, I perceived writing as a magical act and, perhaps, because of those 'vain deluding joys,' as Milton (2001), once penned, very little of the advice I received through peer workshops was taken that seriously. As I matured and developed as a writer, however, the value of those workshops increased dramatically in my estimation, particularly the peer review workshops where I could 'test' my fiction and poetry to get a first-hand view of what worked and what didn't, what impact the piece had upon actual readers and, occasionally, even a great piece of outside advice. With time and experience, my skills and knowledge of creative writing increased, and those notions of writing as 'magic' were gradually replaced with the reality of writing as a process, and the hard work and effort required to produce the best writing I could to connect with real audiences. At that point, the sound advice and suggestions from those peer readers I trusted the most solidified my appreciation of the group workshop, as well as helped to cultivate objectivity towards my work, and, of course, that 'thick skin' so necessary for writer's to develop. As so much of writing is, indeed, a solitary venture with many hours spent alone with one's writing, those creative writing classes and their peer workshops also built a sense of community, and shared experiences with others trying to develop as writers at the same time and going through the same joys, challenges, and frustrations.

Years, and many miles, later, my academic interests and life experiences outside of academia led me to explore writing in various manifestations beyond my training in creative writing, my initial love. In addition to literature and creative writing, my fascination with writing in general resulted in a PhD plan of study that was constructed around gaining familiarity with scholarship about a wide variety of written communication through the study of 'Genre Theory' and 'Writing in the Disciplines' (WID), focusing on Technical and Business Writing in particular. When my studies were interrupted for a number of years, I was thankful to have the employment opportunity to become an actual writing practitioner of sorts in the metal fabrication industry, where I had the chance to experience the world of professional technical and business writing on a daily basis. Through that extended experience outside of academia, I came to appreciate the utilitarian aspects of professional writing, as well as the very real and significant social aspects of professional written communication, including the importance of and demands of collaboration in the workplace.

My re-entry into academia brought with it the opportunity to teach, and eventually serve as the director of writing across a wide spectrum of formats, genres, undergraduate and graduate levels and disciplines from creative writing and composition, writing in the social sciences and humanities, to technical and business communication. Such a vantage afforded me a perspective from which I could examine the shared and unique aspects of various types of writing, discourse communities, and situational exigencies. It also provided me with a full quiver of pedagogical theories and practices with which to approach and apply to each individual type of writing and writers. As an adherent of genre theory, I was extremely careful to recognize and embrace the significant unique characteristics of each type of writing I taught. If, however, a mainstream practice or approach in one pedagogy fit comfortably within another discipline's discourse parameters and could enhance student development within their particular discipline, it only made sense to consider potentially incorporating it. For example, if there is value and significant gain in applying creative writing's peer review workshop practice of collectively analyzing and critiquing a single writer's work into a business course where the class might collectively analyze and discuss an individual writer's bad-news letter or analytical report, that pedagogical practice is certainly at least worth considering as a potential exercise for the business writing course. It was just that reasoning that led me to reconsider the traditional pedagogical approach I had been utilizing in my creative writing courses, and whether with appropriate modification, my application of social 'knowledge' construction techniques via collaborative writing workshops might be useful to the development of my creative writers.

Collaborative Pedagogy in 'Writing in the Disciplines' (WID) Courses

Along with a focus on genre theory, the rhetorical situation, discourse communities and visual design, collaboration has become a significant staple in technical communication and business writing, as well as scientific and social science writing pedagogies. Professionals in these fields (as well as many others) routinely find themselves asked to not only perform roles in collaboration with others as members of a group, they are often required to also work together with others to produce collaborative writing and communication products (Anderson, 1985; Ede & Lunsford, 1983; Lunsford & Ede, 1986; Reither, 1993). As a result, and in an attempt to better develop discipline-specific knowledge production through writing in one's profession, or what Michael Carter (2007) refers to as 'ways of knowing and doing,' collaborative writing projects are a common component of technical communication, business writing, and other professional writing pedagogies. In order to better prepare my own students in such courses for this professional reality, I design and implement regular collaborative group workshops right from the beginning of the semester where students are required to collaboratively apply some concept, technique, or principle from their reading and/or our class discussion, etc. in a document which each group works to construct together, posts to an 'online dropbox' (we use computer classrooms for all of our WID courses), and presents back to the class with each group member sharing a role. Through this direct application of social construction and active learning, students become quite proficient in collaborative work, and are fairly efficient and productive groups by the time I introduce the collaborative project later in the semester. Equally significant, students seem to develop knowledge and skills through these workshops and exercises much more readily than if working alone.

Applying Social Construction to Creative Writing Pedagogy

Borrowing from the successful collaborative writing pedagogies, projects and workshops in my Business Writing, Technical Communication and other WID courses, then, I decided to try similar mini-workshop writing projects in one of my Introduction to Creative Writing courses as exercises for the development of basic skills in poetry, fiction and creative nonfiction such as description, setting, character, action, plot, symbolism, poetic form, meter, metaphor and similes, imagery, tone and so on. Although a number of the students found it somewhat strange at first to attempt creative acts in a group rather than as solitary writers, the vast majority of students soon found the social production of creative writing workshop composition tasks helpful to their understanding of the various fictional elements they worked as a group to produce through their 'mini group compositions.' Likewise, I noticed an increased development rate of student writing skill levels throughout the semester, as well as a considerable elevation in student ability to utilize fictional and poetic rhetoric and technique vocabulary, not only in class discussions but also when students workshopped their individual work.

Encouraged by the success of collaborative workshop creative 'mini-projects' in my more generalized introductory creative writing courses, I decided to apply the same approach in an Introductory Fiction Writing course the following semester. I envisioned the course as an opportunity to gain more direct feedback about what the students thought about utilizing the workshop 'mini group compositions' as a regular classroom activity in a more specialized writing course focused upon a single genre. As with the prior class, the fiction writing students seemed somewhat hesitant at first when I introduced a group workshop where they were to collaboratively compose passages which utilized 'showing' to replace a passage that utilized 'telling' (see Figure 10.1).[1]

As with any collaborative workshop writing or composition task sequence, the workshop above (Figure 10.1) serves as a fair example of increasing the demands upon the workshop groups gradually as the course moves forward. In this workshop activity, for example, each collaborative group is given a scaffold of 'telling' statements to rework and to help guide their new 'showing' passages. Later workshops can place more creative strain upon the groups by increasing their freedom to negotiate what they will write about, but I learned quickly through my business writing and technical communication workshops that it is important to allow students time to acclimate to the demands of collaboration, and to design the workshops to gradually build up to more complex projects.

Similar to the students in my general creative writing introductory class, the fiction writing students seemed somewhat surprised at first to be collaborating to produce actual passages, but within a few workshops, were becoming as proficient in their groups as my WID students in their own discipline-specific collaborative tasks. Perhaps because the students in the Fiction Writing classes are typically more advanced writers of higher class standing, however, I did notice more hesitancy with the first few workshops, most likely as a result of the more advanced students'

> **ENGL 212**
>
> **WORKSHOP 2:** Showing and Telling – Chapter 2
>
> 1. Break up into groups of 2-3.
>
> 2. AS A GROUP, consider the three stories you read for today. Select one example of "showing" you find particularly effective.
>
> 3. Prepare to share your example with the class, complete with a direct "telling" translation of what the author successfully conveys instead through "showing."
>
> 4. NEXT, choose one of the following "telling" passages below:
>
>   AS A GROUP, compose a passage that "shows" the reader what is "told" in each passage, in order for them to "experience" and "feel" first-hand what is being conveyed.
>
>   - The woman was annoying. First, she was younger than I was, and worse, extremely beautiful.
>   - The stranger frightened me. He was imposing and looked plain mean. Even the way he moved was scary.
>   - What I saw next made me sad and guilty at the same time. I held back my tears from streaming down my face when I realized my friend was missing her right hand.
>   - Time moved painfully slow as we waited nervously with anticipation for him to resurface from the water.
>
> 5. AS A GROUP, present the example of "showing" you selected from our text, and also share the "showing" passage your group composed in place of the "telling" passages above.
>
>   *Try to share the responsibility of presenting back to the class by having each member of your group presenting part of what you share with the class.*

Figure 10.1 Showing and telling workshop

heightened sense of creative authorship. Once they became more comfortable in working with the other writers in their groups, became less concerned about any infringement upon their individual creative freedom, and recognized the exercises as opportunities to have some fun with the craft of fiction, their collaborations became predictably much more sophisticated than those in my general Introduction to Creative Writing course. Likewise, as with the previous class, the fiction writing students also exhibited an even greater heightened awareness of the fictional elements and techniques we collaborated on during the peer review workshops of their individual work, and I believe that the students' stories exhibited the fruits of their labor.

Many students from my fiction writing class enjoyed the collaborate exercises so much that two of student groups from the class requested that

I incorporate a collaborative story as one of the major assignments for the next seminar in addition to the more traditional individual story assignments. While I most likely would not incorporate a collaborative graded assignment in a fiction writing class, I am considering the potential for a collaborative project in a screen writing course, a genre where collaboration is more likely in the professional world, or perhaps, a collaborative 'world-building' course in which students could collaboratively create a setting and characters which could interact in a series of collaborative or individual shorts. While it would be inaccurate to state that every single student in the course was so enthusiastic about the collaborative workshop mini-compositions, even those students who didn't fully embrace the exercises appeared to benefit from them. My experience utilizing group workshops to produce written products in my technical communication and business writing courses has confirmed the reality that collaboration will not be embraced, or suit, students with more solitary learning styles and/or less social personalities. Naturally, the same will be inevitable in our creative writing courses.

Student Questionnaire: Pilot Study

In order to discover whether my impressions of student responses to the collaborative workshops I incorporated into my Fiction Writing course, I distributed a voluntary survey via email the semester following the class. Unfortunately, a few of the students had graduated, and/or were no longer enrolled at the school, so I could only obtain responses from about one half of the class (7 respondents). The responses were strictly confidential and although I did not receive responses from every student, a majority of the students did respond and provided what I believe to be an accurate and representative cross-section of the entire group.

Methodology

The semester following their 'Introduction to Fiction Writing' course, students were contacted via email with a request to participate in the survey. Students who wished to participate returned their survey to a collection box anonymously or via email attachment. To keep those respondents who returned surveys via email anonymous, I printed off their attachments and placed them randomly among the others collected without looking at any responses on them.

The survey consisted of 11 questions which the students could respond on either a scale of 1–10, or –5 to +5. The questions were designed to determine what impact the collaborative group exercises had upon the writers' development throughout the semester.

Results

The first 11 survey questions and the student response range and mean average of responses to each question are displayed below in Figure 10.2.[2]

SURVEY QUESTIONNAIRE RESULTS Survey Questions	Response Range	Mean Response
1. How would you rate the level of your skill in fiction writing at the beginning of the semester? *Not Proficient* - ( )1 ( )2 ( )3( )4( )5( )6 ( )7 ( )8 ( )9( ) 10 – *Very Proficient*	4-7	5.43
2. How would you rate the overall level of your skill in fiction writing at the end of the semester? *Not Proficient* - ( )1 ( )2 ( )3( )4( )5( )6 ( )7 ( )8 ( )9( ) 10 – *Very Proficient*	8-10	8.57
3. How would you rate the improvement of your skills in fiction writing throughout the semester? *No improvement* - ( )1 ( )2 ( )3( )4( )5( )6 ( )7 ( )8 ( )9( ) 10-*Vast improvement*	2-10	7.86
4. How would you rate the impact of our collaborative group workshops upon your skills in fiction writing components, techniques, and principles over the semester? *Negative* ( )-5 ( )-4( )-3 ( )-2 ( )-1 ( )*No Impact* ( )+1 ( )+2 ( )+3 ( )+4 ( )+5 *Positive*	+1 to +5	+3.57
5. How would you rate the level of your knowledge of fiction writing components, techniques at the beginning of the semester? *Not Knowledgeable* ( )1( )2( )3( )4( )5( )6( )7( )8( )9( ) 10 *Very Knowledgeable*	3-9	5.43
6. How would you rate the level of your knowledge of fiction writing components, principles and techniques at the end of the semester? *Not Knowledgeable* ( )1( )2( )3( )4( )5( )6( )7( )8( )9( ) 10 *Very Knowledgeable*	9-10	9.43
7. How would you rate the improvement of your knowledge of fiction writing components, principles and techniques throughout the semester? *No improvement* - ( )1 ( )2 ( )3( )4( )5( )6 ( )7 ( )8 ( )9( ) 10-*Vast improvement*	5-10	8.43
8. How would you rate the impact of our collaborative group workshops upon your knowledge of fiction writing components, techniques, and principles over the semester? *Negative* ( )-5 ( )-4( )-3 ( )-2 ( )-1 ( )*No Impact* ( )+1 ( )+2 ( )+3 ( )+4 ( )+5 *Positive*	+1 to +5	+3.14
9. How would you rate the level of your comfort producing writing as a member of a group at the beginning of the semester? *Not Comfortable* - ( )1 ( )2 ( )3( )4( )5( )6 ( )7 ( )8 ( )9( ) 10 – *Very Comfortable*	3-9	5.0
10. How would you rate the level of your comfort producing writing as a member of a group at the end of the semester? *Not Comfortable* - ( )1 ( )2 ( )3( )4( )5( )6 ( )7 ( )8 ( )9( ) 10 – *Very Comfortable*	6-10	8.71
11. How would you classify the use of collaborative group workshops as a class activity? Please rate your experience in the following categories:		
11a. *Not Fun* - ( )1 ( )2 ( )3( )4( )5( )6 ( )7 ( )8 ( )9( ) 10 – *Very Fun*	5-10	7.86
11b. *Not Challenging* ( )1 ( )2 ( )3( )4( )5( )6 ( )7 ( )8 ( )9( ) 10 *Very Challenging*	5-7	6.42
11c. *Not Helpful* - ( )1 ( )2 ( )3( )4( )5( )6 ( )7 ( )8 ( )9( ) 10 – *Very Helpful*	5-10	8.43
11d. *Unproductive* - ( )1 ( )2 ( )3( )4( )5( )6 ( )7 ( )8 ( )9( ) 10 – *Very Productive*	5-10	8.0
11e. *Poor Use of Time* ( )1( )2( )3( )4( )5( )6( )7( )8( )9( ) 10 *Good Use of Time*	5-10	8.43

Figure 10.2 Student questionnaire: Introduction to fiction writing

The two questions directly requesting ratings for the impact of the collaborative workshops on student knowledge and skill in fiction writing concepts, principles, and techniques (Q4 and Q8) utilized a different scale then the other questions(−5 to +5 versus 1–10) in order to provide the respondents opportunities to more explicitly express a negative or positive impact from the workshops.

Discussion of Responses

I must admit, as an instructor I was quite pleased that the survey responses confirmed my own impressions regarding the growth of student skills, and the positive role the collaborative exercises had in that development. More significant for our purposes here, the responses can offer preliminary insight upon the question of whether or not increasing the role of collaborative social construction can be potentially useful in our general creative writing pedagogies.

General improvement of fiction writing skill and knowledge

Although the course was an introductory one to fiction writing, the students in the course came into it with a considerable range of skill and knowledge in fiction writing abilities, knowledge and techniques. When asked in question one (1) in regard to proficiency in fiction writing skill at the beginning of the semester, for example, student responses ranged from 4–7 on a scale from 1–10 (mean 5.43). An even more pronounced range of knowledge of fiction writing components, principles, and techniques at the start of the semester was reported. On a scale of 1–10 from 'not knowledgeable to knowledgeable,' responses ranged from 3–9 (mean 5.43).

At the end of the semester, all respondents reported an increase in both categories. In overall skill in fiction writing at the end of the semester, students reported a mean response of 8.57 (with a range of responses from 8–10), indicating a net increase of 3.14, or 31.4% above their skill levels at the beginning of the semester. Likewise, in overall knowledge of fiction writing components, principles, and techniques at the end of the semester, students reported a mean response of 9.43 (with a range of responses from 9–10), indicating a net increase of 4.0, or 40% above their knowledge levels at the beginning of the semester.

These positive findings correlate generally with the students' own estimation of improvement of fiction writing skills and knowledge in fiction writing components, principles, and techniques during the course of the semester, although when asked directly regarding their improvement over the semester, the student ratings appear to be somewhat inflated. Regarding the improvement of their skill level as a fiction writer over the course of the semester, for example, students reported a mean improvement of 7.86, or 78.6%, but over a somewhat wide range representative of their estimated beginning skills from 2–10. Student improvement in knowledge of fiction writing components, principles, and techniques is similarly rated higher with a mean reported improvement of 8.43, or 84.3%.

Despite these discrepancies, where I suspect the truth lies somewhere between, all of the respondents reported significant improvement over the course of the semester. Our next step will be to analyze their responses to the more direct questions regarding the impact of the collaborative writing exercises themselves.

Impact of collaborative writing workshop exercises

Two questions in the survey directly asked the student writers to evaluate and rate the impact of the collaborative group workshops upon their skills in fiction writing and knowledge in fiction writing components, principles and techniques (Q4 and Q8). As mentioned above, instead of asking students to rate the impact from 1–10, these two questions presented students with a modified range of –5 to +5 in order to avoid responses skewed toward the positive and, thus, better allow respondents to provide a negative impact assessment if such an assessment accurately represented their individual experiences.

The responses to both questions ranged from +1 to +5. The question regarding how the collaborative writing activities had impacted each student's overall fiction writing skills (Q4) averaged a mean rating of positive (+)3.57 (or, + 71.4%), and the one regarding the collaborative writing activities upon each student's knowledge of fiction writing components, principles, and techniques (Q8) averaged a mean rating of positive (+)3.14 (or, + 62.8%). Notably, there appears to be a correlation between those students who regarded themselves most skillful and knowledgeable in fiction writing components, principles, and techniques, with the assessments of the impact of the collaborative exercises. The student responders who rated themselves at higher skill and knowledge levels consistently reported a positive impact, but one lower than those who reported lower initial skill and knowledge levels.

These results would seem to indicate that students found the collaborative writing workshops to have had a considerable positive impact upon their development as writers over the course of the semester.

98 Creative Composition

Student comfort with collaborative writing exercises

Questions 9 and 10 of the survey asked students to rate their comfort level with writing as a member of a group at the beginning and end of the semester. Again, there was a considerable range of comfort at the start of the semester (3–9 on a scale of 1–10), with a mean rating of 5.0. There was a significant shift in comfort with group writing by the end of the semester with a mean rating of 8.71, although the range was still considerable wide (5–10). This would seem to indicate that although most students found group writing considerably comfortable, at least one student was only reasonably comfortable even by the end of an entire semester of group work.

As the sample size of this pilot study is a small one, it is reasonable to believe that a larger study would most likely find a percentage of students who might never be comfortable participating in such group exercises. By the close of the semester, all the students surveyed were somewhat comfortable playing a role in a collaborative writing group, but as in other courses where collaborative writing is required, some students will never feel comfortable in such activities.

Overall student impressions of collaborate writing workshop activities

The final question of the survey (11a–e) was subdivided into five separate categories for students to rate, and was designed to get a sense of how the student writers generally perceived the collaborative writing activities.

Question 11 a–e, for example, asked students to rate how fun, challenging, helpful, and productive they found the group work and exercises. Here too, with the exception of how challenging students found the workshop collaboration activities, student responses ranged from 5–10 on a scale of 1–10. Unlike the responses regarding the positive or negative direct impact of the workshops to individual fiction writing skill and knowledge levels, however, there doesn't appear to be any substantial correlation between the responses of students who rated themselves at higher skill and knowledge levels and those who reported lower initial skills and knowledge. One student responder reported a score of 5 for all the categories of Question 11 and the other responders all recorded varied responses to each category.

Of the categories in Question 11, students rated how helpful the collaborative tasks were, and how good they thought the workshops made of class time, both at a mean score of 8.43 on a scale of 1–10 (not helpful to very helpful; not a good use of time to a good use of time). Students also rated how productive the workshops were at 8.0 on a scale of 1–10 (unproductive to very productive). In terms of how fun they found the collaborative writing activities, students rated the workshops at a mean of 7.86 on a scale of 1–10 (not fun to very fun). Scoring the lowest was the rating of how challenging the workshop activities were. In this category, the students' mean rating was 6.42 on a scale of 1–10, with the range of responses tightly packed between 5–7. While such a score seemed somewhat lower than expected, the level of challenge in most of the workshops were determined by fitting the collaborative activities into the framework of a 50-minute class, with many of the exercises eventually planned to take up to two class meetings from introducing them to the last group presented their compositions, or tasks, back to the class.

Conclusion

While any conclusions drawn from this pilot study must be tempered by the very small sampling size, the findings here certainly suggest there is much potential value in incorporating collaborative writing assignment workshop exercises within some creative writing courses. The students surveyed from my course echoed my own impressions of how instrumental the collaborative exercises were to building their fiction writing skills and knowledge by having them actively apply what we would ordinarily just discuss and analyze in published story selections, prior to encouraging students to apply the fundamental fiction writing components, principles and techniques to their own writing. The traditional pedagogical discussion, imitation and peer review (peer workshop) approach has certainly proven successful for quite some time, and yet we are obligated as instructors to provide the best training we can for our students. If new tools such as the collaborative writing workshop exercises I have described here can help us to accomplish that task, we should most certainly consider them and find out what we can about them. With that in mind, more research should be done on a larger scale to discover whether the promise exhibited in my pilot study will hold up to further scrutiny.

Notes

(1) All references to the ENGL 212 'textbook' [in Figure 10.1 and all workshop exercises in the appendix] are to Janet Burroway, *Writing Fiction: A Guide to Narrative Craft*. 8th. Boston: Longman, 2011.
(2) A special thanks to my graduate assistant, Semontee Mitra, for her excellent work compiling the data from the student questionnaires.

References

Anderson, P. V. (1985) What survey research tells us about writing at work. In L. Odell and D. Goswami (eds) *Writing in Nonacademic Settings* (pp. 1–83). New York: Guilford.
Bruffee, K. (1984) Collaborative learning and the conversation of mankind. *College English* 46 (7), 635–652.
Carter, M. (2007) Ways of knowing: Doing and writing in the disciplines. *Composition and Communication* 58 (3), 385–418.
Ede, L. and Lunsford, A. (1983) Why write... together? *Rhetoric Review* (1), 150–157.
Lunsford, A. and Ede, L. (1986) Why write... together: A research update. *Rhetoric Review* 5 (1), 71–81.
Milton, J. (2001) Il Penseroso. In C.W. Eliot (ed.) *Complete Poems* (Vol. 4, pp. 1909–1914). New York: P.F. Collier & Son.
Reither, J. A. (1993) Bridging the gap: Scenic motives for collaborative writing in workplace and school. In R. Spilka (ed.) *Writing in the Workplace: New Research Perspectives* (pp. 195–206). Carbondale, Illinois: Southern Illinois University Press.*
Rorty, R. (1979) *Philosophy and the Mirror of Nature*. Princeton, New Jersey: Princeton UP.

Appendix I: Student Questionnaire

StudentQuestionnaire: *Creative Writing Collaboration*   **ENGL 212 Spring 2012**

Dear ENGL 212 Students,

This questionnaire below is part of a pilot study to determine how successful collaborate workshop writing approaches can potentially be to aid the development of student skills in creative writing components, techniques, and principles.

As you know, we incorporated many such workshops in our ENGL 212 Introduction to Fiction Writing course last semester. The purpose of this questionnaire is to document your experiences and participation in these workshops, and to determine how useful and effective the workshops were to you in this regard.

I greatly appreciate your willingness to devote your time to complete this questionnaire and allow us to examine its impact upon your fiction writing last semester. I want to assure you that your responses and the use of your work will be completely confidential and put to good use.

Thank you,
Dr. Z

Why should I take the survey?
By taking a few minutes to complete this survey, you are providing invaluable data we can use to better focus pedagogical efforts to better design courses to build student creative writing skills.

Will my responses remain confidential?
This survey is anonymous and great care will be given to protect the confidentiality of your responses.

After collected, the surveys will be kept in a secure location and will only be used for the data collection purposes within the parameters of this study, and not as individual records of any kind.

Can I change my mind about participating after I begin the survey?
Participation in this study and survey is entirely voluntary. You can decide not to participate before, or at any point during the time you spend completing it. You will indicate your consent for us to utilize the survey data you provide through your responses when you return your survey to us, but can choose to halt your participation any time prior to turning it in.

Can I choose not to answer, or skip, a question I am uncomfortable with?
You can freely choose not to answer any question you do not want to. If an answer is not provided, the response will be registered as "no response given."

By submitting this questionnaire, I consent to the use of my responses to this survey for the purposes of this academic study.

Student Questionnaire: Creative Writing Collaboration Workshops

Please respond to the following questions as accurately as possible.

1. How would you rate the level of your skill in fiction writing at the beginning of the semester?
   Not Proficient - ( )1 ( )2 ( )3 ( )4 ( )5 ( )6 ( )7 ( )8 ( )9 ( )10 – *Very Proficient*

2. How would you rate the overall level of your skill in fiction writing at the end of the semester?
   Not Proficient - ( )1 ( )2 ( )3 ( )4 ( )5 ( )6 ( )7 ( )8 ( )9 ( )10 – *Very Proficient*

3. How would you rate the improvement of your skills in fiction writing throughout the semester?
   No improvement - ( )1 ( )2 ( )3 ( )4 ( )5 ( )6 ( )7 ( )8 ( )9 ( )10-*Vast improvement*

4. How would you rate the impact of our collaborative group workshops upon your skills in fiction writing components, techniques, and principles over the semester?
   Negative ( )-5 ( )-4 ( )-3 ( )-2 ( )-1 ( )No Impact ( )+1 ( )+2 ( )+3 ( )+4 ( )+5 *Positive*

5. How would you rate the level of your knowledge of fiction writing components, principles and techniques at the beginning of the semester?
   Not Knowledgeable - ( )1 ( )2 ( )3 ( )4 ( )5 ( )6 ( )7 ( )8 ( )9 ( )10 – *Very Knowledgeable*

Thanks for participating!

6. How would you rate the level of your knowledge of fiction writing components, principles and techniques at the end of the semester?

   Not Knowledgeable - ( )1 ( )2 ( )3 ( )4 ( )5 ( )6 ( )7 ( )8 ( )9 ( )10 – Very Knowledgeable

7. How would you rate the improvement of your knowledge of fiction writing components, principles and techniques throughout the semester?

   No improvement - ( )1 ( )2 ( )3 ( )4 ( )5 ( )6 ( )7 ( )8 ( )9 ( )10-Vast improvement

8. How would you rate the impact of our collaborative group workshops upon your knowledge offiction writing components, techniques, and principles over the semester?

   Negative ( )-5 ( )-4 ( )-3 ( )-2 ( )-1 ( )No Impact ( )+1 ( )+2 ( )+3 ( )+4 ( )+5 Positive

9. How would you rate the level of your comfort producing writing as a member of a group at the beginning of the semester?

   Not Comfortable - ( )1 ( )2 ( )3 ( )4 ( )5 ( )6 ( )7 ( )8 ( )9 ( )10 – Very Comfortable

10. How would you rate the level of your comfort producing writing as a member of a group at the end of the semester?

    Not Comfortable - ( )1 ( )2 ( )3 ( )4 ( )5 ( )6 ( )7 ( )8 ( )9 ( )10 – Very Comfortable

11. How would you classify the use of collaborative group workshops as a class activity?Please rate your experience in the following categories:

    Not Fun - ( )1 ( )2 ( )3 ( )4 ( )5 ( )6 ( )7 ( )8 ( )9 ( )10 – Very Fun

    Not Challenging - ( )1 ( )2 ( )3 ( )4 ( )5 ( )6 ( )7 ( )8 ( )9 ( )10 – Very Challenging

    Not Helpful - ( )1 ( )2 ( )3 ( )4 ( )5 ( )6 ( )7 ( )8 ( )9 ( )10 – Very Helpful

    Unproductive - ( )1 ( )2 ( )3 ( )4 ( )5 ( )6 ( )7 ( )8 ( )9 ( )10 – Very Productive

    Poor Use of Time - ( )1 ( )2 ( )3 ( )4 ( )5 ( )6 ( )7 ( )8 ( )9 ( )10 – Good Use of Time

Thanks for participating!

Appendix II: Sample Workshops

ENGL 212

WORKSHOP 3: Story Form, Plot, and Structure – Chapter 7

1. Break up into groups of 2-3.

2. AS A GROUP, briefly revisit and reconsider the Teolinda Gersao's short story, "The Red Fox Fur Coat" (p. 67). Imagine it as an early working draft of a story **and you are assigned the task of heightening the story's resolution** by reworking the ***plot, crisis, conflict,*** and what Burroway refers to as ***connections and disconnections***.

3. FIRST, **create a modified "working" resolution** for the story that carries more meaning than the present one (woman rediscovers her "animal" body). For example, consider what her discovery could "mean," or might "resolve" in a differently developed draft.

    Examples:

    - The woman overcomes her pronounced denial of herself, and the human organism, as "animal."
    - The woman realizes part of being truly human is learning to celebrate the "animal" inside.
    - The woman discovers that through her imagination she can escape the structure and confines of the contemporary machinations of human existence.

4. NEXT, draft a revised story form by sketching a diagram of an "inverted check mark" similar to the one illustrated by Burroway on p. 258. Be sure to create suitable escalating conflicts, connections, disconnections, and crisis to reach your revised resolution. (See example.)

5. Place your diagram on an overhead transparency to share with the class.

6. AS A GROUP, present your revised story plot to the class, making sure to trace the conflicts, connection, and disconnections leading to your "working" crisis and resolution.

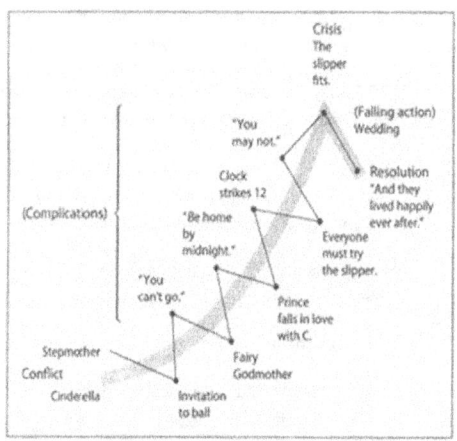

Try to share the responsibility of presenting back to the class by having each member of your group presenting part of what you share with the class.

GROUP WORKSHOP 4: Point of View (Chapt. 8) ENGL 212

1. Break up into groups of 3-4.

2. Review the various 1st and 3rd person points-of-view available for writers to utilize:

    1st Person Narrator
    - Limited Omniscient- Central Character
    - Limited Omniscient- Peripheral Character

    3rd Person Narrator
    - Omniscient
    - Limited Omniscient
    - Objective

3. AS A GROUP, choose one of the works from our readings-to-date, and experiment with alternative point-of-view (we will try to only assign each to one group only):

    - "We Didn't"(*WF* p. 42)
    - "Big Me"(*WF* p. 51)
    - "The Red Fur Coat"(*WF* p. 67)
    - "What You Pawn I Will Redeem"(*WF* p. 265)
    - "My Kid's Dog"(*WF* p. 283)
    - "Everything That Rises Must Converge"(*WF* p. 286)
    - "Missing Women"(*WF* p. 317)

4. AS A GROUP, rework one significant paragraph from the story you have chosen by writing it from an alternative point of view.

    NOTE: *Try not to just pick the easiest change. Try the change you find most interesting in relation to its impact upon the paragraph you have selected (or to the entire work).*

5. If time permits, spend a few moments individually to think about the story idea you are working on right now. Consider what point-of-view you plan on using, and what would change if you told it from a different one.

    Take turns sharing the point of view you are currently using and how the story would be different if you changed the point-of-view.

6. When you have completed your perspective / point of view revisions, each group will
    - Identify the story you are working with
    - Identify the point-of-view utilized in the story
    - **Identify the change you made in viewpoint** (what you changed it to), and then,
    - **Present** both the **original and revised paragraphs** to the class.

Expanding the Role of Social Constructivism and Collaborative Writing

ENGL 212

WORKSHOP 7: Dialogue

1. Break up into groups of 2-3.

2. AS A GROUP, choose two numbers (different from one another) from one to twelve (1-12). Write them down on a sheet of paper (to display to the class later).

3. Next, choose one of the following character pairs and settings (one per group, please):

    - Bob and Eucalyptus at a concert
    - Hannah and June Star at a "sleep-over"
    - Dunn and Harry at a construction site
    - 5 and 7 in the forest
    - Toya and Chum in a museum
    - Mr. Smith and Sally in a hospital waiting room
    - Pepper and Schmidt on a beach
    - Waati and Yuni on a roller coaster

4. For this exercise, imagine your two characters attempting to hold a conversation. Compose a brief fictional scene which primarily utilizes dialogue to convey the two EMOTIONS or "HUMAN CONDITIONS" that correspond to the number your group has chosen.

5. AS A GROUP, prepare to share your dialogue-laden scene with the class. Although we may not be able to hear all of our passages, we will make our way around the room from group to group, listening to one passage from each group until the end of class.

6. AS A CLASS, we will try to identify the "emotion" or "human condition" each group's work conveys.

EMOTIONS or "HUMAN CONDITIONS" KEY:

1. Grief / Sadness
2. Anger
3. Impatience
4. Caring
5. Annoyance
6. Joy / Ecstasy
7. Frustration
8. Interest / Intrigue
9. Desperation
10. Guilt
11. Pain
12. Fear

WORKSHOP 9: Introducing Character

1. Break up into groups of 2-3.

2. INDIVIDUALLY, spend a few moments recalling the character you wrote a paragraph about in Workshop 8.

3. As much as possible, refresh the memories of your group members by quickly reviewing the following information and traits you sketched out about them:

    - Age
    - Gender
    - Appearance
    - Nationality
    - Region
    - Marital Status
    - Education
    - Profession
    - Motives
    - Wants/Desires
    - Habits
    - Likes/Dislikes
    - Attitude
    - Values
    - Misc. Traits

    Additionally, share the paragraph you wrote about your character once again with your group members.

4. AS A GROUP, consider a scenario that would bring all of the group's characters into one story line. Utilizing the following **direct and indirect methods** to reveal as much as you can about your each character, **compose an introductory paragraph or two which reveals the most significant information and traits about all of your group's characters** (as they interact with one another in the same introductory paragraph/s):

    DIRECT:

    Appearance   Dialogue

    Action   Thought

    INDIRECT:

    Authorial Interpretation

    Interpretation By Another Character

5. Prepare to share your passages (including any modifications) with the class. Although we may not be able to hear all of our passages, we will make our way around the room from group to group, listening to one paragraph from each group until the end of class.

6. AS A CLASS, let's enjoy and admire each writer's work as we all consider what we can personally utilize to introduce and develop our own characters.

Expanding the Role of Social Constructivism and Collaborative Writing

WORKSHOP 10: Setting Workshop 1   **ENGL 212**

1. Break up into groups of 2-4.

2. AS A GROUP, choose one of the following stories to base this exercise on (one per group, please):

   - "We Didn't" (*WF* p. 42)
   - "Big Me" (*WF* p. 51)
   - "The Red Fur Coat" (*WF* p. 67)
   - "Fiesta, 1980" (*WF* p. 90)
   - "Following the Notes" (*WF* p. 112)
   - Every Tongue Shall Confess (*WF* p. 100)
   - "Mule Killers" (*WF* p. 138)
   - "Bullet in the Brain" (*WF* p. 147)
   - "Tandolfo the Great" (*WF* p. 151)
   - "What You Pawn I Will Redeem" (*WF* p. 265)
   - "My Kid's Dog" (*WF* p. 283)
   - "Everything That Rises Must Converge" (*WF* p. 286)
   - "Missing Women" (*WF* p. 317)
   - "Who's Irish" (*WF* p. 323)
   - "Reply All" (*WF* p. 332)

3. For this exercise, identify the current setting (time and place) of your chosen story. Next, rework the first paragraph (or so) to set the story in a different location and time.

   Please note: Feel free to rename the characters and make any necessary modifications to your story as part of your setting change.

4. AS A GROUP, prepare to share your revised story paragraphs with the class. Although we may not be able to hear all of our passages, we will make our way around the room from group to group, listening to one passage from each group until the end of class. We will finish them up next class.

5. AS A CLASS, we will try to identify the settings (time and place) each group's work conveys.

SETTING EXAMPLES:

1. A carnival (50-100 years ago)
2. A human settlement on the hostile planet Klaatu (indefinite future – 200 yrs. +)
3. An ocean liner (steam powered - early 20th century)
4. Lost in the desert (during the Gulf War)
5. A medical station / emergency room on a spaceship to Mars (near future – 50-100 yrs.)
6. A jousting contest at the royal palace (Middle ages)
7. On the front line (WWI)

108 Creative Composition

WORKSHOP 12: Fictional Time   ENGL 212

1. Break up into groups of 2-4.

2. AS A GROUP, choose one of the following situations to develop through summary, scene, flash back, and slow motion in this exercise(One per group, please). *Note: you will be creating your own choice of characters for this exercise:*

    - A prisoner tunneling out ofprison breaks through the soil anticipating freedom above.
    - A character trapped in quicksand sinks lower and lower.
    - After a night spent making a crop circle, a character is about to leave the wheat field, but instead, faces the farmer with a shotgun leveled at his/her head.
    - A recently married character runs into an old flame in a grocery store hours after having a big fight with his/her new spouse.
    - During an adult art class, a character discovers the nude model about to disrobe is someone he/she knows.
    - Facing starvation, a character eyes a dying companion, moments away from death.
    - After months of hard labor, a character finally finishes a project, only to feel suddenly hollow inside.
    - Shortly after returning to work from lunch, a character discovers someone has searched through his/her desk.

3. For this exercise, create a timeline of at least five (5) events that have led up to the circumstance you have chosen along with your own central and supporting characters.

4. Next, draft a few paragraphs about your situation in which you incorporate the five events above. In order to do so, convey the events utilizing at least one instance of the following methods available for you to use to portray fictional time in fiction:

    - Summary
    - Scene
    - Flashback
    - Slow motion

    Please note: Feel free to make any necessary modifications to the events if you like.

5. AS A GROUP, prepare to share your story paragraphswith the class during our next class meeting.

6. AS A CLASS, we will try to identify the events each group incorporates in their narrative section, and what method they utilize to convey each event.

11 Grammar and Creativity in Composition: An Unexpected Nexus

Shawn Kerivan

Understanding grammar is a vital component of any first-year composition course. Within the rules of grammar lie the foundations of the clear, concise tenants of composition elements such as punctuation, sentence clarity and subject-verb agreement, to name a few. When William Strunk Jr. and White (1997: 15) advised writers to 'choose a suitable design and hold to it' because 'a basic structural design every kind of writing,' he was advocating for a grammar – not grammar sine arbitus, but a real relationship between the rules that govern language and a way to effectively express ideas through writing. In other words, a link between what's collectively called grammar, and creativity.

Students often arrive at freshman composition courses with little if any comprehension of grammar and its importance. Connecting the grammatical to the creative gives the student a larger understanding of what makes outstanding composition. In *Writing Down the Bones* (1986: 62), Natalie Goldberg addresses the nexus of creativity and the rules of writing by reminding us that we're wired for structural thought: 'By cracking open that syntax, we release energy and are able to see the world afresh and from a new angle.' This reinterpretation of the world is the heart of creativity, and by examining the application of grammar through a semester-long, four-essay curriculum, the steps to this understanding – this nexus between grammar and creativity – can be revealed.

This approach centers around teaching four specific facets within essay assignments: description, compare/contrast, definition and argumentation. The examples used below relate specifically to those rhetorical situations, but the format is easily adaptable to most modalities: narration, example, classification, process analysis and others. Specific elements of grammar connect creativity to composition grammatically. This results in an internalization of the rules of writing, along with a development of an understanding of the creative process.

The first step involves the revelation that grammar isn't an end, but a means to understanding, and that creativity isn't selectively bestowed on some and not others. Couching grammar in the context of 'a basic principle of an area of knowledge' (Soukahov, 1992: 787) – in other words, using different grammars as ways to understand other things – helps disabuse students and instructors of grammar itself as an end. Each of the rhetorical situations below is approached through its own grammar – the things that make it it. The specific facets of essaying (description, compare/contrast, definition, and argumentation) are joined by 'Grammars of Writing,' in which specific grammatical lessons are used to illustrate their connection between composition (the writing process) and the creative process – 'Grammars of Creativity' – which show the methodology behind the creative act, emphasizing the creative reliance and relationship upon and with grammar. The third leg of each cycle is a lesson on the Nexus of Grammar and Creativity – a synthesis of the first two lessons into a real moment of learning.

In the first facet of essaying, description, students are introduced to themselves as writers in a way that shows the person and the writer coming from the same source. Jane E. Aaron (2005) explains description as an understanding of the senses. Everything we know we receive through our senses, and our explanations of what we see, hear, taste, smell and touch become our descriptions. Understanding description helps the writer connect to herself and to the place her creativity comes from. Knowing that there's no division between the student-as-writer and the student-as-self helps begin to break down walls that have been erected over many years. The basics of description – sharing sensory details to communicate an experience – are its Grammar of Creativity. By learning to create simply by observing, smelling, touching, tasting and listening, students master a building block of the creative process. (Notice that the generic reference to 'grammar' – the thing – is avoided, in favor of 'the grammar of _____,' thus creating an understanding in the students' minds that grammar is a means to understanding something, not an end.)

With the creative mastered, Grammar itself can be addressed. For this cycle, the basics are emphasized: parts of speech, parts of sentences, word groups, and sentence types and purpose. By incorporating these lessons during the writing and revising of a descriptive piece, students mimic with basic grammar the approach they're learning with description. They speak sentences every day; learning where those sentences come from offers logical insight into what makes them grammatical. Robert Pinckert (1986: 82) said that students 'want a prescription of what should be done. They want someone to speak with authority and clear up the mess. They want a miracle.'

Aligning creativity and grammar within the context of description is a first step in building the notion that there aren't any miracles.

Grammar and composition come together in this first cycle in a creative nexus exemplified by Corinne E. Hinton's (2010) essay, 'So, You've Got a Writing Assignment. Now What?.' The essay begins on the first day of the semester, addressing the panic students feel when confronted with their first writing assignment: '[I]t's a deep, vomit-inducing fireball that shoots down your body and out your toes.' Humor aside, Hinton provides detailed guidelines that walk the student though the essay process. 'Many students already know and employ many of these strategies regularly; however, few students know or use all of them every time' (Hinton, 2010). Writing, creativity and grammar becomes a process they're already familiar with. Then, they're ready to move on to the next assignment.

In the second facet essay, compare/contrast, students approach compositional elements through a process of comparing and contrasting. The structural requirements of the compare/contrast essay – specific patterns of organization into subject-by-subject or point-by-point arrangements – reinforce the methods acquired in the first essay cycle, and build upon them by requiring more structural complexity. The grammatical focus that supports this expansion of complexity concerns larger sentence-level issues, such as subject-verb agreement, understanding and effectively using pronouns, sentence fragments and run-on sentences. These are all elements of sentence clarity, and 'clarity is achieved through applying logic and organization at all levels of a piece of writing' (Stilman, 2010: 299).

Students experience the connection between grammar and creativity in this facet of essay most keenly in the revision process. Bringing together the new skills of sentence clarity and the structural approach to the compare/contrast writing assignment allows students to implement and understand global and local revisions. In 'Reflective Writing and the Revision Process: What Were You Thinking?', Sandra Giles (2010) uses the process letter as a tool teach students not only the importance of revision, but as a method to achieve the goal: 'Reflection helps you to develop your intentions (purpose), figure out your relation to your audience, uncover possible problems with your individual writing processes, set goals for revision, [and] make decisions about language and style.' Metacognitive techniques benefit the instructor as well as the student by highlighting the areas that need attention. The habit of reflection and revision work hand-in-hand to produce a lifelong skill that will transcend the writing process (Giles, 2010).

In writing definition, students compose with an eye toward argumentation. Through stipulation and limitation, narrowing the message forces students into a precision that requires accurate punctuation. Understanding commas, colons, semicolons, quotation marks and other punctuation marks combines with the explicit needs of definition to form a powerful synthesis of grammar and creativity. This value of this grammar-creativity connection is expressed by Anna Leahy (2005: 307): 'While I don't care much whether students can label phrases and clauses as restrictive or non-restrictive, I am rewarded when some of them realize that commas inserted or deleted change meaning.'

Finally, in argumentation, students assemble the talents acquired during the semester – description, compare/contrast, definition – into a single voice. The compositional elements required for effective argument incorporate the facets of essay already covered. Explorations are formalized through research that supports opinion, and this approach is paralleled in grammar, which emphasizes word choice, sentence style, and usage to create the elements of persuasion necessary to argument. These higher level grammatical concepts live at the core of argument: What could be more important to effective persuasion than word choice and sentence style to achieve a writer's goals?

The confluence of composition and grammar into creativity can be found in Rebecca Jones's (2010) essay, 'Finding the Good Argument OR Why Bother with Logic?' This logic-based discussion of writing arguments highlights the compositional elements crucial to building the kinds of sentences needed to convince an audience – as well as addressing the larger, structural elements through an examination of the role of logic in argument. After a comprehensive discussion of various models of argument, Jones offers that writers 'can be more deliberate in their argumentation by choosing to follow some of these methodical approaches to ensure the soundness and general quality of their argument.'

By combining a strong grammatical approach that relates logically and directly to the facets of composition that are being taught, instructors can create places where creativity manifests itself. A few possibilities have been discussed and proposed here; many others exist, limited only by the imagination of the composition course designer. Creative approaches to composition pedagogy are a powerful tool to unlock the potential of the student writer.

For more detail about this approach to teaching grammar and composition, including sample syllabi and lesson plans, visit grammarandcreativity.blogspot.com.

References

Aaron, J.E. (2005) *40 Model Essays* (p. 21). Boston: Bedford/St. Martin's.
Giles, S. (2010) Reflective writing and the revision process: What were you thinking? In C. Lowe and P. Zemliansky (eds) *Writing Spaces Vol. 1*. West Lafayette, IN: Parlor Press. 193. See http://www.writingspaces.org (accessed February 2013).

Goldberg, N. (1986) *Writing Down the Bones*. Boston: Shambhala.
Hinton, C.E. (2010) So, you've got a writing assignment. Now what? In C. Lowe and P. Zemliansky (eds) *Writing Spaces Vol. 1*. West Lafayette, IN: Parlor Press. 18. See http://www.writingspaces.org (accessed February 2013).
Jones, R. (2010) Finding the good argument or why bother with logic? In C. Lowe and P. Zemliansky (eds) *Writing Spaces Vol. 1*. West Lafayette, IN: Parlor Press. 178. See http://www.writingspaces.org (accessed February 2013).
Leahy, A. (2005) Grammar matters: A creative writer's argument. *Pedagogy* 5 (2), 307. See http://muse.jhu.edu (accessed July 2013).
Pinckert, R.C. (1986) *Pinckert's Practical Grammar*. Cincinnati: Writer's Digest Books.
Soukahov, A. (ed.) (1992) *The American Heritage Dictionary of the English Language* (3rd edn). Boston: Houghton Mifflin Company.
Stilman, A. (2010) *Grammatically Correct* (2nd edn). Cincinnati: Writer's Digest Books.
Strunk Jr., W. and White, E.B. (1997) *The Elements of Style* (3rd edn). New York: Macmillan.

12 Invention in Creative Writing: Explorations of the Self and the Social in Creative Genres[1]

Danita Berg

> A man of imagination among scholars feels like a sodomite at a convention of proctologists. So I keep away as much as possible from buildings named Burrowes South and Goldwin Smith, and their denizens (2001:1).
> – Paul West, *Master Class: Scenes from a Fiction Workshop*

> It's important to understand that there are two aspects to creating truly compelling writing. As (this) book's epigraph (from William Shakespeare's Hamlet) states, what's needed is both method and madness. The method can be learned in an academically rigorous, systematic manner (2009:1, her emphasis).
> – Alice LaPlante, *Method and Madness: The Making of a Story*

In higher education, the notion that creative writing cannot be taught is often perpetuated by those very teachers put in the classrooms to teach it. Creative writing instructors, often 'master' writers (authors who are well-published) might advocate the stance that perhaps the students can work to improve their writing, but only the true talent in the classroom will go on to be authors and only if they learn to emulate the teacher – who absents him- or herself from academic practices even while employed by these institutions to teach students to write.

Certainly a master writer understands his or her own process well enough to create well-crafted works. Yet a master of writing, however artistic his or her inclinations might be, might lack the pedagogical skills to translate the master's writing process to student apprentices – or perhaps the master's process is different from the one that might work for the student. If these masters, with a lack of teaching training, are put in front of the classroom, the often-ensuing lack of pedagogical approaches in creative writing classes 'results in a pedagogy (where) defined learning objectives rarely exist' (Vanderslice, 2008: 70). Students are expected to become inspired, to write naturally, and to bring in finished drafts for workshops with little talk about how to create them. When students fail to bring in finished works, or complain that they are suffering from 'writer's block,' it might be blamed less on their ability to create than the inability of the teacher to explain where to begin.

It's of little wonder that learning objectives exist or, if they do, are ill-defined in creative writing classrooms, considering that the writing processes of master teachers are often described in vague and confusing ways. Joy Williams describes the writing process as 'a spooky, clamorous silence ... A writer turns his back on the day and the night ... and tries, like some half-witted demiurge, to fashion other days and nights with words' (1999: 5–6). Michael Chabon likens his process to being in a war (Shoup & Denman, 2001: 33). Dorothy Allison defines hers as 'you've got all of these balls up in the air, and to get them up in the air, keep everything in your head, is an intense emotional process' (Shoup & Denman, 2001: 51). While these definitions of process might speak to the 'madness' of writing as defined by LaPlante, these kinds of definitions can be misleading or simply perplexing to new writers. While writing can, indeed, be an emotional and sometimes chaotic endeavor, describing it only in these terms does not help the fledgling writer understand how to start the writing process.

It should be pointed out that the institutions where, for example, Williams and Allison have taught are described as some of the best universities, with well-established creative writing programs. Creative writing students admitted to such universities already demonstrate advanced talent and likely understand their own processes. Instructors can claim they had little to do with these students' successes because they merely needed guidance through completed drafts. Even now, the University of Iowa Writers' Workshop, the most renowned college for creative writing, recently claimed sixteen Pulitzer Prize winners and three Poet Laureates among their graduates while proclaiming the program had nothing to do with their students' successes (Menand, 2009: 4).

At institutions such as the University of Iowa, the master-apprentice model may impart considerable benefits; it might be enough to employ the 'traditional' creative writing pedagogy of reading master works for inspiration, responding to craft prompts for practice, and workshopping for ideas for revision. But with the burgeoning of creative writing programs that began during the 1980s and continues to the present, instructors need to question if the master-apprentice model has the same effectiveness for creative writing students admitted to programs that cannot claim the same top-tier status as, say, Iowa, Cornell or Boston University. The teaching strategies that might work in these programs will not work for students who are truly beginners.

Widely published as a poet and literary author and highly respected as a researcher of rhetoric and composition, Wendy Bishop published in 1990 her influential *Released into Language: Options for Teaching Creative Writing*, a work that explores connections between composition theory and pedagogy and creative writing teacher philosophies and classroom practices. Bringing attention to the (potential) problems that can occur when the pedagogical approaches used at one program are uncritically transported to another, the work calls upon creative writing instructors to recognize that the kind of MFA program teaching strategies that seemed to work well for them may not be helpful to 'more varied students drawn from a broader set of open-admissions applicants' (Bishop, 1990: xiv).

According to the Association of Writers and Writing Programs, 800 new programs in creative writing have been developed in higher education since 1975 ('Growth of Creative Writing Programs,' 2012). Not all of the creative writing students in these programs expect – or even wish – to become published authors, but instead simply want to write because they enjoy it. Some students regard creative writing classes as an extension of their learning about written communication, as well as their learning more about themselves and others. All of these students deserve to learn about creative writing at their own pace and to meet their individual expectations.

Adding In(ter)vention to the Master-Apprentice Model

If master writers employed in academia find themselves to be artists more than teachers, still they must prepare to teach – and in a way that all students can understand. The writer-instructor needs to consider his or her own writing processes and, yes, strategies that have proved to be successful, including the study of master works, prewriting and workshopping. However, other strategies can be implemented as well.

Creative writing instructors can assist students in understanding their teaching craft by learning more about invention from compositionists. Richard Young and Alton Becker in 'Toward a Modern Theory of Rhetoric' define invention, a canon of rhetoric, as 'systematic methods of inquiry'

(1965: 127). Invention gives writers the opportunity to find subjects to write about that are meaningful to them, 'to explore for ideas and arguments, to frame insights and to examine the writing situation' (Lauer, 2004: 1). When invention methods are implemented, students are not encouraged towards a cognitive, goal-minded theory of working towards a final product such as a finished draft for workshopping, but instead are guided by their instructors to explore the writing process.

Creative writing instructors might think they are using invention by offering creative writing prompts. But this is prewriting, just one facet of invention. In *Released Into Language,* Bishop somewhat concentrates on prewriting exercises in her chapter 'The Inventions and Variations.' For example, she explains an exercise where she asks students to write passages that incorporate the worst clichés they can think of. While this exercise might teach them to avoid cliché – a craft issue – it does not teach them how to sustain a longer work, nor how to begin one. So, later in the same chapter Bishop describes 'The Muse Activity,' an invention tool of sorts because she asks students to think about where their writing comes from (1990: 64). Discussions of where inspiration comes from – reading other writers, eavesdropping, traveling, people-watching – allow students to consider how they begin their own work (1990: 65). This allows students to more fully understand the entire process of beginning a draft: where the work comes from.

Students Writing for Their Selves

Invention also helps students understand how their 'selves' play into their writing; as Cynthia Selfe and Sue Rodi state in 'An Invention Heuristic for Expressive Writing,' [the] process . . . actively engages students both in examining their experience for that which they find interesting and valuable, and in determining or discovering the most effective way to write about these experiences' (1980: 169). For writers who work in expressivist genres, this approach allows them to consider how their personal experiences might be related to an audience, helping the students create theme and internal conflict by using their own experiences in works that might otherwise be anecdotal or self-serving.

Because creative writing is called 'imaginative' writing; students might fear to draw too heavily from their own lives (excepting the relatively new genre of non-fiction). Burroway and Weinberg warn beginning writers that writing only from personal experience can be a misleading rule (2003: 8) because it limits the experiences that writers can relate on the page. Gardner also believes writing only from self-experience is 'limiting to the imagination'

(1983: 20). However, in the introduction to the popular creative writing rhetorical guide *Three Genres: The Writing of Fiction/Literary Nonfiction, Poetry, and Drama*, Stephen Minot counters that 'using personal experience selectively and honestly is almost a guarantee that your fiction will be fresh and convincing' (2007: 46). For students who are not sure where to begin, starting with self-knowledge can give them a comfort zone within which to explore their craft.

Invention allows students to approach their writing from the 'self' by inviting them to consider their dissonance. Dissonance, as defined by Janice Lauer, is writing to discover what you 'are curious, puzzled, or intrigued (about) . . . (it is) something that you haven't figured out yet. In that frame of mind, you can write to gain insight and to share it with readers' (Lauer *et al.*, 1991: 3). Creative writing students can apply dissonance to writing by creating conflict in their works that stems from their personal issues or from within their communities and cultures. By learning to write about internal or external conflicts in their lives, students discover how to create theme as they work to answer questions about their dissonance.

Questioning strategies also assist young writers in learning how much detail to share. In the chapter 'Toward Understanding and Sharing Experience,' Young, Becker and Pike (1970) say writers can decide which details are 'relevant and interesting' in their writing by answering two questions:

(1) What kinds of details are relevant to understanding an experience?
(2) What kinds of details are likely to be sufficiently interesting to a reader to warrant sharing them with others? (Young *et al.*, 1970: 54)

Creative writers might begin with these questioning techniques when considering which of their personal experiences could translate into story or prose. Questioning can help them decide how much description is needed in their work to translate a scene or character to a reader unfamiliar with the writer's experience.

Questioning also helps them to think critically about where to begin their writing; what experiences might lend themselves to theme, and what be merely amusing or anecdotal. Selfe and Rodi say students 'often fail to carefully consider, weigh, and focus their experiences . . . they fall short of working through these experiences in writing so that their writing becomes imaginative and pleasant to read' (1980: 169). Critically thinking about the experiences with which the writer has dissonance can help him or her decide what he or she needs to write about, rather than writing work that lacks emotional significance.

Selfe and Rodi propose a heuristic technique that places the student writer at a 'fuller, more well-rounded definition of self' by exploring through their lives through their past, present, and future experiences; for instance, how the writer would define themselves at five years old, how others might have seen them physically as a child, and what helped them reach goals ten years ago (1980: 171). This technique could easily be translated to story, as the student writer develops a character who might resemble his or her self while also considers a conflict that centers on how that character resolved conflicts based on his or her social environs, which could help the student create both internal and external conflict and rising action based on their own experiences.

Another technique students can use to examine or question their 'selves,' according to Kenneth Burke, is through the consideration of five elements: the act, the scene, the agent, the agency, and the purpose. Ostrom defines this technique as examining what is being described and what should be done about it (act), where the act takes place (scene), who is acting (agent), how the person is acting (agency) and why he is doing what they're doing (purpose) (2003: 5). This can be turned into a questioning strategy that students can use to consider how to show, not tell. Instructors can use the literary nonfiction piece 'Killing Chickens' by Meredith Hall to show students how this approach can benefit their own beginnings:

> I tucked her wings tight against her heaving body, crouched over her, and covered her flailing head with my gloved hand. Holding her neck hard against the floor of the coop, I took a breath, set something deep and hard inside my heart, and twisted her head. I heard her neck break with a crackle. Still she fought me, struggling to be free of my weight, my gloved hands, my need to kill her...
>
> ...I was killing chickens. It was my 38th birthday. My brother had chosen that morning to tell me that he had caught his wife – my best friend, Ashley – in bed with my husband a year before... When I roared upstairs and confronted John, he told me to go fuck myself. (2007: 5–6)

When students discuss this beginning in class, they consider what is being shown through the active scene: Why does the author begin with killing chickens? How does the act convey, thematically, the purpose of the story? Why is the main character (agent) carrying out the act, and why is this information withheld until the backstory is offered? Through questioning, students begin to understand why the work is started in the middle of the action, and how the act shows the theme of survival of a personal loss.

Students can then work through a journaling exercise, initially flatly or 'tellingly' answering these three questions, considering their selves in their writing. They can begin by writing answers that explain, or tell, the answers to these questions:

(1) What was the first thing on your mind when you woke up this morning?
(2) Identify an event in your life that you are excited about.
(3) Identify an event happening in your life that has you worried, or even scared.

After considering these prompts in expository answers, students can rewrite the answer to one of these questions, showing through scene the act that causes the agency. Through this questioning technique that transforms answers to questions into scenes, students learn to begin their work that shows their overall theme. This shifts the invention exercise to considering the self in writing while also practicing craft. Students are also considering how to show dissonance through an active scene that might begin a longer work. This gives them a place to begin their writing, and a starting point from which their work can grow through consideration of self.

Another creative writing teaching technique teachers can use to help students explore the self through storytelling called character mapping, as illustrated below (Figure 12.1).

Developed by Laurie Hutzler, character mapping explores the topography of character traits that that motivate a person's actions and choices. In this simplified version of Hutzler's process, writers can use the technique to explore their 'selves,' and then apply what they learned to storytelling. Hutzler suggests that creative writers should first learn to map themselves to help them 'start with the personal and move to the universal' (2009). Because the writer begins by learning to understand self as an 'interesting, complex, three-dimensional human being (who) constantly wrestle(s) with

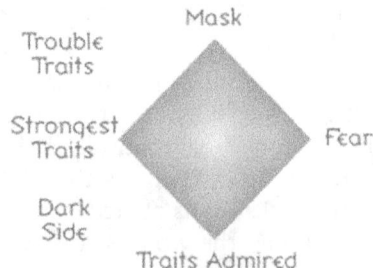

Figure 12.1 The character map: A heuristic tool for invention of story
Source: http://www.ETBScreenwriting.com

a variety of strong emotions and...a whole range of internal conflicts' (2009), students learn how to translate their understanding of self to another character.

The character map allows students to question themselves and to understand how their lives are stories that can be shaped into creative works. The character map is a guide instructors can use to help students consider their own character traits, although they can also use traits they hope to implement into their characters. One by one, students should be asked to consider the following traits for themselves, and to fill them in on the character map. Hutzler recommends naming at least three traits for each question with the exception of question 2:

(1) What is the biggest misconception about you?
(2) What is your greatest childhood fear?
(3) What is your greatest strength or strongest traits?
(4) What are the traits you admire most in other people?
(5) Which of your traits get you into the most trouble?
(6) What traits in other people do you most admire?

After the students answer the questions, the creative writing instructor can explain how this exploration of self can also relate to character:

(1) The 'mask' or misconception: This is how the person represents himself to others, the outer 'shell' or false face the person wears in public (2009). The mask is usually created because of:
(2) The fear: This is something that happened to causes the character to create his or her social facade. According to Hutzler, the fear is created because the writer worries about being unlovable or making a leap of faith towards their 'true self.'
(3) Development of self around fear: This is the defense mechanism the writer has created in order to not deal with the wound. A strong trait creates false pride or a false sense of security, or is what the writer relies on to 'get out of trouble.' Often this trait must be surrendered in order to achieve:
(4) What the person aspires to be. Hutzler calls this the manifestation of the writer's 'truest self.' If the writer can give up the crutch this true self might be achieved; if not, the writer might fall to:
(5) This is the person's Achilles' heel. The writer falls to this trait when he reacts badly to stress, anxiety, worry or fear or, as Hutzler describes it, the ways the character's fear tempts him/her to act badly or clouds the character's better judgment.

(6) The dark side can become apparent in story when the character completely surrenders to the fear, or it might be a trait assigned to the antagonist.

Answers to these questions offer meaningful points of entry into a story that are significant to the writer's sense of self. For example, the first and second points, the mask and fear, could be related to a fictional story or screenplay as a conflicted character and his or her backstory, which would be the first part of the story, or act one. Act two, or the rising action, would center on the character's ability to rise beyond his or her greatest strength or strongest trait to achieve a higher goal. Traits five and six would cause complications in the story, the hurdles the main character would need to confront in the rising action of the story.

The character map allows new writing students to look at their selves and experiences, translating those experiences to fiction or non-fiction; students begin to understand how they play a part into their creative stories.

Though invention techniques, learning about creative writing for the new writer becomes as much about self-awareness as storytelling. This has the added benefit of 'finding your self, your personality,' (Boe, 2003: 32); or, as Carl Jung said, learning about the 'optimum development of the whole individual human being' (quoted in Boe, 2003: 32) through invention and self-discovery.

Invention as a Social Act

Having creative writers consider their selves in their story is certainly a good place to begin. Rhetorician Karen LeFevre points out in *Invention as a Social Act* that the Platonic, or individualistic, view of invention has 'given rise to inventional methods – the use of analogy, freewriting, and clustering – that often help writers to break through the conventional stereotypes of perception and expression, reassuring them that they do have many possibilities and resources within' (1987: 23). However, LeFevre believes that only an individualistic approach to invention 'neglects studies of writers in social contexts' (1987: 23). She says this individualistic approach, looking at writing as a 'private and personal activity' (1987: 23) – often touted by creative writing teachers – makes the writing process seem hidden and mysterious to the writing student. So also placing writing in a social context allows writers to consider the discourse communities in which they live, what Patricia Bizzell names as the social processes 'whereby language-learning and thinking capacities are shaped and used in particular communities' (quoted in LeFevre, 1987: 23). So beginning writers need to also consider how their writing connects them not only to their selves but also to their worlds. Creative writing instructors can lead their students into this consideration of invention when they talk about language (dialogue) and setting, and how characters function in stories considering the social context in which they find themselves.

Burroway defines setting as the illumination of a story's underpinnings, 'a reflection of the emotion or revealing subtle aspects of a character's life' (Burroway & Weinberg, 2003: 173). Characters are a product of their place and culture (Burroway & Weinberg, 2003: 173), and so writers must consider how the social, and not just the 'furnishings' of setting will help to set the tone and emotion of the writing. Considering the social aspect of writing will 'create a world that entices [the reader] in and shows [the reader] what's at stake there' (Packer quoted in Burroway & Weinberg, 2003: 173).

Creative writing instructors can employ beginning through a social context by offering an exercise in the vignette. Vignettes are snapshots of scenes that link together to tell a story – but the link is implied. Writing in vignettes can help to cure a writer who has trouble adhering to the 'show, don't tell' rule, as vignettes are almost all active scenes, with little to no exposition from either the author or story's narrator to explain them. However, they also require the writer to consider how the character would act and react in different social settings, depending on who was in the 'setting' with the character. The beginning writer begins to grasp the social or 'setting' in their work, building upon the characterization invention techniques they learned earlier in the creative writing course. So the writer strives for both invention and craft in one exercise.

Sandra Cisneros's *The House on Mango Street* and Mary Robison's *Why Did I Ever* are strong examples. Each of the stories, built on vignettes, centers on the social; Cisneros's work is shaped around a place while Robison's focuses on characterization (although both works, obviously, employ characterization and setting techniques). In class students talk about how the vignettes, or active scenes, link through different craft elements – characterization (self), setting (social), and so on, to tell the story without exposition.

For example, in Robison's work students can look at the first five vignettes:

1

I have a dream of working a combination lock that is engraved on its back with the combination. Left 85, right 12, left 66. 'Well *shit*, man,' I say in the dream.

2

Hollis and I have killed this whole Saturday together. We've watched all fourteen hours of the PBS series The Civil War.
Now that it's over he turns to me and says, 'That was good.'

Buy Me Something

I end up at Appletree – the grocery – in the dead of the night. I'm not going to last long shopping, though, because this song was bad enough when what's-her-name sang it. And who are all these people at four A.M.? I'm making a new rule: No one is to touch me. Unless and until I feel different about things. Then, I'll call off the rule.

4

Three ex-husbands or whoever they were.

I'm sure they have their opinions.

I would say to them, 'Peace, our timing was bad, the light was ugly, things didn't work out.' I'd say, 'Although you certainly were doing your all, now weren't you.'

I would say, 'Drink!'

5

Hollis is not my ex-anything and not my boyfriend. He's my friend. Maybe not the best friend I have in the world. He is, however, the only. (2001: 2–3)

Students can consider the craft elements brought to each vignette as well as how the character's relationships pose personal and social questions. For example, in *Why Did I Ever* writing instructors can pose the questions:

(1) Why is the symbolism of the first vignette important to set the tone of the work?
(2) How does the main character's relationship with her husband and 'best friend' offer good indirect characterization?
(3) How do the social interactions (or lack thereof) between the main character and her 'best friend' further show who they are?
(4) Why does the work need the social construct of the grocery store to further identify the theme?
(5) Consider the first five vignettes: How do they build on each other to offer conflict/theme, without stating it? How is this 'plotting'?
(6) What is the overall tone of the work? How does Robison establish tone through craft elements, without stating abstractions in exposition?
(7) How do the scenes link in order to convey a theme? What is the theme? How can you tell, without exposition?

After the students talk about how craft elements can link to create a story, they consider one of their own works-in-progress. In their journals, they write five vignettes based on their stories, essentially re-examining – and quite possibly rewriting – their scenes in an active voice. Each vignette focuses on a different craft element: characterization, setting, symbolism, and so on, building the work through a scene with personal or social ramifications. They begin to see their story through not just craft, but also through how their understanding of who they are, who the characters they imagine, and the settings they both know and create can merge together to flesh out a well-rounded scene, using several craft elements.

This is often the exercise that helps students understand the difference between showing and telling; because they have no choice but to write active scenes, they move into showing. It is helps students see they can write beyond their 'selves,' offering up more imaginative considerations of craft in their work. The work begins to expand beyond self to the social. Instead of individual prewriting exercises in characterization, setting and dialogue, they learn to see all of these craft issues as a whole, integrating each invention technique to flesh out story.

Burroway contends that it is the writer's task to write about what you care about (Burroway & Weinberg, 2003: 9). And while skilled writers will eventually move beyond their own experiences to translate creative works, they will struggle enough with craft issues and theme. So while they work on their craft, invention – considering the dissonance in their lives, a thematic source around which to shape their work – gives them a good place to begin.

Conclusion

Master writers can have their place in the classroom, but must learn from other writing disciplines such as rhetoric to become teachers too. If a creative writing instructor is given the title of a master teacher, it should because he or she has mastered not only craft, but also teaching. The master teacher considers the needs of the students and finds several pedagogical approaches that allow them to not only understand how craft issues differ in creative genres, but also how the creative process in writing will always consider the self and community.

A creative writing teacher who understands invention can show students how to begin by helping them considering a student's history: those meaningful events that shaped the student, as an individual or as a member of his community. The teacher can help shape the work, using questioning strategies to probe for dissonance, which gives the writer a place of conflict from where the writing can begin, before the work is written and is given to the workshop for feedback. Helping the student understand the writing process, not just revision but also how writers begin, gives the authority of the writing to the student, instead of to the instructor. The teacher considers not only his or her process, but those processes that have worked for writers at all stages of skill, to enable his students to understand writing beyond art.

The Association of Writing Programs acknowledges that students need to understand this part of the writing process in order to understand their place in the writing world:

> Many students, especially today's students, feel that the world is not of their making, and not theirs to form or to reform; but writing classes often demonstrate the efficacy of the human will – that human experience can be shaped and directed for the good – aesthetically, socially, and politically. (Fenza, 2009)

By offering invention techniques considered by composition theorists, we empower our writers to understand craft as eminent through self, not through rubbing elbows with a successful writer. By removing himself as a master writer to emulate, and giving students invention techniques to help them decide what the students' own stories should be, the teacher becomes more than a master writer, but what Wendy Bishop refers to as a writer/teacher, someone who considers their process as much as they write (Bishop, 1999). For the teacher who is instructing beginning creative writing students, invention empowers students to begin to understand the writing process, as to what makes good story, and will help them avoid writing drafts that have no conflict in them for the first several pages. The writer-teacher gives them the skills to later understand the solitary process, the 'madness' of creativity, and a solid understanding that writing can be borne of inspiration, but is still centered on the self and the society, as invention tools and as places to begin.

Note

(1) Danita Berg's work stems from her 2010 University of South Florida doctoral dissertation work, 'Re-composition: Considering the intersections of composition and creative writing theories and pedagogies.'

References

Berg, D. (2010) Re-composition: Considering the intersections of composition and creative writing theories and pedagogies. Doctoral dissertation, University of South Florida.

Bishop, W. (1990) *Released into Language: Options for Teaching Creative Writing*. Urbana: National Council of Teachers of English.

Bishop, W. (1999) Places to stand: The reflective writer-teacher-writer in composition. *College Composition and Communication* 51 (1), 9–31.

Boe, J. (2003) Storytelling, writing, and finding yourself. In W. Bishop and H. Ostrom (eds) *The Subject is Story: Essays for Writers and Readers* (pp. 30–40). Portsmouth, NH: Boynton/Cook Heinemann.

Burke, K. (1969) *A Grammar of Motives*. Oakland, CA: University of California Press.

Burroway, J. and Weinberg, S. (2003) *Writing Fiction: A Guide to Narrative Craft* (6th edn). New York: Longman Publishers.

Cisneros, S. (1984) *The House on Mango Street*. New York: Knopf Doubleday Publishing Group.

Fenza, D. (2009) About AWP: The growth of creative writing programs. *The Association of Writers and Writing Programs*. See http://www.awpwriter.org/about/our_history_overview (accessed 2 February 2015).

Gardner, J. (1983) *The Art of Fiction: Notes on Craft for Young Writers*. New York: Random House.

Growth of Creative Writing Programs (1975–2012) The Association of Writers and Writing Programs. January 2012. See https://www.awpwriter.org/application/public/pdf/AWP_GrowthWritingPrograms.pdf (accessed 2 February 2015).

Hall, M. (2007) Killing chickens. In S. Minot (ed.) *Three Genres: The Writing of Fiction/Literary Nonfiction, Poetry, and Drama* (pp. 5–8). New Jersey: Pearson Education.

Hutzler, L. (2009) The Emotional Toolbox. *ETB Screenwriting: An Emotional Toolbox Website*. See http://www.ETBScreenwriting.com (accessed 30 October 2013).

LaPlante, A. (2009) *Method and Madness: The Making of a Story*. New York: W.W. Norton and Company.

Lauer, J. (2004) *Invention in Rhetoric and Composition*. West Lafayette, IN: Parlor Press.

Lauer, J., Lundsford, A., Atwill, J., Clemens, T., Hart-Davidson, W., Jacobs, D., Langstraat, L., Miles, L., Peeples, T. and Uber-Kellogg, N. (1991) *Four Worlds of Writing: Inquiry and Action in Context* (4th edn). Boston: Pearson Custom Publishing.

LeFevre, K.B. (1987) *Invention as a Social Act*. Carbondale and Edwardsville: Southern Illinois University Press.

Menand, L. (2009, June 8) Show or tell: Should creative writing be taught? *The New Yorker*. See http://www.newyorker.com/arts/critics/atlarge/2009/06/08/090608crat_atlarge_menand (accessed 1 August 2009).

Minot, S. (2007) *Three Genres: The Writing of Fiction/Literary Nonfiction, Poetry, and Drama*. New Jersey: Pearson Education.

Ostrom, H. (2003) Story, stories, and you. In W. Bishop and H. Ostrom (eds) *The Subject is Story: Essays for Writers and Readers* (pp. 2–9). Portsmouth, NH: Boynton/Cook Heinemann.

Robison, M. (2001) *Why Did I Ever*. New York: Counterpoint.

Selfe, C.L. and Rodi, S. (1980) An invention heuristic for expressivist writing. *College Composition and Communication* 31 (2), 169–174. See http://www.jstor.org/stable/356371

Shoup, B. and Denman, M.L. (eds) (2001) *Novel Ideas: Contemporary Authors Share the Creative Process*. Indianapolis: Alpha Books.

Vanderslice, S. (2008) Sleeping with Proust vs. tinkering under the bonnet: The origins and consequences of the American and British approaches to creative writing in higher education. In G. Harper and J. Kroll (eds) *Creative Writing Studies: Practice, Research and Pedagogy* (pp. 66–74). Clevedon: Multilingual Matters.

West, P. (2001) *Master Class: Scenes from a Fiction Workshop*. New York: Harcourt, Inc.
Williams, J. (1999) Uncanny the singing that comes from certain husks. In W. Blythe (ed.) *Why I Write: Thoughts on the Craft of Fiction* (pp. 5–13). Boston: Little and Brown Company.
Young, R.E. and Becker, A.L. (Winter 1965) Toward a modern theory of rhetoric: A tagmemic contribution. *Harvard Educational Review* 35 (4), 450–468.
Young, R.E., Becker, A.L. and Pike, K.L. (1970) *Rhetoric: Discovery and Change*. New York: Harcourt, Brace & World, Inc.

13 Teaching the Exploratory Essay as Pedagogy, Process and Project

Sonya Huber and Ioanna Opidee

As teachers, we wish for our students to develop the capacity to think for themselves – more often and more intensely, more critically and creatively. We want our students to ask better questions and actively seek answers. Their ability to do this depends, perhaps, on their genuine curiosity and desire to learn, question and *know,* so we wish for them to cultivate that desire and tendency as well. We want them to appreciate the fine art and craft of inquiry and knowledge-generation, to envision themselves (and, thus, act) as authors of their own learning, committed to the lifelong process of it. We want them to discover meaningful connections between course material in our classes and those of others, as well as their personal and professional lives and the greater world beyond.

As teachers of *writing,* we wish to receive papers that are clearly and thoughtfully written, with purpose and cohesion; we want to read papers with life and energy that showcase authentic intellectual curiosity, creativity and engagement with the subject matter. We recognize these papers immediately when we seem them. In short, they have *substance.*

And yet, too often, we receive lifeless, dull, canned papers, or papers written sloppily, without care. Too often, we complain that our students don't, in fact, seem to think for themselves, that all they care about are grades, that they don't take control of their own learning.

Rather than simply exhorting our students to write better, and to think and to care more, we propose the exploratory essay – not only as an assignment but as a teaching stance and organizing principle for a writing course. Ultimately, as we will explore, this requires a shift in our understanding of the writing teacher's role in the classroom and a renewed focus on the process of discovery as experienced through writing itself. This shift attends to both the writing and the broader 'wish list' of educational goals described above; through this process, we support students in growing as thoughtful and skillful writers, thinkers and scholars who are genuinely engaged in the process of learning.

Teaching and Valuing Risk

When we model the essay in class as a cognitive and pedagogical stance, we give students a lived experience of intellectual and emotional risk. The essay not only provides us with a model of digression but also stresses the importance of holding open a space for inquiry in which the outcome is not assured. Much like scientific innovation or creative work, essay writing in the Montaignian tradition begins with an impulse or an interest and a willingness to follow that interest.

We can reach the goals of a composition class through a nontraditional route using the exploratory essay as path and guide, and we can achieve our desired outcomes by inverting our approach to teaching writing from an initial focus on form to one of content. In the process, we challenge outsiders' perceptions of both composition and creative writing, who may 'cast creative writing as a decorative opportunity, with no practical import, serving a few genius students, and composition studies as a training regimen for school and vocational skills,' as described by Douglass Hesse (2010: 44). He continues, 'Both fields are better served by a richer view of writing that articulates the values of a creative, productive art, "practical" in much wider terms than would be imagined ... A life activity with many interconnected manifestations.'

The fact that composition is often positioned so far from exploratory writing will not surprise those who have taught composition and felt the pressures of composition framed as a service course in which students are expected to learn transactional, transferrable skills to employ in other courses where content is presumed to be delivered. Among other transferrable skills, composition is assumed to improve the *readability* of students' texts. If a student turns in a paper riddled with incomplete sentences or grammar errors, our colleagues in other disciplines may ask, 'What are they *teaching* over there in freshman comp?' A second transferrable skill, more complex and with greater implications for epistemology and modes of inquiry, is a disproportionate focus on the much-exalted *thesis statement,* couched in the larger agenda of establishing, as William Zeiger writes, 'a premise, implicitly or explicitly, with which presumably the audience agrees' (1989: 236) within a paper that 'then attempts to transmit the force of that agreement to a conclusion with which, presumably, the audience would not have agreed initially' and in a voice of 'intrusive rigidity' (1989).

Although this style of writing might be painful enough to read, it is likely even more painful – and counterproductive – for students to write. The larger question of whether this stance serves students is articulated by Nancy Sommers, who has watched her students marshal quotes in support of a thesis and, in the process, 'disappear behind the weight and permanence of their borrowed words... allowing sources to speak through them unquestioned, unexamined' (1999: 180).

What we suggest in place of this – in many cases, exclusive – emphasis on *argument* is an essayistic stance, in the sense of the essay as an *experiment* or *test,* grounded more solidly in the *question* than the *statement.* Like Pat C. Hoy, we see value in trying to turn students 'from a precise thesis to a supple idea' (1989: 289).

An exploratory essay, rather than driving into a topic from one direction like a battering ram, may use several woven approaches and areas of research or inquiry. This approach uses several effective rhetorical strategies. It sets up a contract with the reader in which the writer commits to openness and thoroughness in pursuit of a question. One of the givens of the essay is range of motion, and this range of motion can increase reader interest and even makes a case for the urgency of the text itself. What is being communicated through form and language is that the conclusion cannot wholly be guessed from the introduction. The form of the exploratory essay encourages the reader to stay engaged with the text by promising not a restatement and marshalling of evidence but instead a willingness to incorporate the unexpected.

The essay engages readers because the audience is invited into an unfolding inquiry. The essay's often-dialogic form admits weaknesses and pursues questions, which may make it a much more natural and intuitive form for student writers who often feel too uncomfortable with their authority to write about subjects they may not fully understand. In offering an invitation to *consider* a topic, the essay models for student writers the rhetorical strategies of give-and-take as a way to build reader investment. The essayist, rather than building defenses against reader 'attacks' to a thesis, inhabits the imagined mind of the reader and empathetically imagines a question from many readers' points of view. This is only possible because the essay's tasks may include the acknowledgement and exploration of these points of view, but the essay is not tasked with resolution or destruction of these alternate viewpoints. The essay's invitation, according to Chris Anderson, 'is not "watch me write," but "join me in thinking"' – which is precisely what we ask our students, and hope that they will ask each other, to do (1989).

Cultivating Writer Engagement through Digression

The engine of an essay is the writer's own engagement with the question at hand – in other words, on the student writer's ability, tendency, and inclination to *care*. We define 'caring' here as engaged investment. Contrary to what may seem obvious, we have found that caring *is,* in fact, a skill that can be taught. On the first day of class, Ioanna Opidee has begun telling her students that the most challenging aspect of her course may be her expectation that they all must *care* – about the subject matter, course material, their own learning, and even each other as peers and colleagues. This is not something they're expected to come in with on day one; it's a skill and practice they are expected to actively develop over time, with visible support and guidance from their professor. Teaching the exploratory essay as a process and product as well as a stance is one key way to do so.

The intermediate practice of essay writing requires writer investment in a question rather than in a more narrow 'case' to be built. The development of the question gives student writers impetus to pursue the question into doubt, and this is the geography we aim to help our students navigate. The ability to grapple with doubt produces mature writers and thinkers who are able to confront complexity in their work and in the world. The questioning impulse and the ability to 'lean into' doubt are hallmarks of the exploratory essay, requiring the central element of digression as seen in the essays of Montaigne and many others since his time.

However, digression itself is often misunderstood. Rather than pursuing tangents with a facile distractability, the art of association – and the ability to follow those associations – allows a student to seek connections between what they care about and what they may not, initially, moving incrementally toward synthesis. 'The chief role of the digression,' Phillip Lopate points out 'is to amass all the dimensions of understanding that the essayist can accumulate by bringing in as many contexts as a problem or insight can sustain without overburdening it.' It 'scoops up subordinate themes in passing,' and 'must wander off the point only to fulfill it' (1994: xl).

Digression is a skill and mode more likely to be championed in a creative nonfiction course that includes a focus on the literary essay – the essay *as literature* – than in a composition course, where the thesis-driven, argument-based essay is forefronted. But digression can be pointed out, questioned, examined, and ultimately practiced in the composition classroom as well, and not necessarily so that every composition student will assume and try on the role of literary writer but for a more widely practical and concrete reason: pursuing a topic that might seem peripheral but that a student intuits to be connected helps a student writer to develop skills in discovering connections that might not be readily apparent and in looking beyond the obvious and superficial. Synthesis in student thinking and writing is a higher cognitive function that requires the ability to balance and tolerate ambiguity and doubt. Training students to think as essay writers – in the exploratory and creative, rather than expository and solely argumentative, sense – helps them to become not only stronger writers but stronger thinkers and scholars; thinkers and scholars who can identify strategies and habits of mind that will allow them to suspend judgment and determinations long enough to make these connections meaningfully.

Our goals, as instructors of both creative nonfiction and composition, is to develop and support students' ability to engage in dialogue and discovery; this, rather than mere readability, is a higher-order transferrable skill necessary for complex and relevant communication.

A central outcome from student practice in the exploratory essay is an increased range of motion and agility in writing; both are teachable skills. Writing teachers do recognize this facility as good writing when they see it, but composition courses are often structured under the assumption that students will develop separate skills in separate genres by practicing each of those genres. The portfolio is a move toward combining those genres and a recognition that a student must be able to switch between them. The genuine essay, however, foregrounds agility and range of motion with the demand for a constant careful focus on whether new questions have arisen, where they might lead, and whether the assumptions of the piece of writing still hold. Flexibility is woven into the DNA of the essay. The essay may offer a completely 'bottom-up' approach to fostering cognitive flexibility in our student writers.

Re-Envisioning 'Argument'

For teachers and for students, a central risk in writing the essay is the very real possibility of a complete 'turn' of one's thesis. In the research essay as traditionally framed, a thesis revealed to be incorrect is often interpreted to be a failure because its hypothesis was not supported by the data. Lab reports or scientific studies, however, often acknowledge that a failed hypothesis offers a range of rich data and the opportunity for publishable research. Why have our fields of inquiry diverged so strongly, with the student writers in a computer lab expected to find success at every turn, and the students in the biology lab carefully observing, considering and learning from the outcomes of both experiments that meet their expectations and those that don't?

In reframing our teaching of writing to include re-consideration of one's thesis, we are modeling a version of the writing task in which students are rewarded for openness to their research and to their evolving thoughts and reactions. In the process of documenting their 'lab work' and discoveries carefully, their job is not to choose a 'correct' thesis and to support it but to investigate and weigh whether their initial hypothesis is correct. Along the way, they challenge even the fundamental assumptions of their initial ideas, including the influences and biases that led to the surprising conclusions and discoveries. The more we can track and foreground this process of discovery in the classroom and focus on observation rather than judgment based on a 'good' thesis, the more we train student writers in the practices of thought agility and true reflection.

A teaching stance that genuinely invites and encourages students to essay in the Montaignian sense of exploration and intellectual experimentation requires looking differently at argument, reading past and through confusion, prioritizing thoughtfulness above and beyond the lower-order skill of readability. In a way, we should be encouraging students to make a mess on the page at one developmental step toward achieving greater range and reach in the end, much the way an athlete training with weights must shred muscle tissue in order to build muscle.

Assigning and Assessing the Exploratory Essay

We can say we want our students to be more thoughtful and open to new ideas, we can preach to them about the importance of process, and we can even assign the exploratory essay as described above, but when our rubrics – reflections of what we value and reward in our courses – and our teaching stance do not align with that, students will read these boundaries and learn from them as well as from the explicit content and frames offered in our course. As essayistic teachers of writing, on the other hand, we aim to reward risk and inquiry, and we believe we can create and teach assignments that focus on and allow us to seriously assess process as well as product.

On a concrete level, one of Sonya Huber's major goals for evaluating a major revision to an essay is the degree of risk involved and the student's willingness to let go of initial assumptions and methods in order to try a second approach for a revision. Under that shifted rubric, an 'A' revision for a final portfolio is one evaluated by its degree of re-vision rather than the degree to which the student has merely polished or elaborated upon the thesis in the previous draft.

By devoting serious time and attention, in our assignments and in-class activities, to exploratory thinking and writing, we can highlight and help students experience a sense of *urgency* as they write. In Sonya's classes, students are asked to write initial 'rants' about assigned readings or class discussion topics. The students are encouraged to share their real and non-academic feelings and thoughts, including boredom, unexpressed frustration, or 'dislike' for an idea. Students often find that, in being allowed to vent and explore these initial reactions, they are able to slowly unfold a thoughtful and scholarly reaction to a reading out of what they had previously assumed to be an irrelevant emotion. Training students in careful reflection means putting the focus on the assets within them and using those assets and reactions in the service of the writing process. Collecting individual reflections at various points of the writing and discovery process can allow a student to review his or her own reactions and engage in the meta-cognitive act of making meaning out of one's own changing perspectives, discerning patterns and posing questions about the reasons for the changed perspectives over time. An essayistic approach incorporates an 'inside-outside' perspective that moves back and forth between such internal reactions and information from outside or from another view, and as students are encouraged to include all this information in their drafts and in their discovery processes, they will be more likely to develop the agility and fearlessness that is a quality of the best exploratory essays. We encourage students to develop a sense of themselves as thoughtful 'travelers,' who are comfortable crossing into unknown terrain, collecting artifacts – information, insights, curiosities and questions from other disciplines and contexts – for closer examination along their journey or back at home base.

One might ask whether such intensive practices of reflective and open-ended writing are limited to the small writing-workshop classes and whether this model would be prohibitively time-intensive for the lecture or for the teacher of several sections of composition. The practices of a dynamic lecture may include a dialogue with students aiming partially to expose the underpinnings of assumptions, as influenced by the Socratic Method. When modeling the essayistic mode of inquiry, however, an instructor may seek not to pursue contradiction but to highlight open questions in which individual students may seek to formulate answers through a variety of means. Instead of a conversation in which the lecturer explains, the teacher in this case models a mode of thought that involves tracking the threads of ideas as they come up in class discussion, possibly via a whiteboard. The essay, rather than seeking closure, arrives at sense and meaning through consideration of disparate but intersecting threads that the writer can combine and juxtapose in order to find fruitful questions spurring on a continued inquiry.

The 'Personal' in the Essay

Essaying as a teaching stance moves beyond the inclusion of a personal narrative assignment in a composition class. Reformulating one's class on an essayistic template focuses on crafting an invitation to students to mine their interests, identities, background, and experiences as material for serious inquiry and reflection. Doing this, Kurt Spellmeyer argues, we are 'calling attention to the writer's situatedness,' (1989: 270) and we 'permit our students to bring their extratextual knowledge to bear' upon course material (1989: 275).

As Jim W. Corder acknowledges, 'The personal essay is not the exclusive place, but it is a place for us to begin to know ourselves and show ourselves to each other rather than confronting each other with definitions and theses, wanting... to be authoritative before or at each other' (1989: 313). It is, as William Zeiger writes, an 'egalitarian medium' that is 'flexible enough to tolerate ambiguities' (1989: 236). The ambiguities highlight the complexity of subject matter and questions, encouraging students to suspend their resolutions and continue imagining possibilities – which is at the heart of creative thinking.

Wendy Bishop argues that 'we all need to essay our lives' (2003: 267), which means to delve well below the surface of experience in order to investigate significance and relevance – and this can extend as well to the texts and contexts we take up in our courses. Phillip Lopate speaks of the 'vertical dimension' (1997: xxv) of the form, which provides a vehicle for teaching students to 'think for themselves,' as introduced above – more often and more intensely. By assigning this type of writing, we help students cultivate habits of mind that will serve them well as writers who are able to formulate their own questions and to pursue their sites of engagement, both within and beyond the academy.

Writing and Engaged Thinking

An additional outcome for students, and one that is most difficult to put into concrete outcomes, is the central skill of self-listening. This skill underpins both agility of thought and dialogic connection to reader. The essay cannot capture thought itself, but it takes the shape of thought; essayist Phillip Lopate described the task of the essayist as capturing 'the mind at work' (1999: 337) on the page. Because thought is flexible, loose, and branching, the essayist must develop the skill of paying careful attention to his or her own racing thoughts, developing the skill of catching intuitions and questions and seeing those small threads as productive and creative opportunities and spurs for future writing and research. This self-listening is often thought to be a non-teachable skill because it is confused with creativity itself, but the tuning in to one's thought patterns in order to essay allows students to truly access their own minds in a way that is not fostered through a writing approach that privileges external over internal sources. We are not advocating here for a turn away from external sources and research. Rather, we are recommending that with sharpened cognitive skills, students' abilities to engage with those external sources will be vastly increased. These engaged writers – those given permission and support to find their interests in the world at large – will develop into engaged, flexible thinkers and citizens better able to confront the questions and dilemmas of a rapidly changing world.

References

Anderson, C. (1989) Error, ambiguity, and the peripheral: Teaching Lewis Thomas. In C. Anderson (ed.) *Literary Nonfiction: Theory, Criticism, Pedagogy* (pp. 315–332). Carbondale, IL: SIU P.

Bishop, W. (2003) Suddenly sexy: Creative nonfiction rear-ends composition. *College English* 65 (3), 256–275.

Corder, J. (1989) Hoping for essays. In C. Anderson (ed.) *Literary Nonfiction: Theory, Criticism, Pedagogy* (pp. 301–314). Carbondale, IL: SIU P.

Hesse, D. (2010) The place of creative writing in composition studies. *College Composition and Communication* 62 (1), 31–52.

Hoy, P.C. (1989) Students and teachers under the influence: Image and idea in the essay. In C. Anderson (ed.) *Literary Nonfiction: Theory, Criticism, Pedagogy* (pp. 287–300). Carbondale, IL: Southern Illinois University Press.

Lopate, P. (1997) Introduction. *The Art of the Personal Essay: An Anthology from the Classical Era to the Present.* New York: Anchor.

Lopate, P. (1999) What happened to the personal essay? In R.L. Root and M. Steinberg (eds) *The Fourth Genre: Contemporary Writers of/on Creative Nonfiction* (pp. 337–344). Boston: Allyn and Bacon.

Sommers, N. (1999) I stand here writing. In R.L. Root and M. Steinberg (eds) *The Fourth Genre: Contemporary Writers of/on Creative Nonfiction* (pp. 177–184). Boston: Allyn and Bacon.

Spellmeyer, K. (1989) A common ground: The essay in the academy. *College English* 51 (3), 262–276.

Zeiger, W. (1989) The personal essay and egalitarian rhetoric. In C. Anderson (ed.) *Literary Nonfiction: Theory, Criticism, Pedagogy* (pp. 235–244). Carbondale, IL: SIU P.

14 Beyond Argumentation: Toulmin's Model as a Dialogic, Processual Heuristic

Debra Jacobs

Writing students are most likely to encounter Stephen Toulmin's model of the 'layout' of arguments when, not surprisingly, the focus of instruction is on argumentation. In that context, the model often serves as a way to test the logical validity of an argument. Although teaching students to assess the soundness of arguments is important, the tendency to align such assessment with (quasi) formal logic contradicts Toulmin's efforts to provide a non field-specific model for analyzing arguments, whether in the context of reception or production. In fact, given Toulmin's objective of providing an analytic model that can be applied to arguments of any field, including the practical arguments of everyday life, confining the pedagogical usefulness of Toulmin's model to just the teaching argumentation per se neglects the far wider applicability the model has as an analytic and inventional heuristic.

Granted, the formulaic appearance of Toulmin's model does not help it to establish a strong first impression as a portable inventional aid (Figure 14.1).

It is ironic that the model Toulmin proposed to demonstrate the limited usefulness of formal logic for accounting for arguments would appear so *logical*, especially considering that the traditional approach to teaching argumentation with reference to logic and 'rational' reasoning (consider, for example, the fallacies) does not easily facilitate teaching the applicability of Toulmin's model to the wide-ranging arguments that Toulmin conceived the model to accommodate.

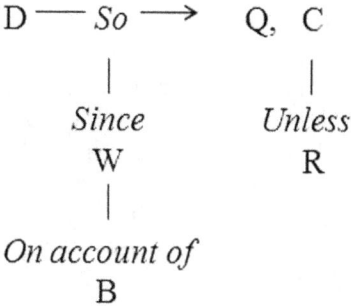

Figure 14.1 Stephen Toulmin's argument model

Of course Toulmin's model can be useful for teaching the elements of an argument as closely associated with logic. Toulmin did not deny the value within certain contexts of bringing the methods of logic to bear on the study, formulation or analysis of arguments. It was, rather, the scope of logic that Toulmin questioned:

> When we ask how far the authority of the Court of Reason extends, therefore, we must put on one side the question how far in any field it is possible for arguments to be analytic: we must focus our attention instead on the rather different question, to what extent there are already established warrants in science, in ethics or morality, in law, art-criticism, character-judging, or **whatever it may be**; and how far the procedures for deciding what principles are sound, and what warrants are acceptable, are generally understood and agreed. (Toulmin, 2003: 162; emphasis added)

Liberated from the field of logic, arguments so conceived are amenable to being taught in any field whatever. Indeed, according to Toulmin's conception of a general jurisprudence, discernments of validity can occur so long as there is 'common ground on which to argue': 'Two people who accept common procedures for testing warrants in any field can begin comparing the merits of arguments in that field' (Toulmin, 2003: 162). Potentially present in virtually any statement that seeks or presupposes assent, arguments are amenable to being taught within any writing context whatever. After all, statements that seek or presuppose assent occur in discourse of any aim, and so too, then, do arguments – whether explicitly or potentially, whether relatively fully elaborated or highly truncated.

Starting from Conclusions

As those familiar with the Toulmin model know, it provides a layout of six elements of an argument – claim (C), qualifier (Q), data (D), warrant (W), backing (B), and rebuttal (R) – in a manner that indicates how the elements relate to each other. The model depicts an argument developing as a forward progression that concludes with the claim. The issuance of a claim, then, suggests that some amount of processual reasoning has occurred – unless, as Toulmin notes, 'the assertion was made quite wildly and irresponsibly' (2003: 90). In fact, since it is the conclusion of an argument, a claim all by itself indicates the potentiality of the other elements. Consider, for example, this assertion from the 'Champion of the World' chapter of Maya Angelou's *I Know Why the Caged Bird Sings*: 'It wouldn't do for a Black man and his family to be caught on a lonely country road on a night when Joe Louis had proved that we were the strongest people in the world' (1993: 134). Issued as a statement that seeks or presupposes assent, this assertion is a claim, albeit not one excerpted from an argumentation essay. Just as other elements of a fully expressed argument are potentially present by virtue of a claim of traditional argumentation (such as 'Social media are a bane to education'), it is not difficult to recognize that other elements of an argument are just as potentially present by virtue of this 'caught on a lonely country road' claim.

Given the potential presence from a claim of the other elements of an argument, student-generated claims can serve as an effective starting point for engaging students with Toulmin's model. The processual activity of generating the other elements provides an inductive instructional approach rather than what is afforded by a top-down presentation of Toulmin's model all at once. Certainly, learning the elements of an argument can benefit anyone who has an interest in language and communication. But what is more relevant to my treatment of Toulmin's model for the purposes of this chapter is that engaging students with the model processually develops their ability to utilize the model as an inventional strategy that not only assists with filling out a given argument but also provides opportunities for critical reflection on aspects of subjectivity disclosed in arguments.

Beginning with student claims as a means for introducing students to Toulmin's model has the advantage of providing a starting point that students quickly understand and appreciate without the hindrance that presenting the model all at once can create. This approach also allows for engaging students with using the model with or without reference to the instructional context of argumentation. In fact, even using the term *claim* is not necessary to begin with the brief directive that students jot down a few assertions that express viewpoints, opinions or beliefs they hold. Typically, students will be able to recall actual assertions they've recently made. To assist, I provide a couple examples of my own, such as, most recently, these:

- 'East Bay's spring little league program is better than its summer program,' said to a neighborhood parent who, knowing I had a son in little league, asked for my opinion.
- 'Crate training is an effective way to housebreak dogs,' stated to a dog rescue volunteer who was following up on an adoption application I had submitted.

And these are a few of the assertions written down by students, following suit, in my class:

- 'Matt Christopher books can help get middle school boys to enjoy reading,' said by a student to his sister, whose son disliked reading.
- 'It's best not to relax a young girl's hair,' said by a student to a friend who was trying to decide whether or not to use a relaxer on her daughter's hair.
- 'It's not ethical to eat meat,' said by a student to her parents when they questioned why she had become a vegetarian.

Like mine, these students' assertions were representative of utterances they recalled having recently made, beneficial because the brief instructional activities for engaging students with the Toulmin model unfold with greater ease and more meaningfully if the students' assertions express a viewpoint to which they have some commitment. Commitment to an assertion suggests that there are underlying values, beliefs, experiences and so forth that in some way connect to it. As other elements of an argument become articulated processually, such aspects of subjectivity can serve as focal points of inquiry, facilitating critical reflection and leading, perhaps, to attenuated commitments – whether strengthened, weakened, or simply better understood – to the claim or other elements of the argument.

Challenging Assertions, Discerning Subjectivity

Again, an assertion that seeks or (rightly or wrongly) presupposes assent – a *claim*, if that term is being used with students – to which there is some commitment, indicates the potentiality of the other elements of an argument. Engaging Toulmin's model processually to determine and express those elements (re)enacts the dialogic character of issuing an argument, something that Toulmin treats concretely (if not explicitly). Beginning with the initial assertion, the dialogic character occurs as clarification- or challenge-type questions are raised and answered. For a claim, Toulmin offers (2003: 90), 'What have you got to go on?' The question is meant to elicit information – a reason, a detail, a piece of evidence – that supports the claim, hence providing a data element to the argument. But notice that there is something more specific asked than what just *any* evidence there might be to support a claim. The question asks the person who issued the claim to disclose his/her own thinking.

As before, one or two illustrative examples help students to follow suit. Asking myself 'What have you got to go on?' with reference to my 'East Bay's spring little league program is better than its summer program' claim, I responded with, 'The summer program emphasizes competitiveness.'

The information I offered as support for my claim shed light on the subject matter of the claim, namely that little league programs entail competitiveness to varying degrees and that East Bay's summer program makes competitiveness a prominent feature. But issuing that information as a reason for the claim also shed some light on me personally; I apparently think that the extent to which competitiveness is made prominent should serve as an important criterion by which a little league program is evaluated and, further, I appear find competitiveness to conflict with an ideal I must have about little league.

Taking a few moments to note these observations in writing, I encourage students to do likewise as they reflect on their own statements.

The act of articulating what is disclosed throws those aspects of subjectivity into relief, enhancing self-awareness and making self-reflection more likely. For the Matt Christopher assertion, the student provided 'Matt Christopher books are America's best-selling books about sports written for middle school boys' as support; for the ethical diet assertion, the student stated, 'Eating animals is a choice, not a necessity.' As much as they provide subject matter information, these data statements suggest something about the students who issued them, such as a belief that a sports subject matter can make a difference in whether or not a boy will enjoy reading a book and a conception of ethics that includes the circumstance of choice, respectively. And just as there seemed to be an as-of-yet-unstated 'more' behind my claim–data statements that would help explain the connection I was seeing between competition and program quality, these students' claim–data assertions suggest a similar kind of something-more.

An argument in a form even as brief as what is now two statements, claim and datum, continues to announce its dialogic character, as another question 'waits in the wings,' so to speak. The new clarification- or challenge-type question asks about what bearing the datum has on the conclusion, as in the question (Toulmin, 2003: 91), 'How do you get there?' How, for example, does the student get to 'can help get middle school boys to enjoy reading' from 'best-selling books about sports written for middle school boys'? What am I assuming about competition that I think 'entitles' or 'authorizes' me (Toulmin's words) to conclude that the spring program is better?

A response to a clarification/challenge question about how a data statement supports a claim – 'How do you get there?' – produces the warrant element of Toulmin's model, a statement of a principle that connects the data element to the claim. Responding to 'How do you get there?' for my little league argument, I stated, 'Competition in youth sports takes away from enjoying the sport,' as a warrant. For the Matt Christopher argument, the student produced 'Boys like reading fast-paced, action-packed books about sports.' Notice that these propositions match Toulmin's description of warrants as 'general, hypothetical statements' (Toulmin, 2003: 91). From my experience, the same can be expected of the warrants created by most students when following a processual approach, significant because no explicit instruction has to be given that names or formally characterizes the elements. Notice also that what is stated in the warrants, beyond serving as explanations for what bearing the data has on the claims, further illuminates the values/beliefs disclosed thus far.

If students are to be encouraged to think critically, it is important that they learn to bring disclosed aspects of subjectivity into focus, something that articulating thoughts in writing helps to accomplish. To invoke Michael Polanyi's theory of knowledge (1974), students have some degree of subsidiary awareness of values, beliefs, and other aspects of subjectivity that participate in shaping their arguments. Subsidiary awareness, however, does not constitute actually thinking about those aspects. To become a focal point for conscious, critical thinking, a subsidiary form of knowledge needs to become what Polanyi calls 'articulated' knowledge. The dialogic character of issuing an argument, made prominent by teaching Toulmin's model processually, facilitates such transformations.

At each point in generating another element of an argument, a challenge raised about the last element prompts students to generate the next element, demonstrating that the dialogic relationships among the elements can serve a heuristic function. But students also come to recognize that the pauses at each juncture additionally open up opportunities to consider what aspects of their own subjectivities have been disclosed – or haven't been, as the case might be. The student whose claim concerned relaxing a young girl's hair, for example, paused to reflect on her commitment to a data statement she had composed about lye as a main ingredient in hair relaxers. The 'what have you got to go on' question elicited a response, 'The lye in relaxers causes irreversible chemical damage to hair follicles,' which shed light on the subject matter of the claim: lye is an ingredient that should indicate caution when deciding whether to use a hair relaxer. Were the student interested only in issuing relevant support for her claim, the response to the challenge question demonstrated quite successfully the heuristic potential that the dialogic relationships among elements of an argument make available. But because the student took advantage of the opportunity for critical self-reflection also made available, she determined that she did not wish to 'own' what was suggested by her making the ingredient of lye an important consideration. Here is what the student wrote for her self-reflection at this juncture:

> I chose to use the health of a young black child's hair as the main supporting point for my claim. But that suggests that relaxing a girl's hair would be okay if it didn't get damaged. That's not what I think. I think that relaxers damage a young girl's self-esteem the same way that putting on makeup or covering her face completely (for non-religious reasons) would suggest to her that she must possess some undesirable trait that needs to be concealed.

The student explicitly identified aspects of subjectivity perceived from her subsidiary awareness, shifting, for the moment, her object of focal attention. Such shifts, which are moments of self-awareness, open up opportunities for interrogating one's own beliefs, values (or value hierarchies), accepted personal/cultural narratives, and so forth – one's own 'personal knowledge,' to use Polanyi's terminology.

Consider the issuance of an argument that, produced for the sheer purpose of convincing another, reflects little critical self-awareness:

> 'It's really an awfully simple operation, Jig,' the man said. 'It's not really an operation at all.'
> The girl looked at the ground the table legs rested on.
> 'I know you wouldn't mind it, Jig. It's really not anything. It's just to let the air in.'
> The girl did not say anything.
> 'I'll go with you and I'll stay with you all the time. They just let the air in and then it's all perfectly natural.' (Hemingway, 1998: 212)

The speaker's claim, the proposition the argument supports (and the statement to which the speaker wants Jig to assent) is '[Y]ou wouldn't mind it, Jig.' A reason – the data element – is offered: 'It's really an awfully simple operation,' a reason the man repeats ('It's not really an operation at all'). When the man states that 'it's all perfectly natural,' the statement that serves as the warrant element of the argument, he discloses what bearing he believes (or presents himself as believing, at any rate) his reason has on the claim. Typically, a warrant expresses a justifying principle that the person issuing the argument thinks the reader/listener likely believes to be true and relevant, as well. An implication drawn from the speaker's warrant, therefore – and this implication is made stronger by the fact that the speaker stated the warrant explicitly – is that Jig surely already agrees that something natural, such as that which is *not really* an operation, should not bother her. To back up the warrant (to provide evidence that 'it' is natural), the speaker offers, 'It's just to let the air in,' which like the data statement is repeated again. A qualifier, the element of an argument that indicates the extent to which the speaker believes a claim to be true, is not present. In this case, the absence of a qualifier is in keeping with the speaker's wording of the claim (his certainty expressed by '*I know* you wouldn't mind it'). Nor is there an expressed rebuttal, a statement that would acknowledge a condition (or more than one) that would render the claim false. Nevertheless, the reassurance the speaker offers, 'I'll go with you and I'll stay with you all the time,' serves as a refutation of a would-be rebuttal, indirectly disclosing that the speaker realizes he might be wrong about Jig's not minding 'it,' in which case, even if she did, everything would still be fine because he'd be there with her.

This brief excerpt from 'Hills Like White Elephants' reflects, perhaps, the implicit knowledge Hemingway had about the structure of an argument. Just as likely, though, it shows that his keen powers of observation enabled him to write highly realistic dialogue, including dialogue that entailed the presentation of an argument. Toulmin formulated his model of an argument based on his extensive observations of actual arguments, resulting in a schematic representation that is able to accommodate arguments expressed in science or in law, in philosophy or in everyday conversations. Expertly utilized in much of Hemingway's writing, a dialogic mode of story-line development discloses a great deal about subjectivity – about values, beliefs, motivations, and so on. Conceived as dialogic, so too do the elements of an argument.

The processual approach to teaching Toulmin's model that I have been describing can be used to introduce students to all six elements argument identified by Toulmin. For brevity's sake, I provide the model below (Figure 14.2) with challenge questions included. The questions for data, warrant, and backing are those offered by Toulmin. I have created questions for claim, qualifier, and rebuttal based on Toulmin's descriptions.

Neither this model as such nor all of its terminology need to be provided to students when they are first introduced to Toulmin's model,

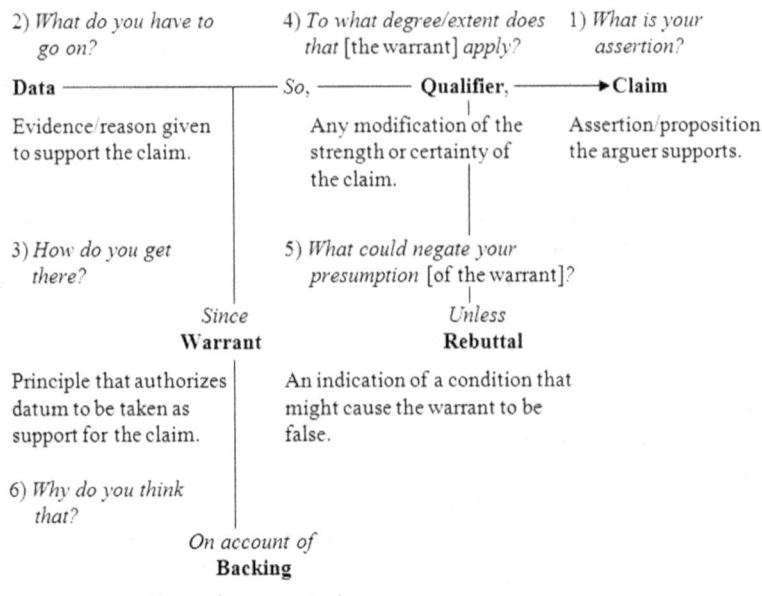

Figure 14.2 Processual approach to teaching Toulmin's model

especially if one of the pedagogical goals is to encourage critical self-reflection. Once students have engaged in instructional activities that help them to recognize the dialogic, processual character of issuing an argument, they are much better prepared for understanding the model and the fuller usefulness it offers for analyzing and producing arguments.

But what makes working with the model so worthwhile is that continued practice expands a writer's heuristic repertoire, the stock of thinking strategies a writer possesses, whether when actually composing or not. A writer benefits from learning to recognize and articulate all six elements of an argument according to Toulmin's model. The benefits extend beyond gaining the ability to supply the elements of an argument or to generate content for developing those elements, although these compositional skills are certainly important. Surely as important to writing teachers, however, is the self-awareness that a writer can gain from the issuance of an assertion that is a claim. Pursued processually by Toulmin's model, such an assertion presents dialogic opportunities for giving aspects of subjectivity focal awareness, a focus necessary for critical reflection.

References

Angelou, M. (1993) *I Know Why the Caged Bird Sings* (reissue edn). New York: Ballantine Books.
Hemingway, E. (1998) Hills like white elephants. In *The Complete Short Stories of Ernest Hemingway* (Finca Vigia edn, pp. 211–214). New York: Simon and Schuster.
Polanyi, M. (1974) *Personal Knowledge: Towards a Post-Critical Philosophy* (corrected edn). Chicago, IL: University of Chicago Press.
Toulmin, S. (2003) *The Uses of Argument* (updated edn). Cambridge: Cambridge University Press.

15 Leave it to the Imagination: Service Learning as Part of an Undergraduate Creative Writing Curriculum

Scott J. O'Callaghan

Many first-year writing programs feature service learning as a means of making writing public and having an impact beyond the classroom, showing students that their words make a real difference in the world. Miller (2002) has pointed to how service learning in the first-year writing classroom can work 'as a sort of apprenticeship in which students develop pre-employment skills' (Miller, 2002: 43). Service-learning opportunities allow students to make connections between classroom learning and future employment skills. Such opportunities are places for students to see writing differently.

For ten years, I taught within an undergraduate creative writing major at Southern Vermont College, a small, private, liberal arts college with a career-enhancing focus. This program regularly featured service learning in its two introductory courses. Students in the first creative writing course – one that served as both an introduction to the major and as a general core offering for non-majors – regularly organized and ran a creative writing contest for elementary school children in Bennington, Vermont. The college students in this course's sequel, taken by majors in their second semester in college, offered a contest to a very different audience: the college community. Originally intended as a contest for students, the contest expanded when a student in the inaugural group asked why the contest couldn't offer a second section for faculty, staff and administrators.

These projects invert the usual pattern in writing classes, where teachers assign and evaluate writing. Instead, students developed the prompts and the means for judging the writing that followed. In their second semester of college, students were judging the writing of faculty and staff using criteria that these new-to-college students developed collectively. Across two semesters, they built skills by not only doing their regularly assigned writing but also developing the means to critique others' work and articulate differences. Further, these contests allowed new students to learn about the town community as well as the college community, better understanding community needs in the process, while offering a way to support the work of writers in both places.

I have successfully used the sequence of assignments I describe here in both a creative writing and a public speaking course, with only the contest details themselves changed. It can work similarly well in first-year writing courses.

While some creative writing teachers will claim that neither creativity nor writing can be fully taught, I would argue that writing teachers can create a climate in which students' contributions to learning can be made public and visible, that such learning can have a positive impact on community members. Students need authentic audiences for their work, and helping students to become the ones making decisions about writing assignments and judging them only adds to students' authority. What's more, empowering students to make key decisions and to position themselves as the assigners and judges of writing, in a real-world, meaningful context, inverts a common pattern of instruction, one often found in introductory courses.

Developing Each Contest

Each semester's contest was a one-semester project, one undertaken by the class as a whole and counted as one part of the course's overall requirements. This focus allowed students to work together on one task, bringing together students in a way that I believe helped with student retention and allowed for greater student engagement with their peers, the creative writing program and the local community.

Students and I began work on each contest on the second day of classes. Students brought in a list of potential prompts and a list of skills they could bring to the contest. I wanted students to think about how they could contribute, immediately. Their ideas for the contest prompts formed the basis of discussion over the course of what could be two class sessions. In these discussions, students thought about the needs of their audiences, thought about what would make for engaging writing, and eventually developed the parameters for the individual contests. Each contest yielded at least two prompts. For the elementary school contests, we ran two groups, one for third and fourth graders and another for fifth and sixth graders. The two groups wrote to different prompts, generated by my class. With the college contests, we always offered at least two different prompts to the full community, in the hope that some choice would encourage more people to submit writing.

Within those initial discussions, my role was to gather options where the class could see the full range, either on a whiteboard or projection screen. I encouraged students to elaborate on their own ideas and encouraged others to offer their comments. Where we could, we combined ideas and refined core impulses. My voice was one among many. In places, I could offer advice on what seemed to work earlier, but each class made its own decisions. After multiple votes, the class decided on its prompts. Outside class time, committees of students developed the texts that would become the full prompts themselves and the guidelines for submitting entries.

Distribution to area teachers or to the college community followed. In our earliest contests, a flyer with cover letter was the extent of our communication with area teachers, often followed by emailed reminders as the deadline approached. Later classes used means like videos that could be shared with prospective participants, audio podcasts or online wikis that students and teachers could consult.

Determining Criteria and Judging

When the college students sent out their invitations for the contest, many of them believed that their job was done, for a time. Instead, I assigned two of their prompts within my own class. Everyone wrote to one prompt initially, submitting entries anonymously. Students had the experience of reading through the group of entries, ranking their favorites and then voting. For this first attempt, I tabulated the votes within the class; students did not discuss their results until all votes were in. From this process, students discussed what they valued as they read their peers' entries. As a class, they developed criteria that they could use in future voting.

Because some classes decided that they wanted to offer more than one contest prompt, the second time that my students wrote to their own prompts, those classes of students faced a choice of what prompt they would write to. When the class's entries came in, students were judging both prompts as a mixed group, much as they would later in the semester. Further, on this second attempt at judging, students worked in groups, using the criteria that the class developed after the first prompt. Now, students had the experience of making decisions together. They also had the criteria to help them find common ground as they evaluated. From the discussion that followed, criteria were often further refined.

Students learned a great deal about their prompts from this process. Some prompts were far harder to write to than expected. Some groups realized how much range or how little range their prompts offered contest participants. In this process, students shifted roles between the ones who had developed the prompts, to the ones now writing to that task, and then back out to the ones evaluating the work of their peers. Students experienced what it was like to assign the writing, do the writing, and then judge it, a process unfamiliar to many of them. No longer passive recipients of assignments, these students saw something of the other side of the teacher's desk.

Because of the preparation that students did in writing to the class prompts and judging their peers' work, many of them felt very secure when it was time for actual judging. Each class had at least two groups of entries to be judged, either separate groups of elementary school students, in the first class or college students separate from college faculty, staff and administrators. Having these groups allowed me to be able to divide the class in a way that asked everyone to judge writing. Groups were large enough to foster diverse opinions, but not large enough to allow students to hide. Since I was the only one who saw entries with names on them, students did not initially know whose contest entries had won.

Giving Awards and Reflecting

Soon after each contest's entries were judged, we held awards programs to celebrate entries and announce winners. Elementary school students and their families were invited to come to our college campus. For many, this was their first visit to any college campus. In the case of the contests within the Southern Vermont College community, the awards program was a chance to celebrate writing done by students, faculty, staff members, and administrators.

As each class planned their contest awards program, I offered to do the same task every time. My job would be to thank everyone at the end, highlighting all the hard work that participants had done. That was it, I told each class. They would have to do all the rest: everything from the welcome, through the lists of names, awards certificates and winners alike. We allowed room for more confident public speakers to take more speaking-intensive roles like outlining the contest's goals or describing the process by which the class made its decisions.

After several contests passed, one guest observed that it would have been good to hear the winning entries. From that time on, students read pieces of writing from all the winners.

In both the fall and spring semesters, timing the contests was often a tricky process. During the fall semesters, we had to be careful not to go too late into the semester, or the awards program would be lost in the shuffle between Thanksgiving and the December holidays. In the spring semesters, going too late into the semester meant risking conflict with end-of-year banquets, convocations and pre-Commencement events. Furthermore, I wanted to be sure to leave time for reflection before each contest was done.

At the end of each contest, all students wrote reflections that were roughly five pages in length, addressing three topics. First, students needed to account for what they contributed to the contest overall. Students described all that they did as the contest took shape up through what they did during the contest reception. Second, I asked students to consider what changes they would offer future classes, as they looked back over their own experiences. Finally, I asked students to write about what they learned from the contest, overall. At once, I wanted students to reconsider their own contest and to look ahead to the future.

These reflections had several audiences. For me, these reflections were a place to offer final comments and grades to the members of the class. They were a project to be graded, a course component. Students also knew, though, that their writing would be shared with the campus Director of Community Engagement, and as such, any writing that students did here could be incorporated into grant applications or other writing from the Director. Where contests involved area schools, reflections might be shared with cooperating teachers or principals. Finally, students knew that their reflections could be shared with future classes, especially suggestions based on their experiences. Having these audiences helped students to write more specifically and to more concerns than their grades alone.

In these reflections, many college students, most of them in their first year, commented on reading writing from those younger or older than themselves. College students were amazed at what elementary aged students wrote. Other groups of college students considered their peers, including previous 'generations' of these introductory classes. Those students who judged the writing of college faculty, staff, and administrators were often at once critical and appreciative, simultaneously. *This* is what a faculty member's writing looks like? It seemed much closer to being part of a spectrum that included students' own first-year college writings. Through the experience of the contests, students saw themselves as part of larger communities of writers.

Service Learning and the Writing Class

Describing how service learning has functioned within her own program, Miller (2002: 50) writes that students 'came to a broader understanding of community/public literacy and how it differs from the academic literacy in which they had been immersed'. Service learning opens up a space for students to see what they have learned in class through a different perspective.

I would argue that the Southern Vermont College practice of inviting students to lead such contests across two consecutive semesters, potentially, led to development opportunities for students that standalone opportunities would not. From a programmatic standpoint, too, students moving to sophomore status, beyond these introductory courses, had an investment to return to the contest held on campus as participants. Having helped to run the contest as first-year students, these advanced majors wanted to compete with their peers.

According to best practices in teaching, service learning must be equally service *and* learning. Students should see the connection between what they learn in class and what they do in their service work. Many introductory writing students struggle with finding their voices and attempting to meet the requirements of new situations, audiences, and assigned tasks. I can think of no better way to help students better understand this process than to invert the usual pattern, thereby empowering students to be the ones assigning writing tasks and then judging the performances.

Reference

Miller, H. (2002) Writing beyond the academy: Using service-learning for professional preparation. In C. Moore and P. O'Neill (eds) *Practice in Context: Situating the Work of Writing Teacher* (pp. 42–54). Urbana, IL: NCTE.

16 Show, Don't Tell: Using Graphic Narratives to Teach Descriptive Writing

Tammie M. Kennedy and Tracey D. Menten

Description is an important feature of all writing genres. Like exposition, narration and argumentation, it is one of the four modes of discourse that writers employ as a rhetorical strategy to achieve a certain goal or effect on readers. We ask students to write description to make the abstract more concrete, recreating people, objects, actions, places, situations, events and experiences that resonate with readers. Description can be used to organize an entire essay or as a strategy that supports an essay's larger purpose. It can also be objective or impressionistic. For example, writers often use objective description to identify the facts of a crime scene or to report on the results of an experiment. Their goal is to act like a kind of camera, capturing the data of the situation without introducing their reactions or feelings about it so that the reader can 'see' the object or event without having been there. Impressionistic description employs more artistic freedom, focusing on the observer's experience and intentions. This type of description appeals to the reader's emotions, attempting to make him or her feel or experience something more than just 'see' the facts of it.

In composition courses, we ask student-writers to use both kinds of description to support their arguments, embolden their narration and illustrate results, concepts and theories in their essays. However, while descriptive writing can be found in all kinds of texts (e.g. fiction, lab reports, advertising, police reports, poetry, journal writing), student-writers often produce descriptive writing that is underdeveloped, vague and incoherent. For example, the description is filled with facts or topic sentences that read more like an outline of possibilities than a descriptive passage that provides a movie of the event that places the reader emotionally, perceptively, and contextually at the scene. In short, the translation process between the writer's observation and the descriptive details composed for the reader is short-circuited, creating a gap between the reader and writer, as well as between the words and mental images conjured on the page. As a result, the persuasive power of description is minimized and the reader is less engaged and informed.

To better illustrate the gap that often emerges in the translation process between observation and remembering and crafting effective description, let's look at a scenario we share with our students:

> Remember your first kiss. Squint your eyes if you need to 'see' it again. Make a note of each distinctive detail: location (movie theater, closet, front door, bedroom, swing set); specific background elements of that location (LeBron James poster, summer time, streetlight, orange sofa missing a cushion, other spin-the-bottle contestants, Hello Kitty bedspread); what you and s/he were wearing (Walgreens flip flops, acid wash jeans, 'I'm with Stupid' T-shirt); sounds (Britney Spears' 'Toxic,' friends giggling, birds chirping, cherubs singing, bells ringing); textures (chapped lips, sweaty foreheads, pimply noses, locked braces); and smells/tastes (Axe cologne, chlorine from the pool, car exhaust, Juicy Fruit gum, cherry lip gloss, garlic and onions).
>
> Now that you have conjured up the memory, write a descriptive paragraph that communicates this scene to a reader, translating the mental images into words that convey a central image or impression and provide enough information for readers who were not there.

Not so easy. Right? While students remark that the guided exploration of the memory is helpful in recalling specific details before they draft the description, they also lament that the words on the page pale in terms of the rich images they 'see' in their minds. For example, after attempting this prompt, students made the following kinds of observations: 'I don't really have a point-of-view. Should I write the description based on how I experienced the kiss then or now?' Others noted that while they had the general scene down, it was mostly riddled with 'facts' or 'statements' that didn't begin to 'capture the emotions of the experience,' even if they weren't trying to sound 'distant or objective' about the kiss. Some were very aware that the description lacked a focus or dominant impression, which they traced to a lack of 'organization or flow' in the way they described the kiss. Many expressed frustration in depicting this event, which they remembered well but 'couldn't quite capture in words the way they wanted.'[1]

Despite all the vivid images that flutter in the mind's eye or the imprint of perceptive details that accompany close observation, crafting those images with concrete, significant details that address the senses in an organized manner and resonate with the reader creates a never-ending challenge for most writers. In fact, one of the trickiest tenets of writing to teach is description, or what we often explain as 'Show, don't tell.' Student-writers frequently find this guideline difficult to implement effectively in their writing, regardless of genre. Furthermore, many of the writing activities instructors use to augment effective descriptive writing in the invention and revision process – i.e. focusing on specific details, employing more than one sense, replacing 'to be' verbs with vivid verbs – often don't translate as successfully as we hope in student-writers' drafting and revising processes. Even if the descriptive details are strong, the particulars also must support a larger rhetorical or imaginative purpose in the essay. For example, referencing the earlier 'first kiss' scenario, there are questions that need to be considered in order to articulate a larger context for the description: Is there a hidden story behind this image? How did you feel during the kiss? What happened before the kiss? What happened after? What had you forgotten until you started remembering the kiss? What are some of the other images that come to mind when you think of the events and feelings and conflicts that surrounded the actual kiss? What might your readers need to know in order to understand the dominant impression of the kiss you are trying to convey?

Children learn to connect words to images during the nascent phases of language development. Graphic narratives recall a time when students were learning to read and their books were full of pictures. The combination of words and pictures taught them not only to read the words but also to inscribe the subject and actions with feelings, thoughts, and contexts that helped to establish and reinforce meaning. In other words, the pictures helped to flesh out the job the words were supposed to be doing, which was to describe what was happening to the subject, around the subject, or within the subject. Therefore, when teaching students how to write descriptively, it makes sense to return a familiar genre and skill set: reading picture books.

Graphic narratives such as *Persepolis, Fun Home, Stitches, Maus, American Born Chinese, Jimmy Corrigan: The Smartest Kid on Earth,* and *Blankets* help to illustrate that effective descriptive writing stems from creating powerful sensory images in the mind of the reader that bring the depiction to life. In order to create these images – visual and textual – the writer crafts sequential mental images in the minds of readers so they can walk in the writer's shoes and watch the movie of the event or experience from the writer's perspective. Like film, graphic narratives often solicit an immediate reaction from the reader because the images produce such powerful, long-lasting impressions in the reader's mind – the goal of effective description. Plus, most student-writers are already familiar with graphic narratives as readers, so they can apply these lessons adeptly to their own compositions.

In this chapter, we demonstrate how using graphic narratives in the composition classroom can address the translation gap that emerges between observing the person, place, object or experience and effectively communicating that mental picture to the reader through description. Ancient rhetorician Hermogenes wrote that description brings 'before one's eyes what is to be shown' (quoted in Crowley & Hawhee, 2004: 418). However, student-writers often express difficulty in recreating the memory of their observation of the object, person, place or experience in a way that conjures the same mental image for the reader. Therefore, student-writers need more help in learning how to recreate mental images effectively that fulfill reader expectations and support a larger rhetorical purpose. Once they are able to deploy description more deftly, they will be able to write with more confidence across a range of writing genres and rhetorical situations.

What is a Graphic Narrative?

While most student-writers know what description is, the term 'graphic narrative' might be a bit more elusive despite their familiarity with comic books and other graphic literature. Hillary Chute and Marianne DeKoven (2006: 767) describe graphic narratives as 'narrative work in the medium of comics ... [composed in] frames and gutters ... [that] calls a reader's attention visually and spatially to the act, process, and duration of interpretation' (2006: 767). The 'images are not illustrative of the text, but comprise a separate narrative thread that moves forward in time in a different way than the prose text, which also moves the reader forward in time' (2006: 769). Lisa Hoashi (2007: 159) refines Chute and DeKoven's definition from a writer's perspective: 'Fluent in two languages – one textual and the other graphic – [the writer] plays with the tension created by two simultaneous narratives, developing new ways to tell [a] ... story'. For simplicity's sake, we will use the following **definition** throughout the rest of the chapter: *A graphic narrative tells a story, not only through words that are carefully chosen and crafted but also through images that are equally revealing and well chosen.*

Students in writing courses are already immersed in a visual world where images shape their perceptions of reality and themselves and 'show' them how to think and behave. In fact, the pervasiveness of visual culture and mixed media has already changed the ways most student-writers develop and communicate their ideas about people, cultures, history and social interactions.

Many of them are already knowledgeable about sequential narratives, such as comic books, video games and Anime, which underscore the ways they think about the relationship between words and images. As a result, they have an innate understanding of how drawings together with words can accomplish more than just complement or substitute for each other. These texts help to disrupt the division between word and image that W.J.T. Mitchell (1996: 47) describes as 'the relation between the seeable and the sayable, display and discourse, showing and telling.' Many, too, have already read graphic narratives such as *Maus, Persepolis* or *American Born Chinese*, which are commonly taught in high school. By drawing on student-writers' literacy practices with graphic narratives, they are better able to create and revise descriptions successfully as well as critique and revise these writerly choices. The tangibility of how words and images create certain effects in graphic narratives offers not only a poignant touchstone for teaching descriptive writing in composition classes, but also provides another rhetorical tool that student-writers may take with them after the composition course ends.

Description as Image-Making

To introduce student-writers to the idea that effective description needs to create a particular image and effect in the reader's mind, it is useful to study examples from various graphic memoirs. Marjane Satrapi's (2003) *Persepolis* works well and many of the images from the text can be found on the internet.

Reading Activity

Ask students to read the first two chapters of *Persepolis* (Satrapi, 2003: 3–17), 'The Veil' and 'The Bicycle,' before class. In order to focus their attention on the interplay between image and text, instruct them to pay attention to how the author's composition of images, frames and text shapes the 'dominant impression' (mood, tone, feeling, perspective – principle effect the author wants to create for the reader) of the chapters. Ask student-writers to articulate *how* the author constructs the piece. For example, how does the author present her persona narrator (both visually and textually)? What does she include? What is missing? How does the child's point of view shape the story and/or the reader's reaction? How does she use the cell space to denote time, emphasis and movement? How does she use color? Students can prepare a short summary of how Satrapi constructs the chapters before class, or work in small groups to generate some preliminary ideas for class discussion.

In-Class Activity

After discussing their analysis of both chapters and *how* Satrapi constructed the text and its effect, student-writers complete the following exercise:

Step 1: Draw a line down the center of a piece of paper. On the left, describe the plot or dominant impression of the chapter, 'The Veil' using **only words**.

Step 2: On the right side of the page, describe the plot or dominant impression of the chapter, 'The Bicycle' using **only images**.

Next, discuss the following questions:

- Which response was easier to create – using only words or using only images? Why?
- Does the fact that the text is a graphic memoir make it easier or more difficult to respond using just words or images? Why or why not?
- Would responding have been easier using both words and images? Why or why not?
- Which approach would make it easier for someone who had not read the chapters to understand the gist of the work? Why?

After the discussion, we ask students to summarize one of the chapters again. However, this time we tell them they may use *both* words and images to do so. As student-writers summarize one of Satrapi's chapter, using both words and images, they begin to notice how their previous descriptive summaries may change from words to images and vice versa. On one hand, this exercise helps student-writers recognize where they struggle to develop description effectively with no accompanying images to help flesh out the gist of the content. On the other hand, this activity assists student-writers as they identify where their description is successful, noting how they were able to translate the summary into words with less reliance on visuals. Moreover, this activity helps student-writers understand how description, even when using only words, creates visual images in the minds of their readers – a feat that takes a great deal of thought and finesse.

Words, Images, or Both? Description and 'The Charlie Brown Effect'

Student-writers often produce one-dimensional descriptive passages that mostly 'tell' about the experience, place, person or object. Such a one-dimensional rendition limits their rhetorical credibility with readers and diminishes the effect of employing descriptive details. Furthermore, without being conscious of it, student-writers often over-rely on using one sense – what they can see and put easily into words. Student-writers need to be reminded that touch, sound, taste and smell offer powerful ways of knowing and understanding the world, which help to form the mental pictures that materialize from their description. Using graphic narratives reinforces these core ideas about description, demonstrating that readers need a range of details to comprehend a situation. For example, in comic strips, readers rely on the characters' facial expressions, thought-balloons, visual style and cell space to understand and imagine what is taking place. The same is true for effective descriptive writing, which relies on a layering and sequencing of specific, sensory details and figurative language to achieve a particular purpose.

The following activity helps student-writers better appreciate how the use of sequential images functions in the same way as the words they choose to describe something. 'The Brain: The Charlie Brown Effect' by Carl Zimmer (2012), a former comic book artist who is now a neuroscientist, provides an important platform for discussing how images and text produce a certain alchemy for the reader. Understanding the relationship between effective description and its effect on the reader is essential for student-writers who are learning to write reader-based texts in their composition classes.

Before class, instructors should prepare envelopes that contain four or five *Peanuts* comic strips of their own choosing from Charles M. Schulz's (2004) *The Complete Peanuts Vol. 1*. Instructors should cut the strips into individual horizontal panels and black out any text. It is helpful to select narratives that range from simple to more complex. They should also assign Zimmer's short article for students to read before class.

In-Class Activity

Step 1: After discussing Zimmer's article, hand students one of the pre-prepared envelopes and ask them to place the panel strips in the proper narrative order intended by the author (students may work alone or in small groups).

Step 2: Once the students believe they have the strips in the correct order, project an image of the comic strip as it was originally published so that students can check their work.

Step 3: Ask students to summarize the narrative of the comic strip on a separate piece of paper. Invite them to describe how the characters are feeling and what they are thinking, as well as the general plot points.

Students should be able to describe in specific detail what the characters are feeling, thinking and doing. If students are struggling with these descriptions, demonstrate how to read the facial expressions and movements of the characters (e.g. 'What do these lines behind Linus indicate about his movement?').

Step 4: After repeating this process for multiple comic strips, it is important that students recognize how many words they used to describe stories that were originally told completely without words. Students are then encouraged to discuss how easy and/or difficult it was to place the panels in the correct order, what made it more difficult as the number of panels grew or the narrative got more complex, how the grammar of the images works much like the grammar of words and how, without the use of words, the students were able to extract so much story from such a small number of descriptive details contained in the images.

Some students who put panels in the incorrect order might argue that their version of the story is more compelling than, and just as valid as, the original version. This situation facilitates some interesting conversation about the author's intent, creating a dominant impression and the reader/writer relationship. Furthermore, this discussion is useful for highlighting key ideas about descriptive language, such as how images can create a variety of descriptions, just as words can create many different meanings and images in the reader's mind.

Visual Storytelling: Collecting, Sorting, and Locating the Poignant Details of Description

Another challenge of writing effective description is resisting the inclination to rely on too many surface-level details, or just to 'throw a bunch of stuff' into the paragraph or scene. These impulses stem from two key problems: First, students often halt the collection of details prematurely without exploring their observational and memory data with enough depth and breadth. Second, once they generate a plethora of details, they often have trouble crafting their description around a central idea or dominant impression for the reader. Student-writers need to become more skilled at collecting enough details for their descriptive writing, as well as how to sort through and select the most poignant details to craft their descriptive prose. Both strategies help them produce description that isn't dull and one-dimensional, or that reads like an incoherent rambling of details that readers don't understand or need. While composition classes focus on choosing vivid language, descriptive details and using more than one sense in descriptive writing, these guidelines are easier to explain than perform on the page, especially during the brainstorming phase. What follows is an example of how we support student-writers in the invention, drafting and revising processes.

We compare the descriptive writing process (invention, drafting, revision) to producing a stellar graphic memoir. On one hand, graphic memoirists spend a great deal of time collecting all of the memories, images, words, perspectives, scenes, feelings, colors and shapes that inform their story, mining every detail they can muster. From this perspective, it's better to have 'too much' content than not enough. On the other hand, to compose the book, the graphic memoirist must select and organize the details they want to express to support the overall story they are telling. There are too many moments, ideas and experiences to use. If all the content and details were used, the narrative would not be focused enough to convey a main idea that the reader could grasp. In other words, before writers like Marjane Satrapi can create a graphic narrative that people are going to want to read and discuss, she had to assume the roles of Brilliant Detective and Brilliant Editor of her life experiences, memories and observations.

To help demonstrate the importance of both the brainstorming and editing processes, we do a short demonstration in class. We say 'childhood' and ask student-writers to 'watch' what images and details appear in their minds. We then ask them to write down as many details as they recall, not censoring or stopping their flow until we call 'time.' After we call 'time,' we instruct students to write down all of the details they have forgotten. This second prompt inspires them to dig deeper, looking between, behind and beyond the first rush of memory images. After the activity, student-writers often comment that they experienced instant blankness followed by a barrage of memory images flashing through their minds almost too quickly to capture. They also say the 'forgetting' prompt helped them remember even more details.

Next, we narrow the topic and say, 'Third grade.' Students follow the same procedures as described above. With a narrower focus, student-writers might remember their school picture, the classroom pet or who their best friend was. For example, Tammie remembers the 'banana curls' she sported in the photo and the fact that her mom accidently singed her scalp with a curling iron that morning before the big photo shoot. Tracey remembers the gorgeous, healthy plant she had to care for over winter break, forgot to water, and returned, yellowed and dying.

After a brief discussion about the kinds of details they recalled during the exercise, we ask student-writers to jot down which images they would have captured with a camera or how they might create a scene in a graphic narrative or movie to represent that memory. These instant 'snapshots' help student-writers start to narrow the scope of their description, creating a way to locate and select the kinds of details needed to provide the reader a cogent sense of what they are attempting to describe instead of a disjointed mass of details. This brief demonstration prompts student-writers to consider that effective description stems from carving out enough time to collect enough detailed memory or observational 'footage,' as well as to select and edit the materials they have observed or uncovered.

To reinforce the complex process involved during the invention and editing process, the activity below helps student-writers practice generating memory material from a photograph, opening up to all of the memories and sensations that accompany the picture, and then selecting a memory to work with for a descriptive assignment. Working with a photograph in conjunction with the mental images and descriptive phrases that emerge mirror how graphic narratives employ two languages to describe something and convey meaning to readers. The activity also provides a tangible approach to assessing how well they have described the memory for a reader by employing a graphic narrative format.

Invention Activity: 'Photographic Memory'

Step 1: Ask student-writers to select a personal photograph that triggers an emotional reaction.

Step 2: Ask them to create a list of five actions that led up to the moment in the photograph as well as five actions that followed it. Start each item on the list with a verb (e.g. 'Taking final exams,' 'Sitting in the hot sun,' etc.).

Step 3: Have student-writers brainstorm a list of thoughts and feelings about the photograph, as they relate to the five senses (e.g. 'The stiff, scratchy feeling of the dress shirt and necktie made me even more uncomfortable than being at my first funeral and seeing a dead body'). Instruct them not discount anything that pops in to their heads (e.g. I felt fat that day in my new dress). Write it down. If they are stuck, read over the list of before/after actions in Step 2, imagine themselves back in that moment, and describe what was happening using sensory details. Instruct student-writers that they need to try to remember what they have forgotten when they first look at the photo. In other words, dig deeper. A useful cue is to say, 'I had forgotten that ...' and list anything that comes to mind. Tell them to keep remembering. More details will surface, if they keep remembering.

Step 4: Ask student-writers to pair actions (Step 2) to thoughts/feelings (Step 3). There may be multiple thoughts/feelings with the same action. However, student-writers will need to start making choices in order to narrow down their topic into something manageable to compose a short descriptive scene or paragraph.

Step 5: Have student-writers write a descriptive paragraph or scene using one 'strand' from the memory to tell a story about the photo that provides the reader a dominant impression. Remind them to 'show, not tell.'

Step 6: Once students have generated some descriptive text based on the photographic memory activity, they need to assess how effectively they have described the memory for a reader. Employing graphic narrative strategies works well as they assess the effect of their description. Ask students to draw at least six panels on a separate sheet of paper. Before you ask them to translate the descriptive paragraph or scene into at least a six-panel comic layout, it is important to address both their anxieties about drawing as well as the basics of layout. Many student-writers are intimidated by having to draw, but many are just as intimidated by writing in a traditional fashion. Reassure them that stick figures are fine, and all they need is 5th grade art skills. If they need a refresher of what graphic panels look like, the student-writers can review the Satrapi chapters again as well as the student graphic that we annotated (Figure 16.1).

With a stronger appreciation of how the narrative, gutters, and cells must work together, students have an easier time translating their descriptive paragraph/scene into a one-page graphic narrative.[2] As they translate their descriptive words into a graphic narrative, remind them they are not allowed to invent details, but they can make inferences based on descriptive details. If colors are mentioned, they can use color in the panels. If there is dialogue, they may use it in the graphic narrative as well. As they create the graphic narrative, instruct them not to focus on the quality of their drawings, but rather on the details that they are able to create using their descriptive writing. Ask them to make a note on the actual text where they have trouble translating the text as well as where it is easiest to create the images.

Step 7: Ask student-writers to discuss or write a short reflection about the experience and how it might inform their strategies for writing description. For example, where in the text was there too much tell and not enough show? How could those areas be improved? How might they rework those sections for the revision? Analyze the sections that worked well and identify specifically what about the

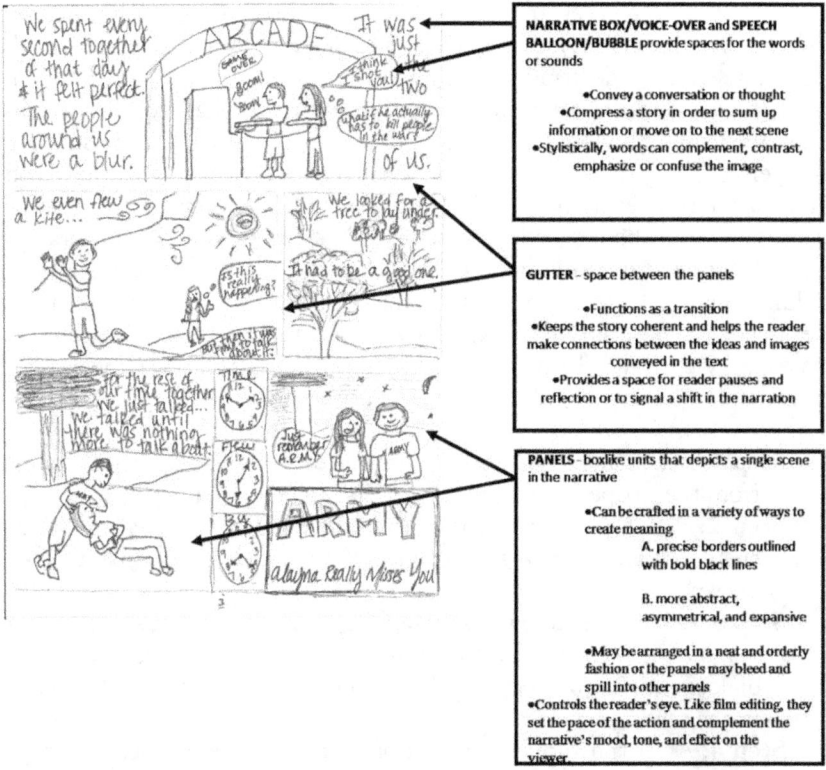

Figure 16.1 A.R.M.Y.

language in those sections produced more show and less tell. Then, have student-writers revise the original descriptive passage of the memory based on what they learned from this activity.

Revising Description: A Translation Activity for Peer Review

Student-writers often fill in the gaps of their own work, thinking that what they have described is perfectly clear because the image is vivid and specific in their own minds. That is why peer review is so important. Student-writers need a representative reader to point out what has not translated onto the page from their mind and offer specific comments that help them consider the necessary revisions. Using graphic narrative strategies to assess rough drafts provides another way to facilitate productive peer review and more effective descriptive writing.

When students bring in their first draft of a paper that requires description, we usually review the basics of descriptive writing. Often, students are perfectly capable of articulating what makes for effective description. In fact, we frequently note the sighs and rote replies as we name the five senses and talk about specific details. However, while student-writers cognitively understand the premises of description, their papers often are riddled with 'tell' and explanations that make it difficult for a reader to get inside the descriptive passages. To help them locate these problematic passages, we 'show' them what their description is actually conveying to a reader.

Step 1: Ask student-writers to select one descriptive paragraph or scene from their papers and highlight or draw a box around it.

Step 2: Pick a partner for peer response. Student-writers should ask their partner to draw a panel grid of six panels on a separate sheet of paper.

Step 3: Ask partner to illustrate graphically the descriptive scene or paragraph chosen by the student-writer, using *only* the details, action, and dialogue included. They should not add anything that is not included in the text.

Step 4: After the allotted amount of time, have the partner return the draft to the author, along with the graphic translation of the text they created. Ask the partner to discuss his/her process: What was difficult to illustrate? Why? What was effective about the description that made it easy to translate? How effective was this scene? What is missing?

Student-writers typically find the graphic representation of their descriptive paragraph or scene illuminating. They are intrigued by how few specific details are in the passage and how little description is actually there. The exercise also helps them to better comprehend how what they see in their minds is not actually on the page. For example, in one student-writer's descriptive scene about dancing with her new boyfriend, she wrote that he 'stuck out his arm when he asked me to dance.' While that image was perfectly clear in her mind, her partner did not know how to illustrate 'stuck out his arm.' This recognition provided a tangible example of what gets lost in translation from the writer's memory or observation to the words crafted on the page.

Step 5: After completing the graphic translation, ask student-writers to examine their draft again and employ Lee Gutkind's 'Highlighter Test' (quoted in Moore, 2007: 39):

- Read through your entire draft. Each time you read a sentence or paragraph of summary – 'My parents got divorced when I was in fifth grade and I was miserable because I had to change schools' – leave it unhighlighted. **'Tell'**
- Whenever you run across a scene, a portion of the draft when there is action, when the reader is given a moment-to-moment description of an event as if it were happening right then – 'When my mom started being the only one who picked us up from school, her jaw was always clenched as if she were swallowing a scream' – highlight that section. **'Show'**
- Are there more highlighted than unhighlighted sections? 70–30% ratio? Although one cannot assign a mathematical formula to effective writing, Gutkind argues that this 70/30 ratio of description (tell) to exposition (show) provides a useful guideline for thinking about revision (quoted in Moore, 2007: 40).

Ask students to discuss their results. This highlighting process is a useful way to reinforce some of the concrete lessons learned from the graphic translation exercise. It also helps student-writers start to locate some of the areas in their text that might need more attention, especially revising key paragraphs or scenes that need to be more descriptive.

Conclusion

Introducing graphic narratives into our writing classes has proven to be effective in many ways. Not only does the genre draw on student-writers' literacy practices, but it also provides a tangible way to 'show' students where their description falls short in achieving its desired effect. Moreover, even when we are not focusing on employing graphic narrative techniques in the invention, drafting, and revision processes, we find that students often use this strategy without being prompted. Some actually 'storyboard' their descriptive papers and paragraphs before they draft; many more use the graphic narrative as a heuristic to guide their revision strategies on different kinds of writing projects. Using graphic narratives in the writing classroom also provides a shorthand vocabulary for student-writers where in addition to asking such questions as 'Does the descriptive paragraph include sensory-based, specific details,' we can also add, 'Would it translate graphically'? Such an addition often resonates with student-writers, helping them better appreciate and implement the strategy that writer Dinty W. Moore (2007) implores descriptive writers to master: 'Show the most, tell a little, and never explain.'

Notes

(1) Thank you to all of our students at the University of Nebraska at Omaha and Omaha Central High School who helped us to think through these ideas and provided feedback to the various activities we have employed in the following courses: Autobiographic Reading and Writing; Modern Familiar Essay; Writing Graphic Narratives; Composition I; English 3–4; and Theory of Knowledge. You were all wonderful collaborators!
(2) Scott McCloud's book *Making Comics: Storytelling Secrets of Comics, Manga, and Graphic Novels* (2006), New York: Harper, is a very useful resource to teach about reading and writing graphic literature. He also has two TED Talks on comics, which students find helpful. See http://blog.ted.com/2009/01/13/understanding_c/ and http://www.ted.com/talks/scott_mccloud_on_comics

References

Chute, H. and Dekoven, M. (2006) Introduction: Graphic narrative. *Modern Fiction Studies* 52 (4), 767–82.
Crowley, S. and Hawhee, D. (2004) *Ancient Rhetorics for Contemporary Students* (3rd edn). New York: Pearson/Longman.
Hoashi, L. (2007) Fluency in form: A survey of the graphic memoir. *The Missouri Review* 30 (4), 159–174.
McCloud, S. (2005) The visual magic of comics. See http://www.ted.com/talks/scott_mccloud_on_comics (accessed February 2005).
McCloud, S. (2006) *Making Comics: Storytelling Secrets of Comics, Manga, and Graphic Novels.* New York: Harper.
McCloud, S. (2009) Understanding comics. See http://blog.ted.com/2009/01/13/understanding_c/ (accessed January 2009).
Mitchell, W.J.T. (1996) Word and Image. In R.S. Nelson and R. Schiff (eds) *Critical Terms for Art History* (pp. 47–57). Chicago: University of Chicago Press.
Moore, D.W. (2007) *The Truth of the Matter: Art and Craft in Creative Nonfiction.* New York: Pearson/Longman.
Satrapi, M. (2003) *Persepolis: The Story of a Childhood.* New York: Pantheon.
Schultz, C.M. (2002) *The Complete Peanuts Vol.1.* Seattle: Fantagraphics Books.
Zimmer, C. (2012) The brain: The Charlie Brown effect. *Discover Magazine,* December 2012. See http://discovermagazine.com/2012/dec/29-the-charlie-brown-effect (accessed January 2013).

17 A First-Timer's Approach to Teaching in a Non-Traditional Setting

Connie Langhorst

My first teaching opportunity occurred when I was a student in a low-residency MFA creative writing program. The program director tasked pedagogy students with leading a workshop and challenged us to *be creative*. My classmates, all teachers and local to the program, secured teaching opportunities in a traditional setting. This was not my experience.

Taking the director's challenge to heart, I focused on finding a non-traditional setting for my workshop. This led me to the public library in Gulfport, Florida, an artsy community near my home and alma mater (Eckerd College). I met with the administrator and, after reveling in our shared passion for writing (and what better place to do this than in a library), she agreed to the event and provided a tour of the facility, during which she mentioned that the library hosted a weekly writers group. I felt a phantom nudge. The director's challenge came to mind. *Be creative*. I asked if I could schedule the workshop around an upcoming writers group meeting and, if so, offered to allow its members to select the topic. The group embraced the idea. My workshop had a home, an audience, and a name: 'Discovering Your Story: What Makes a Good Story.'

On event day, I posted a welcome sign, arranged the tables to facilitate face-to-face dialogue, and displayed some of my favorite books on the craft of writing. So the books would be available for checkout from the library, I provided the administrator with a list of titles prior to the workshop, including *Writing Fiction* (Burroway, 2003), *The Practice of Creative Writing, A Guide for Students* by Heather Sellers (2008), *Bird by Bird* by Anne Lamott (1994), *Writing True: The Art and Craft of Creative Nonfiction* by Sondra Perl and Mimi Schwartz (2006), *On Writing: A Memoir of the Craft* by Stephen

King (2000), and *Writing Down the Bones: Freeing the Writer Within* by Natalie Goldberg (1998).

The display was a conversation starter. A popular item was my memoir. I included it with the thought that it would afford a measure of credibility (however meager) regarding my status as an author. The book motivated attendees to engage with each other and express their publishing aspirations, which created a buzz in the room before the workshop started. I referred to the display during my lecture and offered the books to the participants for closer inspection. The tactile experience of sharing, writer-to-writer, appeared to resonate. The attendees eagerly looked at the dust jackets, leafed through the pages and jotted notes.

With little advance knowledge of their writing ability, I followed a process approach to structuring my workshop, which, according to 'What You Need to Know About Theory (For Now),' from Brock Dethier's *First Time Up: An Insider's Guide for New Composition Teachers* (2005) (one of my pedagogy strand textbooks), addresses, as a central question, 'What does the writer do to create a good written product?'

Attendees were asked to bring two double-spaced typewritten pages of a story-in-progress for review. To create a 'caring and sharing' environment, I explained that I was teaching the workshop as an assignment and asked them to keep this in mind, as they would be asked, at the end, to evaluate the workshop content and my teaching ability. After an overview and summary of my educational and writing background, participants were invited to introduce themselves and provide a brief statement about their story-in-progress and any angst they were experiencing with completing it. My teacher-in-training skills were called into action as I had to guide the conversation around the room to keep things moving.

The group, as an acronym, embodied the United Nations of writing. Various ethnicities and ages were represented. The oldest, without provocation, disclosed that he was 90 years young. Several identified themselves as members of the library's writers group. There were fiction writers, nonfiction writers and a science fiction writer.

To push all of the genre buttons, I used tried-and-true exercises learned on my own writer's journey, starting with a question to help the participants identify their voice as a writer. I asked them to describe their image of a writer and enumerate what gets in the way of being successful at writing. A discussion ensued, concluding with the assertion, agreed by all, that life intervenes in our creative pursuits. Writer's block came up as an issue. Anticipating this, I produced a one-inch by one-inch picture frame without a picture in it and suggested, when struggling with what to put on the page, that instead of staring into the void of a computer screen, it can be helpful to narrow focus from the vastness of a blank page to a smaller space: a paragraph, a sentence or a word. I gleaned this example (from a lecture or textbook) and used it, because, from time to time, it was an effective tool for my own writing. As another suggestion for invigorating creative flow, I shared the idea of writing outdoors, by hand, as opposed to inside on a keyboard.

Utilizing an exercise on scaffolding from Heather Sellers' book, I demonstrated how building a story is like constructing a house: both require a strong foundation and good building materials. In her example, another writer's text is used, line by line, to create one's own piece. 'You know the system of platform constructed around the building site, as the new floors are built? That's scaffolding ... That's the function of the text we use to launch our imitations' (Sellers, 2008: 42–43).

I led a roundtable discussion aimed at identifying story elements, including tension and conflict, action, character development and dialogue, and recited famous (and favorite) author quotes, including, 'Your story must accomplish something and arrive somewhere' from 'Mark Twain's Rules for Writing, or Fenimore Cooper's Literary Offenses' (Twain, quoted in Campbell, 2010) and Chekhov's 'If you say in the first chapter that there is a rifle hanging on the wall, in the second or third chapter, it absolutely must go off. If it's not going to be fired, it shouldn't be hanging there' (quoted in Selvidge, 2006: 78).

We did some sensory exercises, including one from Janet Burroway, in which I asked the group to put themselves in the mind of a character from their story-in-progress and brainstorm with a focus on setting (Burroway, 2003). Building on an exercise titled 'Follow the Scent,' from Naomi Epel's *The Observation Deck: A Tool Kit for Writers* (1998), I asked participants to associate a scent with the character/setting and write a one-sentence summary on the effectiveness of this detail. I then invited them to share their summary by reading it aloud as part of a peer review session. As an outcome, one participant indicated that his story had 'turned a corner' and, to his relief and excitement, was going in a new direction. Another stated that the exercises led her to a new story idea.

After a short Q&A session, I summarized the learning objectives, thanked everyone for attending, and distributed handouts, including 'Mark Twain's Rules for Writing' (a personal favorite) and a list of titles included in the book display. I provided my email address and encouraged participants to contact me if they had questions or needed assistance or encouragement with their story-in-progress. I then asked them to complete a post-workshop survey, explaining that their feedback would be included in a critical paper submitted to the program director to fulfill the requirements of the assignment. All of the participants complied.

Their responses to the survey suggested that the workshop was appreciated. The book display, exercises and handouts were acknowledged as highlights. All of the attendees felt the 90-minute format was too short. They recommended a three-hour workshop or ongoing series of workshops. My teaching ability was, across the board, assessed as being 'very good.' Some wrote glowing comments to this effect. (I weighed the possibility that their response to this question might be jaded by the immediate afterglow from the camaraderie that comes from being in the company of other writers.) One respondent indicated that she felt others monopolized the time (although, my observation, as the instructor, was that she was the one who had to be monitored for her repeated attempts at lengthy soliloquies about her writing). The same respondent raised a good point, suggesting five-to-ten minutes of one-on-one time to discuss each story-in-progress. Her suggestion resonated as an idea for future workshop planning.

After the workshop, I personally thanked the administrator and followed up with a handwritten thank-you note. She reciprocated, inviting me to return to the library to teach future workshops. Before writing the critical paper, I reread the survey responses and took a moment to concentrate on the sensation of breathing, something I learned from a passage in Epel's book: *'The word inspiration comes from the Latin root spirare, to breathe. It also contains the root of the word spirit.* When you feel stuck or are looking for inspiration, take a few minutes to breathe. Flush out old, tired ideas by exhaling fully' (Epel, 1998: 82).

Inspired by the positive survey feedback, I took a few breaths. I met the program director's challenge to be creative in leading a workshop and, as a consequence, was no longer a 'first-timer.' After a cleansing breath, I realized I had the confidence, desire, ability – and the spirit – to teach.

References

Burroway, J. (2003) *Writing Fiction: A Guide to Narrative Craft* (6th edn). New York: Longman.
Campbell, T. (2010) Mark Twain's rules for writing, or Fenimore Cooper's literary offenses, *how to be a writer*. See http://writerblue.com/2010/06/mark-twains-rules-for-writing-or-fenimore-coopers-literary-offenses/ (accessed June 2013).
Dethier, B. (2005) *First Time Up: An Insider's Guide for New Composition Teachers*. Logan, UT: Utah State University Press.
Epel, N. (1998) *The Observaton Deck: A Tool Kit for Writers*. San Francisco, CA: Chronicle Books LLC.
Goldberg, N. (1998) *Writing Down the Bones: Freeing the Writer Within*. Boston: Shambhala Publications, Inc.
King, S. (2000) *On Writing: A Memoir of the Craft*. New York: Scribner.
Lamott, A. (1994) *Bird by Bird: Some Instructions on Writing and Life*. New York: Anchor Books.

Perl, S. and Schwartz, M. (2006) *Writing True: The Art and Craft of Creative Writing.* New York: Houghton Mifflin.
Sellers, H. (2008) *The Practice of Creative Writing: A Guide for Students.* Boston: Bedford/St. Martin's.
Selvidge, L. (2006) *Writing Fiction Workbook.* Raleigh, NC: Lulu Enterprises.

18 In It for the Long Haul: The Pedagogy of Perseverance

Anna Leahy

Recently, I talked with my fiction-writing colleague Jim Blaylock[1] about what it takes to be a writer. Beginning a semester, we saw great potential in our students but agreed that we couldn't predict which students would do well over the course of the semester, let alone over the long haul of a career. 'As a student, I'd never felt I was the best writer among my peers, but I'm still writing,' I said. He replied, 'Writing means doing the work.' That comment reminded me something another colleague, fiction writer Richard Bausch (no date), had written:

> The thing that separates the amateur writer from the professional, often enough, is simple [sic] the amount of time spent working the craft. You know that if you really want to write, if you hope to produce something that will stand up to the winds of criticism and scrutiny of strangers, you're going to have to work harder than you have ever worked on anything else in your life hour upon hour upon hour...'

My colleague and I concluded that perseverance is at least as important as talent for the long haul of a writing career. Then, we each headed home to write. I also wondered, at the time, whether writing in more than one genre has helped me sustain the effort over time or divided my focus, whether variety has made it easier to do the work and helped me gain perspective on craft, even though MFA programs and individual creative writing courses often encourage focus on a single genre.

Within days of that encounter, I read an interview of Tracy Kidder and his editor, Richard Todd (2013). Kidder says: '[T]here were a lot of people who had more interesting lives than I had, people who were smarter and quite possibly with more talent. I thought, I'm just going to work as hard as I can and make up for whatever deficiencies I have in that way' (37). Todd adds, 'This reliance on talent is deadly in any field...Musicians practice. That's the only way they get good' (37).

Malcolm Gladwell (2008), in *Outliers,* offers an overview of this relationship between talent and perseverance, also using musicians as the example. Referring to a study by K. Anders Ericsson *et al.,* Gladwell writes, 'The students [violinists] who would end up the best in their class began to practice more than anyone else...In fact, by the age of twenty, the elite performers had each totaled ten thousand hours of practice' (Gladwell, 2008: 38–39). All violinists in the study had started playing when they were five years old, but by age nine, some practiced more than others, and those who practiced more became significantly better in the long run. Among violinists and pianists, the Ericsson study 'couldn't find any "natural," musicians who floated effortlessly to the top while practicing a fraction of the time their peers did' (Gladwell, 2008: 39). Sticking with a specific endeavor over time matters.

Psychologist Angela Duckworth (2009) calls this *grit,* after the girl in the film *True Grit.* In her TedTalk, Duckworth says, 'There is no domain of expertise that has been studied where the world-class performers have put in fewer than ten years of consistent, deliberate practice to get to where they are.' Capacities like grit allow us to take advantage of our talent. We all 'know many, many extremely bright people who don't have the capacity to stay on task towards one goal.' In her talk, she repeats *eventually,* emphasizing the long haul necessary for creative success.

In his book *Where Good Ideas Come From,* Steven Johnson (2010) shows that, though Charles Darwin felt as if his theory of evolution 'at once struck' (Johnson, 2010: 79), it actually arose over a long period of observation and documentation. Creative insight often emerges from what Johnson calls *the slow hunch.* He writes, 'Sustaining the slow hunch is less a matter of perspiration than of *cultivation.* You give the hunch enough nourishment to keep it growing, and plant it in fertile soil, where its roots can make new connections. And then you give it time to bloom' (Johnson, 2010: 78). Cultivation – of a hunch or of talent – matters whether you are a musician or a scientist.

This notion of cultivation is akin to the sort of concentration that poet Jane Hirshfield (1997) advocates in *Nine Gates:* 'By concentration, I mean a particular sense of awareness: penetrating, unified, and focused, yet also permeable and open' (Hirshfield, 1997: 3). She writes of '[v]iolinists practicing scales and dancers repeating the same movements [...]. They are learning how to attend unswervingly, moment by moment, to themselves and their art; learning to come into steady presence, free from the distractions of interest or boredom' (Hirshfield, 1997: 4). Patience is what she means – and self-awareness.

These notions about practice and concentration bring me back to my pondering of how genre fits into the equation. Certainly, practice within a genre is necessary to develop expertise, and one cannot divide one's focus among many pursuits and expect to become very good at all of those pursuits. Still, a violin is a string instrument, so the craft of playing the violin likely makes an expert violin player far better at playing piano or cello than I am. I am most deeply trained as a poet. Still, poetry uses techniques found in other genres, and by taking seriously other genres as a writer, I find that I come back to poetry with a new appreciation, a sense of its possibilities, pleasures and demands. Albert Einstein practiced violin for hours on end for years, though his major contributions were to physics. That gaining of perspective – that moving among genres to practice and understand each – creates self-awareness, introduces challenges and circumvents writer's block or a taking for granted that can occur in an immersive experience.

That cultivation over time, that focus or immersive experience, is the very quality that Nicholas Carr (2010) worries is undermined by contemporary life. In *The Shallows*, he writes, 'Now my concentration starts to drift after a page or two. I get fidgety, lose the thread, begin looking for something else to do' (Carr, 2010: 5). He's continually tempted to hop to something new. Carr blames the internet, which speeds up research and puts socializing at our fingertips. 'Calm, focused, undistracted, the linear mind is being pushed aside by a new kind of mind that wants and needs to take in and dole out information in short, disjointed, often overlapping bursts…' (Carr, 2010: 10). Distraction and immediate gratification become significant obstacles to the long haul of a writing life.

These obstacles put grit at risk. Some writers give up when the going gets tough. Even genre-hopping, if it becomes a skimming of or skimping on craft by the writer, might be a version of giving up that is founded in distractedness and the need for immediate reward or validation. Hirshfield, though, notes, 'Difficulty itself may be a path toward concentration – expended effort weaves us into a task, and successful engagement, however laborious, becomes also a labor of love… Difficulty, then, whether of life or of craft, is not inherently a hindrance to an artist' (Hirshfield, 1997: 5). That is, an obstacle is not a problem and might be an opportunity if the artist sticks with the task when the going gets tough – or when the distraction gets easy.

Hirshfield's assertions about difficulty presage Duckworth (2009), who says, 'Having perseverance in the face of adversity…setbacks, failures, that's important.' Or as Johnson puts it, 'Being right keeps you in place. Being wrong forces you to explore' (Johnson, 2010: 137). Even as I write this essay – or rather, as I'm distracted from my work by an internet search – I find nonfiction writer Phillip Lopate (2013) online, saying, 'Strangely enough, doubt need not impede action.

If you really become friends with your doubt, you can go ahead and take risks, knowing you will be questioning yourself at every turn, no matter what.' Mistakes, doubts, and obstacles become important components of perseverance, especially in creative endeavors, because challenges create new possibilities and unexpected connections. The challenges of writing in more than one genre include making connections instead of losing the thread, as well as making mistakes from which you can learn across projects or ideas.

Considering all this when setting goals for writing instruction can reshape our teaching. If perseverance is as important as Blaylock, Bausch, Gladwell, Duckworth, Johnson and Hirshfield think it is, we must prioritize that capacity as a goal. The academic environment, of course, works against the cultivation of grit. With any given student, we have only a few hours each week for maybe fifteen weeks, not ten years. Moreover, mistakes seem more easily added up as faltering grades than as the path to success. Cultivating grit in students is no easy task, but we can articulate existing practices and develop pedagogical approaches that encourage perseverance as well as the balance between concentration and openness.

We assume practice is embedded in our courses, as students *do* writing. But that assumption may be hidden from students, so our first step in a more perseverance-oriented pedagogy is to make grit part of the course conversation and a conscious choice. My students' attitudes shifted when I started talking about the practice of writing as akin to the practice of musicians and athletes. These analogies made sense to them, and they began to talk of writing talent as something that had to be cultivated. To this end, I've developed two specific activities, one for a single class meeting and the other as an extended out-of-class task. Though I discuss the way these activities work in my poetry courses, these activities can be adapted across types and levels of courses and across genres.

Many of us use writing exercises in class, but probably few of us repeat the same exercise with the same class. Why not repeat an exercise to emphasize that writers solve similar problems over again in different ways? One day, I explained so-called rules for a nonet – a nine-line poem in which the first line has nine syllables and each subsequent line has one fewer syllable than the line preceding it.[2] When my students finished writing a nonet, I asked them to do it again, like dancers repeating the same movements. I myself wrote one nonet every day that week. Why not ask fiction-writing students to draft three versions of the same scene, one after the other, perhaps shifting point of view to practice that aspect of craft? Why not ask composition students to write a descriptive paragraph of their kitchen, then do that again and again? Tony Barnstone teaches a fixed-forms poetry workshop in which he requires each student to write multiple sonnets.[3] A writer's first thoughts and words on a topic are rarely her most brilliant, but the real point of this approach for writing pedagogy is to cultivate in students a habit of concentration, practice, and perseverance.

To make this point about sticking with a task on a grander scale, I developed a draft-a-day blog project.[4] My own blogging – committing to at least one polished post with my co-writer every week – has made writing a habit of mind in ways I couldn't have predicted. The regularity of blogging means that I'm working on it in my mind even when I'm not writing. So a version of the following appears on my recent syllabus:

> Each student will set up a private Wordpress.com blog and will post a draft there every day for a month. If you need prompts, take a look at the end of each chapter in *The Poet's Companion*,[5] which is on reserve at the library. If you miss posting a draft on a given day, you must post two separate drafts the next day to catch up. If you do this more than three times or if you miss two days in a row, your project score will be negatively affected. While it is possible to queue up posts ahead of time, the goal of this project is to cultivate a daily poetry writing habit over time.

The blogs are private, with myself invited as a reader and perhaps classmates invited as commenters, so that the work remains practice towards those 10,000 hours needed to achieve expertise. The point is *doing* and *doing* some more.

In addition to basic practice, writing instructors can cultivate perseverance by requiring extensive revision. My students revise, workshop and revise again some – but not all – of the poem drafts from the blog. As I've written elsewhere (2010: 63–77), 'Revision is indeed a common part of the creative process and, in the case of the workshop, encourages the divergent thinking and experimentation necessary for innovation.' In a course that requires revision, the early danger is the following:

> Suggestions for revision, to some students, appear to be harsh criticism of initial ideas and feelings...However, while revision appears to put students' self-esteem at risk, students build confidence as they write versions of poems and stories that they didn't know they could, as they move out of complacency and accomplish something that they don't just feel but can see, hear, and share. (Leahy, 2007: 64)

The benefit of revision is that students become aware; they define and overcome obstacles and discover unanticipated connections or new approaches. They practice; they stick with a poem over time.

In this way, revision encourages the cycle that neurologist Alice Flaherty (2004) discusses in *The Midnight Disease:* 'When someone is highly motivated to do something, that person is likely to learn to do it well, and when someone can do something well (especially when it wins praise), the ability to do it often increases the drive to do it' (Flaherty, 2004: 52). Rarely is a first draft of a poem or novel the end for a serious writer. Revision and experimentation – ongoing practice – encourages improvement. Awareness of that improvement fuels more practice.

Other capacities cultivate perseverance in general and revision in particular. Curiosity can make those ten years of practice rewarding along the way. Not long ago, I talked with a student about a draft of her poem that had begun to develop the bullet train as a metaphor. 'What do you know about bullets? What do you know about trains?' I asked. Then, instead of pointing her to other poems – to reading in the genre – I pointed her to a visual dictionary,[6] which offered images and terminology about the subject matter with which a poet might play: *trigger, barrel, chamber, vertical damper, hand rail, air deflector*. I want my students to become permeable to the unexpected and simultaneously to focus more deeply. I also suggested my student talk with my colleague in creative nonfiction, Tom Zoellner,[7] whose latest book is about trains. Research opportunities abound, and different genres handle similar topics differently. Poets and fiction writers, after all, get ideas or instigations from news stories, fairy tales, animal shows on the *Discovery* channel – from a variety of fields and texts. My hope was that, in talking to another writer and an expert about trains, but someone who worked in a different genre, my student could figure out ways her poem might become distinctive as a poem. I expect my students to investigate subject matter and language and to cultivate for themselves curiosity about the world as well as about the genres in which they choose to write.

One activity I use to teach curiosity about craft and language involves bringing in my *Chicago Manual of Style* and discussing several rhetorical moves, an activity I initially developed to address specific grammar problems in students' work but that is surprisingly successful in encouraging curiosity. I wax enthusiastically about restrictive appositives, for instance. While some students learn the difference between *Robert Burns, the poet* and *the poet Robert Burns*,[8] that isn't exactly the point. Knowing something they hadn't known an hour earlier makes them want to know more. This grammar lesson piques their interest in how language works, and that interest generates further attentiveness to grammar – language devices – they can learn and use themselves. Proof that this activity had an effect: several students secured their own copies of *The Chicago Manual of Style*, and two had used their phones to order before they'd even left the classroom.

Will these two students go on to publish? I don't know. Only time will tell. Most creative writing students won't rise to the top of the field. That fact, however, makes perseverance even more important to consider when we teach. No matter what our students become, grit fosters success. And perseverance allows some of us to stick with writing – and teaching – for a lifetime.

Notes

(1) James P. Blaylock is the author of more than 20 books, including *Homunculus* (1986, Ace Books, New York) and *The Aylesford Skull* (2013, Titan Books, London).
(2) This form can be found in Brewer, R.L. (2012) Nonet Poems: Poetic Form. *Writer's Digest* (July 17). See http://www.writersdigest.com/whats-new/nonet-poems-poetic-form (accessed 1 February 2015).
(3) I visited Tony Barnstone's fixed-forms workshop on April 9, 2014.
(4) I discuss (with co-author Douglas Dechow) this draft-a-day project in much greater detail in a chapter entitled Leahy, A. (2015) Concentration, form, and ways of (digitally) seeing. In M.D. Clark, T. Hergenrader and J. Rein. *Creative Writing in the Digital Age* (pp. 29–44). New York: Bloomsbury.
(5) Addonizio, K. and Laux, D. (1997) *The Poet's Companion: A Guide to the Pleasures of Writing Poetry.* New York: Norton.
(6) I use the *Ultimate Visual Dictionary 2000.* New York: DK Publishing, 1999.
(7) Tom Zoellner is the author of *A Safeway in Arizona* (2011) Viking Books, New York, *Uranium* (2009) Viking Books, New York and *The Heartless Stone* (2006) St. Martin's, New York.
(8) This example appears on page 153 of *The Chicago Manual of Style*, 15th edition (2006, 15 September, University of Chicago Press: Chicago, IL).

References

Addonizio, K. and Laux, D. (1997) *The Poet's Companion: A Guide to the Pleasures of Writing Poetry.* New York: Norton.
Bausch, R. (no date) Letter to a young writer. National Endowment for the Arts. See http://www.nea.gov/national/homecoming/essays/bausch.html (accessed 14 January 2014).
Blaylock, J. P. (1986) *Homunculus.* New York: Ace Books.
Blaylock, J. P. (2013) *The Ayesford Skull.* London: Titan Books.
Brewer, R. L. (2012) Nonet poems: Poetic form. Writer's digest (July 17). See http://www.writersdigest.com/whats-new/nonet-poems-poetic-form (accessed 1 February 2015).
Carr, N. (2010) *The Shallows: What the Internet Is Doing to Our Brains.* New York: Norton.
Duckworth, A. (2009) True grit: Can perseverance be aught? TEDTalk (October 18). See http://tedxtalks.ted.com/video/TEDxBlue-Angela-Lee-Duckworth-P (accessed 14 January 2014).
Flaherty, A. (2004) *The Midnight Disease.* New York: Houghton Mifflin.
Gladwell, M. (2008) *Outliers.* New York: Little, Brown.
Hirshfield, J. (1997) *Nine Gates: Entering the Mind of Poetry.* New York: HarperCollins.
Johnson, S. (2010) *Where Good Ideas Come From.* New York: Riverhead.

Kidder, T. and Todd, R. (2013) Authenticity applies. Interview by Elfrieda Abbe. *The Writer* 126 (3), 32–37.
Leahy, A. (2007) Creativity, caring, and the easy 'A'. In K. Ritter and S. Vanderslice (eds) *Can It Really Be Taught? Resisting Lore in Creative Writing Pedagogy* (pp. 55–65). Portsmouth, NH: Heinemann.
Leahy, A. (2010) Teaching as a creative act: Why the workshop works in creative writing. In D. Donnelly (ed.) *Does the Workshop Still Work?* (pp. 63–77). Bristol: Multilingual Matters.
Leahy, A. and Dechow, D. (2015) Concentration, form, and ways of (digitally) seeing. In M. D. Clark, T. Hergenrader and J. Rein (eds) *Creative Writing in the Digital Age* (pp. 29–44). New York: Bloomsbury.
Lopate, P. (2013) The essay, an exercise in doubt. *The New York Times*, February 16. See http://opinionator.blogs.nytimes.com/2013/02/16/the-essay-an-exercise-in-doubt/ (accessed 1 February 2015).
The Chicago Manual of Style (2006) (15th edn). 15 September, Chicago, IL: University of Chicago Press.
Tom, Z. (2006) *The Heartless Stone*. New York: St. Martin's.
Tom, Z. (2009) *Uranium*. New York: Viking Books.
Tom, Z. (2011) *A Safeway in Arizona*. New York: Viking Books.
Ultimate Visual Dictionary 2000. (1999) New York: DK Publishing.

Index

Academia, xvii, 90, 116
Audience, xiii, xx, 14, 27, 41–44, 51–52, 56–57, 70, 72, 79–85, 89, 111–112, 117, 130–131, 148–149, 152–153, 169
  audience awareness, xiii, 50, 57, 80–82
Analysis, 13, 20, 31, 35, 61, 65, 68, 72, 80–81, 83, 90, 97, 99, 109, 138–139, 146, 159, 164
  Self-analysis, 78
Argument, 2, 4, 10–11, 13–14, 31–32, 44, 63, 68, 70, 72, 82–84, 112, 117, 131–134, 138–146, 154
  argumentative, xvii, 54, 133
  argumentation, 82–84, 109–112, 138, 140, 154
  counterarguments, 4, 82
Association of Writers and Writing Programs (AWP), 116, 126

Bacon, Francis, 2–3
Bishop, Wendy, xi, xii, xiii, xv, xvi, xviii, xix, xx, 24, 53, 116–117, 126, 136
Brainstorming, 38, 40–41, 69, 162–163, 171
Burroway, Janet, 99, 103, 117, 123, 125, 169, 171

Collaboration, xiii, 87–88, 90–94, 98
  collaborative writing, 32, 34, 68, 71–72, 87–89, 91–92, 94–99, 101, 103–108
  collaborative pedagogy, 91
Composition classroom, xi, xii, xiii, xviii, xix, 8, 24, 47–48, 53–55, 57, 59, 132, 157
Composition studies, xiii, xviii, xx, 39, 60, 69, 130

composition pedagogy, 31, 54, 112
Compositionists, xvii, xviii, xx, 12, 40, 57, 61, 116
Constructivism, xiii, 87–88
Craft of writing, xvi, xviii, 52, 87, 169
Creative nonfiction, xii, 2–3, 6, 35–36, 41, 43–46, 91, 132–133, 179
Creative writing classroom, xii, xiii, xix, 82, 88, 115
Creative writing studies, 60
  pedagogy, xiii, 47, 87, 91, 96, 115
Critical Engagement, 20, 60
  critical response, 22–23
  critical thinking, 12, 35–36, 73, 143
Critique, 56–57, 62–63, 149, 158
Curate, 63, 69
  curating, xiii, 60, 63, 67–68, 72, 74
  curatorial stance, xiii, 59–64, 68–69, 72–73
Curriculum, xii, xiii, xv, xviii, 61, 109, 148
  writing-across-the-curriculum, xiii, 35–36, 39, 46

de Montaigne, Michel, 2–3, 5, 8, 132
Descriptive writing, 25, 109–110, 112, 154–168, 177
Description, 43, 66, 69–70, 91, 110–112, 118, 154–168
Dialogic, 4, 63, 71–72, 131, 136, 138, 142–146
Disciplines, xiv, xvi, xix, xx, 68, 130
  disciplinary alliance, xix, xx, 35–36, 72
  disciplinary boundaries, xvi, xvii, xix
  writing-in-the-disciplines, xiii, 36, 39, 41, 45, 88, 90–91, 125, 135

Discourse community, 36, 38–39, 55
Discovery, 35, 38–43, 45–46, 60, 63–65, 103, 122, 129, 133–135

Elbow, Peter, xviii, 14, 69
Essaying, xiii, 1–5, 7–8, 110, 136
  to essay, 1–4, 134, 136–137
Ethnography, 13, 61
Experience-based writing, 12–13
Experimentation, xi, 1, 3, 40, 44, 54, 69, 82, 85, 104, 131, 133–134, 154, 178–179
Exploration, 21, 41, 112, 121, 131, 134, 155
  exploratory essay, 68, 129–135
Exposition, 123–124, 154, 167

First-year composition, xv, xvi, 2, 24–25, 27, 45, 109, 148–149, 152
Freewriting, 25–27, 38–41, 46, 79, 122

Genre, xvi, xvii, xviii, xx, 2–8, 11–14, 24–25, 28, 35–36, 41, 44, 49, 51, 59, 61, 69, 73, 79, 85, 87, 89–90, 92, 94, 117, 125, 133, 154, 156–157, 167, 170, 174, 176–177, 179
  subgenre, 2, 8
  genre theory, 90–91
Goldberg, Natalie, 109, 170
Grammar, xvii, 109–112, 130, 161, 179
Graphic narrative, 156–158, 160, 162–164, 166–167
Gutkind, Lee, 167

Hampl, Patricia, 36
Harris, Joseph, 11, 13–14
Harris, Judith, 53
Hemingway, Ernest, 32, 144–145
Higher education, 18, 114, 116

Imagination, xvii, 52, 65, 67, 78, 112, 114, 117, 148
Inquiry, 4, 12, 41, 60, 62–63, 66–68, 73, 80, 116, 129–131, 133–136, 141
Invention, xi, 6, 11, 35, 54, 114, 116–118, 120, 122–123, 125–126, 138, 140, 156, 162–163, 167

Journaling, xv, 39–41, 46, 56, 63–65, 72, 79, 119, 125, 154

Lamott, Anne, 169
Leahy, Anna, 112, 178
Lopate, Phillip, 3–5, 7, 41, 69, 132, 136, 176

Mayers, Tim, xviii, xix, 60
Minot, Stephen, 118
Moore, Dinty W., 71, 168
Moxley, Joseph, 53
Murray, Donald, xviii, 36
Myers, D.G., 18

Objectivity, 13, 89, 154–155

Pedagogy, xiii, xiv, xvi, xix, 20, 31, 47, 54, 57, 60, 72, 80, 90, 112, 115–116, 129–130, 169–170, 177–178
  collaborative pedagogies, 91
Personal essay, 3, 7, 136
Personality, xix, 14, 49, 122
Pinckert, Robert, 110
Poetry, xvii, 20, 24–25, 28, 31–34, 40, 53, 59–67, 73, 89, 91–92, 115–116, 154, 175–179
Politics, xviii, 12–13, 64, 126
Process, xiii, xv, xvii, 1–7, 11–13, 25–28, 36–37, 40–41, 43–44, 46, 48, 52, 54, 63, 65–66, 71, 79, 83–84, 88–89, 109–111, 114–115, 117, 120, 122, 125–126, 129–132, 134–135, 140–141, 143, 145–146, 149–153, 155–157, 161–163, 167, 170, 178
Publishing, 16–20, 116, 133, 170, 180

Reflection, 2, 7, 12, 21–22, 28, 35, 41, 47, 52–53, 57, 60, 66–67, 71–72, 82, 111, 123, 134–136, 141–142, 144, 146, 151–152, 164
  Reflexivity, 21–22,
Research essay, 61, 68, 72, 133
Revision, 26, 32, 35, 38, 40, 57, 66, 83, 111, 115, 126, 134, 156, 162, 164, 166–167, 178–179
Rhetoric, xvi, xix, 2, 16, 21, 36, 44, 69, 82, 84, 92, 116, 118, 122, 125, 157, 160
  rhetorical situation, xiii, xix, 6, 57, 59, 68, 73, 83, 91, 109–110, 157
  rhetorical analysis, 68, 72, 131

Rhetoric *(Continued)*
  rhetorical argument, 13
  rhetorical strategies, 82, 131, 154, 156, 158, 179
Ritter, Kelly, xvii, 51

Scaffolding, 12–14, 37, 45, 63, 92, 171
  Academic scholarship, xix, 35, 44, 60, 82, 90
Self-awareness, 56, 122, 142, 144, 146, 175–176
Self-discovery, 41, 45, 122
Service-learning, 27, 61, 148, 153
Shields, David, 1–3, 6–8
Social media, 54, 61, 140
  blogs, 54, 61, 72, 178
  text messages, 24, 62
  Twitter, 24–25
Stegner, Wallace, xv, 81, 85

Subjectivity, 140–146

Toulmin, Stephen, 138–143, 145–146

Uppal, Priscilla, 73

Vanderslice, Stephanie, xvii, 51, 115
Visual storytelling, 161
Vygotsky, Lev, 37, 40–41

Writing across the curriculum, xiii, 36, 39,
Writing in the disciplines, xiii, 36, 39, 41, 45, 88, 90–91, 125, 135
Workshopping, 3, 39, 73, 81–83, 87–108, 115–117, 126, 135
Writer's block, 30, 115, 170, 176

Zeiger, William, 130, 136

For Product Safety Concerns and Information please contact our EU Authorised Representative:

Easy Access System Europe

Mustamäe tee 50

10621 Tallinn

Estonia

gpsr.requests@easproject.com

www.ingramcontent.com/pod-product-compliance
Lightning Source LLC
Chambersburg PA
CBHW070609300426
44113CB00010B/1467